A BLUE NEW DEAL
Why We Need a New Politics for the Ocean

CHRIS ARMSTRONG

YALE UNIVERSITY PRESS
NEW HAVEN AND LONDON

For information about this and other Yale University Press publications, please contact:
U.S. Office: sales.press@yale.edu   yalebooks.com
Europe Office: sales@yaleup.co.uk   yalebooks.co.uk

Set in Adobe Garamond Pro by IDSUK (DataConnection) Ltd
Printed in Great Britain by Clays Ltd, Elcograf S.p.A

Library of Congress Control Number: 2023931096

ISBN 978-0-300-25974-2 (hbk)
ISBN 978-0-300-27040-2 (pbk)

A catalogue record for this book is available from the British Library.

10 9 8 7 6 5 4 3 2 1

A BLUE NEW DEAL

CHRIS ARMSTRONG is professor of political theory at the University of Southampton. An expert on issues of justice and conservation, natural resources and the climate, he is the author of *Global Distributive Justice, Justice and Natural Resources* and *Why Global Justice Matters*.

Further praise for *A Blue New Deal*:

'This thoughtful tome is a must-read for anyone who cares about ocean and marine life.'
Sunday Express

'Some 70 per cent of the earth's surface lies under water. Chris Armstrong's *A Blue New Deal* is an important look at the climate and industrial devastation hitting oceans.'
Martin Chilton, *Independent*

'An intriguing new book ... Using an array of political and oceanographical literature, Armstrong details how humans are on the way to wrecking our marine environment through everything from overfishing to climate change.'
Bill Bowkett, *Reaction*

'A valuable and a thought-provoking read, providing a great introduction to current issues in ocean governance.'
Mélodie Ruwet, *Environmental Politics*

'Indispensable. A must-read for anyone who cares about the ocean and understands the integral role it plays in our lives. This book is also a strong reminder that doing better and leaving no one behind in the process is a choice we can and should make for the sake of our present and our future.'
Dr Asha de Vos, founder of Oceanswell

'Chris Armstrong delivers a deep dive into a complex and crucial ocean narrative. *A Blue New Deal* is a gripping read, providing a well-argued vision of a just future for nature and humanity in the largest liveable space on earth.'

Torsten Thiele, founder of the Global Ocean Trust

'*A Blue New Deal* is a timely contribution to one of the most important issues facing us all, written with an appropriate sense of urgency but also as a result of deep and wide scholarship. I hope, for all our sakes, it reaches a wide readership.'

Ray Monk, author of *Ludwig Wittgenstein: The Duty of Genius*

'*A Blue New Deal* is the first systematic look by a political theorist at the most important and most endangered global commons. Not only does Chris Armstrong provide a brilliant critical account of the origins of the failing oceanic governance, he also offers forward-looking guidance on how to design reforms towards justice and environmental sustainability. The range of issues addressed (from workers at sea, marine animals, small island states, seabed minerals) and a broad and practice-based approach to justice makes this book a must both for policy-makers and political theorists.'

Dr Petra Gümplová, University of Erfurt

'*A Blue New Deal* shows how our treatment of the sea aggravates both climate change and socioeconomic inequalities. It is rare for a book written by an academic to be so rich in facts and arguments and yet also fun to read. A must-read for academics, policy-makers and activists alike.'

Dr Dimitrios Efthymiou, Goethe University Frankfurt

CONTENTS

ILLUSTRATIONS

ACKNOWLEDGEMENTS

While completing this book I've learned from many wonderful scholars who have written on the ocean, its ecosystems and its role in human societies. Some of them are no longer with us (including Rachel Carson, Elisabeth Mann Borgese and Alastair Couper). Others are working in oceanography today (including Sylvia Earle and Callum Roberts), or in law, history and the social sciences (including Philip Steinberg, Peter Payoyo, David Abulafia, Laleh Khalili, Liam Campling, Alejandro Colas and Surabhi Ranganathan). I'd like to express my admiration for their contribution to our understanding of the sea and its connections to society. My own background is in philosophy or political theory, and immersing myself in these literatures has been a hugely rewarding experience. I believe strongly that the ocean needs advocates in all walks of life, across academia as well as outside of it, and if this book helps in its own way to open up vital debates about the ocean's future to a wider readership, I will consider my time to have been well spent.

For her wise counsel and her enthusiasm for the project right from the beginning, I'd like to thank Jo Godfrey, my editor at Yale University Press. For written comments on various chapters, I'd like to thank David Owen, Paula Casal, Jeff Sebo, Kian Mintz-Woo, Jamie Draper, Eloise Harding, Lior Erez, Ben Saunders, Alex McLaughlin and Stefan Andreasson. I was able to present draft chapters, in some cases virtually, at the University of Waterloo in Canada, Pompeu Fabra University in Barcelona, the University of Palermo, the

Netherlands Institute for the Law of the Sea in Utrecht, the Goethe University in Frankfurt, the Hebrew University of Jerusalem, the University of Bern, the Mercator Research Institute on Global Commons and Climate Change in Berlin, and the Institute for Futures Studies in Stockholm. I'd like to thank the audiences at all of those places for their helpful comments and questions, and for their encouragement that this was a book worth writing. I was very fortunate that the book-in-progress was selected for the annual York Political Theory Manuscript Workshop. The Workshop took place in March 2021, and I am very grateful to Monica Brito-Vieira and Gabriele Badano for making that happen amid the challenges of the pandemic. Cara Nine, Dimitris Efthymiou, Torsten Thiele and Petra Gümplová provided thought-provoking and generous responses to various chapters, and along with the other participants managed to make the event a stimulating and productive one.

In the years 2018–19, I was lucky enough to hold a British Academy/Leverhulme Senior Research Fellowship on the theme of ocean justice. I'd like to thank the funders for that opportunity, which allowed work on this book to begin in earnest. I am also grateful to the *Journal of Political Philosophy* for permission to reprint material from my paper 'Abuse, Exploitation and Floating Jurisdiction: Protecting Workers at Sea' in Chapter 6, and *Renewal: A Journal of Social Democracy* for permission to draw on my paper 'A Blue New Deal?' in writing Chapter 9.

Finally, I want to thank my family for the support they've given me. The project has always struck my children Felix, Leonard and Yasmin as timely, interesting and important (perhaps by contrast to my previous books!). Over the past few years they've come to me with countless stories and ideas. After reading pieces about whales, or overfishing, or plastic pollution, they've asked, 'Are you going to talk about this in your book?' And I've been able to reply, 'Yes!' Sophia, too, has put up with my distractedness with great forbearance, and has encouraged me throughout that the topic was worthy of the effort. I would like to dedicate this book, with love, to Sophia, ocean-lover extraordinaire.

GLOSSARY

The Area	The deep seabed lying underneath the High Seas. It falls under the authority of the International Seabed Authority rather than individual states.
Area Beyond National Jurisdiction (ABNJ)	The portion of the ocean that is beyond state control, comprising both the High Seas and the Area.
Biodiversity Beyond National Jurisdiction (BBNJ)	The wildlife and genetic material to be found in the Area Beyond National Jurisdiction. An international treaty regulating its use is in preparation.
Continental Shelf	The portion of the sea floor ranging for up to 200 nautical miles from the shore (and in some cases for 350 nautical miles or more), within which the local coastal state has jurisdiction over natural resources.
Exclusive Economic Zone (EEZ)	An area of the sea ranging for up to 200 nautical miles from the shore, within which the coastal state has jurisdiction over natural resources.

Exclusive Flag State Jurisdiction (EFSJ)	The legal doctrine that the flag state alone has authority over a vessel at sea.
Flag of Convenience	A Flag of Convenience country will exert lacklustre oversight over the activities of vessels sailing under its flag. Flags of convenience therefore provide legal cover for illegal fishing and the abuse of workers' rights.
Flag State	The country under whose 'flag' a vessel is sailing. This state should exercise legal oversight over crew and passengers.
Freedom of the Sea	The legal doctrine that, outside of states' territorial seas, all nations should be free to engage in fishing, navigation and other peaceful uses of the ocean.
High Seas	The portion of the ocean that does not fall under the authority of any state.
International Seabed Authority (ISA)	The body established under the contemporary Law of the Sea to regulate seabed mining in the Area.
Marine Protected Area (MPA)	A zone in which at least some commercial activities are limited in order to protect ocean ecosystems. The most strongly protected zones are known as Marine Reserves.
Nautical Mile	A common unit of distance at sea. One nautical mile is 1,852 metres, or 1.151 regular miles.
New International Economic Order (NIEO)	A vision of a more egalitarian and participatory world order, espoused by many countries emerging from colonialism in the 1960s and 1970s.

Regional Fisheries Management Organisation (RFMO)   A body that allows its member states to negotiate limits on fishing. Dozens of RFMOs govern fish in different areas on the High Seas, and sometimes apply to different species.

Territorial Sea   The portion of the ocean falling within 12 nautical miles of a coastal state, within which the laws of that state are generally assumed to apply.

UNCLOS   An abbreviation for the United Nations Convention on the Law of the Sea. Often considered a 'Constitution for the Ocean', it was signed in 1982 and finally came into force in 1994.

INTRODUCTION

Seven-tenths of the earth's surface lies under water. The great world ocean represents the vast majority of our planet's habitable space, and we depend on it in ways we may never have paused to reflect on. It is home to perhaps two million species, the bulk of them still unknown to science.[1] But despite all that, anyone keeping track of contemporary politics could be forgiven for wondering if the ocean is there at all. Remarkably few of our governments contain Ministries for the Ocean (South Korea and Canada are rare exceptions),[2] and our politicians rarely campaign on ocean-related issues (though fishing did emerge as an issue during the 2016 Brexit referendum). The ocean is governed by a complex body of international law which the average citizen probably knows little about. Going about your busy life, you might be tempted to file the ocean, its politics and the Law of the Sea in a mental box along with gravity or the internet: things that go on working whether you think about them or not. Its immense size, and its permanence, might fool you into believing that the ocean is immune to degradation.

Such an assumption would be profoundly mistaken. We cannot assume that the ocean will simply go on doing its work of supporting life on earth, or providing us with plentiful supplies of natural resources. Even if it is not going anywhere, the ocean is in crisis. The past three decades have witnessed greater changes to the ocean's ecosystems than have occurred in all of human history to date.[3] But the kinds of physical and chemical changes that are now under way – including warming, acidification and the growth of ocean 'dead zones' with little or no oxygen – are not wholly unknown. To scientists studying our planet's past, they are actually ominously familiar. Each has been associated with the mass extinction events that have punctuated our planet's long history. Earth has faced at least five of these events to date, and each time biodiversity has plummeted as organisms struggle to adapt to a changing environment. The fifth mass extinction event took place around 65 million years ago, and was triggered by a massive meteorite impact. The destruction that followed wiped out the dinosaurs, and countless other species besides. Many scientists believe we are now in the early stages of a sixth great extinction.[4] The difference this time is that it is not a natural catastrophe: it is a largely man-made one.

Climate change in particular is rapidly turning the ocean from a source of sustenance and wealth into a threat to lives and livelihoods. Whole countries might vanish as sea-level rise redraws the atlas of our world. When we factor in pollution, overfishing and habitat loss, we confront a perfect storm of problems that we have not yet proven ourselves a match for. Whether we manage to weather this storm, or even turn back the tide of destruction, will depend on our actions in the coming years. The first step is to shake off the notion that the ocean is simply too vast to be damaged by human actions. Like the banks before the last financial crisis, it is not 'too big to fail'.[5] We need to think seriously about how the ocean that protects us in so many ways can itself be better protected, and there is no time to waste.

There is also a second ocean crisis, which is partly wrapped up with the environmental one. It is a crisis of inequality. In recent years marine scientists have pointed to a 'Blue Acceleration' – a step-change in the intensity of resource exploitation at sea.[6] To an ever-greater degree we are now turning to the ocean for the raw materials that fuel our economies, and as we become more and more dependent on the ocean, there will be both winners and losers. The battle lines are already becoming clear: as fishing becomes ever more industrialised, small-scale 'artisanal' fishers are struggling to compete with vessels that use satellite technology to locate fish, and mile-wide nets to haul them in. The fossil fuel industry has turned to the seabed in search of still more oil and gas – even though we already have more of both than we can burn without hurtling the world towards climate catastrophe. The proceeds of these economic activities flow largely to the haves, rather than the have-nots. High-tech products like laptops and rechargeable batteries depend on minerals – including cobalt, nickel, manganese and lithium – that are increasingly scarce back on dry land. As it happens, those minerals lie liberally scattered across the deep seabed. Harvesting them, though, would require mining technology that is far out of reach of anyone apart from very wealthy corporations.

Given that our economies are already witnessing the return of inequality on a scale not seen since the Victorian age, this opens up a very real danger. The wealthiest 10 per cent of the world's population now consumes roughly half of all planetary resources, owns more than half of its wealth, and is responsible for almost half of all carbon emissions.[7] People from the global North (from countries, that is, like the US, the UK, Canada, Germany or Australia) are heavily overrepresented within this elite group, just as people from the South are overwhelmingly overrepresented among the world's poor. But inequality is not a purely North–South issue. For one thing, the top 10 per cent is an increasingly globalised class, with more and more rich individuals from China, India and the countries of the Middle East now entering its ranks, and even finding their way into the global top 1 per cent.[8] At the same time, the economic tides of recent decades have seen many people in the global North – and especially the working classes, the unemployed and ethnic-minority communities – fall behind in the race for economic security. In that sense our politics is one in which the 10 per cent are pitted against the 90 per cent, and in which the former, regrettably, have come to exert an outsized influence on our politics, setting the rules of the game in their interest rather than those of the majority. There is a very real danger that a new gold rush on the ocean floor would make these gulfs of wealth and power still worse.

To get an insight into what is going wrong in ocean politics today, consider a little-noticed news story from February 2019. The tale occurs at a meeting of the Council of the ISA, in Kingston, Jamaica. The ISA, or International Seabed

Authority, is the global institution that regulates the mining of the deep seabed. Seats at the table are held by nation-states, from large countries like the United States or Russia, through to small island states like Nauru and Kiribati, each of them concerned, in principle, to ensure that any seabed mining is conducted sustainably and fairly. As the representative from Belgium began to talk, a murmur passed around the room. For the Belgian representative was not, as would be expected, a diplomat or legal official from that country. Instead he was a private citizen, who happened to be an executive from a Belgian seabed mining corporation. At the same meeting, the government of Nauru in the South Pacific was represented by another executive, the CEO of a mining company registered in Canada.[9] If an entire country can delegate its decision-making power at an important global body to the head of a private corporation – answerable to no one but his shareholders – something has gone badly wrong. That opens the door to the politics of the 10 per cent, not the 90, and to a politics in which the destructive consequences of corporate exploitation of the ocean are quietly placed to one side. As we will see, there are serious concerns about the likely environmental impacts of seabed mining, which may well mean it should never take place. In that context, to ask a seabed mining executive to participate in formal international discussions about the future of the seabed is to send a fox to guard the henhouse. Though it raised eyebrows at the time, the story is all too indicative of an ocean politics that is far removed from the heat and light of public debate, and where the relationship between governments and corporate interests has become altogether too close.

For another glimpse of what is going wrong in ocean politics, consider the 'marine genetic resources' of the deep ocean, which is populated by many creatures adapted to living in inhospitable conditions with little heat or light. Many scientists believe that the genetic codes of these creatures will be key to important medical advances of the future: perhaps the genes of a jellyfish could, if sequenced and reproduced in a laboratory somewhere, provide effective treatments for conditions such as cancer or multiple sclerosis. Who, if anyone, ought to be able to acquire and own those genetic sequences? If a corporation owned them, it could patent any medicines that emerged from its research and name its price. If the whole international community owned them, it could allow the genetic information to be used widely, and use any proceeds to tackle global problems such as poverty, climate change or plastic pollution. But out there on the 'High Seas' – the portion of the ocean that no country controls – the rule in play is actually 'first come, first served'. One single company has registered 47 per cent of all patents arising from marine genetic resources.[10] Countries that cannot afford to invest in high-tech genetic laboratories, meanwhile, have gained nothing.

The central claim of this book is that, to prevent further environmental damage and widening inequality, we need a new ocean politics. Moving onto a different path is possible, and necessary, and the first step is to recognise that the current politics of the ocean is not fit for purpose. The institutions and laws that govern the ocean are too fragmented, too weak and too amenable to powerful vested interests to turn the tide of inequality and the destruction of the marine environment. The new ocean politics, by contrast, would place equality and sustainability at its heart. And rather than being the preserve of elites, with key decisions taken behind closed doors – which often conceal an excessively cosy relationship between politicians and powerful economic interests – a new ocean politics would have to involve citizens everywhere in the governance of our shared ocean. It would protect the vulnerable, whether this means those whose homes and communities will be threatened by sea-level rise, the workers at sea who face some of the worst working conditions in the world, or those – such as future people, and animals – who are so often forgotten by our legal and political institutions. And it would seek to ensure that the benefits of any sustainable ocean industries were widely shared, rather than being monopolised by a few corporations from the global North.

By the end of the book, I will have painted a radical new vision in which fully 80 per cent of the world's ocean is strongly protected from human inter-ference, and allowed to recover its ecological richness, becoming the remark-able haven for biodiversity it once used to be. Insofar as sustainable ocean industries are possible, they would, on this vision, be oriented not around corporate enrichment but around securing social and economic benefits for the many. The ocean can play many roles in our lives: providing comfort and tranquillity, sustaining vibrant natural spaces, supporting livelihoods for many millions of people and opening up ways of decarbonising our economies. To find our way to a new ocean politics, though, we need to tackle powerful vested interests which would wreak the same destruction in the ocean that they have on dry land. Instead of blindly sailing towards ecological destruction and spiralling inequality, we can – and must – change course. This book shows how we can do so.

In setting a course for a new politics for the ocean, the book has five major ports of call. First, it will demonstrate the centrality of the ocean to our future, and the future of the planet. In Chapter 1, we will learn about the many ways in which life as we know it is sustained and protected by our ocean, which performs a variety of ecosystem roles that we often take for granted. But we will also see that its ability to sustain lives and livelihoods is now under threat from a variety of environmental challenges that we have not yet proven ourselves capable of dealing with. This first chapter will also show just how the ocean economy has become so unequal – more unequal, in many ways, than our land-based economies. In setting out these twin threats of growing inequality and environmental destruction, it will make clear the challenges that a new ocean politics will have to meet.

Second, it shows how we have come to this point. Chapters 2, 3 and 4 describe the three great visions that have shaped ocean politics until now, based respectively on freedom, enclosure and equality. It is only by delving into the history of ocean politics that we can understand how and why we have ended up with legal and political institutions that have failed, so far, to arrest the twin crises of environmental destruction and spiralling inequality. Chapters 2 and 3 show how the politics of freedom and enclosure have led us to our current predicament. Chapter 4, by contrast, examines an alternative, more egalitarian model of ocean politics which emerged from the global South in the 1960s and '70s. By taking a closer look at the evolution of ocean law and governance, these chapters allow us to identify paths not taken, including alternative models of ocean politics that could have shifted us onto a course of greater equality and greater sustainability and which can continue to inspire us today.

Third, the book identifies key principles of ocean justice capable of guiding us when we confront the challenges of the future. Chapter 5 outlines seven principles, focusing on our common stake in the ocean, democratic inclusion, the ocean as a space of rights, sustainability, fair benefit-sharing, fair burden-sharing and fair transitions. Any vision of a new ocean politics will require a clear moral compass, and these seven principles can guide us on the path to a new, more egalitarian and sustainable ocean politics. Taken together, they inform the arguments of the rest of this book.

Fourth, it addresses some of the key vulnerabilities of the people, and animals, whose lives are closely entwined with the ocean. Chapter 6 focuses on the human rights of people working in fishing. Workers at sea can find themselves exposed to especially dreadful forms of abuse and exploitation. The chapter shows why they are so vulnerable to such abuses, who bears moral responsibility for their situation, and what we can do to better protect their rights. Chapter 7 concentrates on the rights of marine animals. The ocean is first and foremost a home to many other species, and their interests should be at the heart of the struggle for ocean justice. This chapter argues for the protection of an important set of rights for all cetaceans, that is, whales, dolphins and porpoises. This is just an opening salvo in the case for animal rights at sea, though, and the chapter shows how we could go about building a defence of key rights for many other marine creatures. Chapter 8 then discusses the challenge sea-level rise poses to people living in small island states. Triggered by climate change, rising tides threaten the lives and livelihoods of millions of coast-dwellers. In some cases – most obviously the small island states that dot the Pacific and Indian oceans – they threaten the very existence of political communities, given that these islands could be completely submerged even by a modest degree of sea-level rise. Will climate change wipe those states from the map? Or is there a chance that the inhabitants of small island states could continue to enjoy statehood and political community even if sea-level rise comes to pass?

This chapter addresses what we owe individual islanders, by way of safe refuge overseas. And it also shows how we can help them to sustain their political communities even if sea-level rise does inundate their islands.

Finally, the last two chapters take a more systematic look at the future of ocean politics. They reveal how our current institutions of oceanic governance are failing us: split into a variety of different bodies, each operating under different principles (and often beholden to specific interest groups), they do not appear capable of putting us on the path towards equality and sustainability. If we can, and should, govern the ocean differently, the final objective of the book is to show how.

Chapter 9 introduces the idea of a Blue New Deal, which is the name we can give to a suite of policies aiming to tackle both inequality and environmental degradation simultaneously. It shows how countries can – and in some cases already have – put in place policies that regenerate coastal communities as well as coastal ecosystems. It identifies key priorities for a Blue New Deal, and some of the most promising success stories to date. But it also shows that each country cannot be left to pursue its own Blue New Deal alone. In the global South, communities face a tragic choice between environmental protection and the desire to escape from poverty. A global Blue New Deal would have to unlock new sources of funding capable of dissolving that tragic choice, and making the New Deal policies work for everyone. Chapter 9 shows how that could happen.

While these policies would be a major boon to the future of coastal regions worldwide, they would not take us all the way to a genuinely new global ocean politics. Chapter 10 takes us beyond the policies of a Blue New Deal, presenting a radical argument for a new World Ocean Authority capable of turning ocean politics on its head. Rather than a patchwork of ocean zones, some protected better than others – and most not protected at all – it presents a vision in which 80 per cent of the ocean would be strongly protected. The World Ocean Authority would be charged with defending the lion's share of our great ocean, involving ordinary citizens in its governance for the first time, and protecting the interests of future people and the animals that actually live in it. The vast majority of economic activities would be outlawed, with a strong emphasis on environmental protection instead of exploitation. When we turn away from our current approach of exploiting the ocean first and worrying about the consequences later, we could see an extensive rewilding of the ocean within a single human generation. Only a radical approach along these lines can do justice to the centrality of the ocean to all life on earth.

This book is animated above all by a belief that the time for serious discussion about the future of our world ocean is long overdue. Activists, politicians and concerned citizens are slowly waking up to this fact. My aim is to inspire greater discussion about justice in the blue part of our planet, and to open up a sense of possibility about the options open to us. Can we shift ourselves onto a different trajectory, in which the ocean remains a haven for biodiversity, and supports people's livelihoods around the world rather than enriching a privileged few? That question could hardly be more urgent. To resort to a tried-and-tested maritime metaphor, turning around a super-tanker is a very slow process. In an age of dangerous climate change – in which we have perhaps a decade to drastically reduce our economies' dependence on fossil fuels – there is no time to waste in rethinking the demands we place on the ocean.

1

THE CRUCIBLE OF LIFE

Life on our planet, most scientists believe, originated in the ocean, and for nine-tenths of its history it could only be found there.[1] Even now the ocean remains vital both to human existence and to planetary health more broadly. It performs key functions which help make earth (unlike the vast majority of worlds we have discovered so far) hospitable to life. But the ocean is being pummelled by many overlapping environmental challenges. Subjected to more and more intensive economic activity, its fragile ecosystems are under increasing pressure. This chapter illustrates some of the ways in which our lives and livelihoods are dependent upon a healthy ocean, as well as some of the environmental and social challenges we face, which now pose serious threats to a healthy, just and prosperous planet.

THE OCEAN AS LIFE-SUPPORT

Without our ocean, it is hard to see how advanced forms of life could ever have emerged on our planet, or survived for so long. One of the most important roles it plays is as a moderator of temperatures. The sun floods the nearer limits of the solar system with enormous amounts of heat energy. Our ocean absorbs the bulk of the energy that reaches earth, and it does so while actually changing temperature relatively little. Its high 'heat capacity', as scientists put it, allows the blanket of water covering seven-tenths of our planet to protect us from fluctuations in temperature. That's why on a very hot day we run from the scalding sand into the cool sea – both have been absorbing heat energy from the summer sun, but the sand heats up rapidly while the sea does not. To see what our world might be like without the sea, consider the moon, which lacks large bodies of open water. Pick a spot on its naked surface one night, and think about it rotating away from the sun and back again. As it turns from shadow into light, it will fluctuate wildly in temperature, rocketing between minus 280 degrees and plus 260 degrees Fahrenheit (or minus 173 and plus 126 Celsius). Earth's climate is much gentler – thanks mainly to the ocean.

Extremes of heat and cold are also moderated by great ocean currents, which constantly push water away from the equator, towards the poles, and back again. Just one of them, the Gulf Stream, transports 550 trillion calories of heat energy across the North Atlantic *every second*.[2] Without these currents, the tropics would be unbearably hot, and our North and South vastly colder. Europe, where I live, would probably be a frozen waste. Our own bodies rely on a similar process: the circulation of blood (which is roughly four-fifths water) protects us from extremes of heat and cold, levelling out our temperatures whatever the weather is doing. The ocean is our planet's great physical equaliser, moderating what would otherwise be intolerable extremes.

It also drives weather patterns and the global water cycle. Huge amounts of water evaporate from the ocean every day, fall as rain and rush through rivers back into the sea. Every drop of water you drink will, on average, have been cycled through the ocean more than a million times during the earth's long history. The ocean is also the origin of most of the world's storms and weather patterns. These can be both blessing and curse. In India and in the great Sahel region of Africa, crops providing nourishment to hundreds of millions rely on great monsoons originating out at sea (anyone visiting India during monsoon season is unlikely ever to forget the sheer quantity of rain involved). Storms can also threaten lives and livelihoods, and are more and more likely to do so in an era of accelerating climate change. In many places, though, the ocean offers its own protection: natural features including coral reefs and kelp forests shelter the land from storms and extreme wave patterns.

The ocean also has a crucial relationship with our atmosphere. The fact that we can breathe at all owes a good deal to the activity of tiny ocean organisms called phytoplankton. They release an estimated 70 per cent of the world's oxygen – far more than plants and trees back on dry land, which our teachers once told us were the 'lungs of the earth'. They also cycle nitrogen, which is crucial to plant life. If ocean warming and acidification were to cause a collapse in plankton populations, the consequences for life on our planet could be dramatic.[3] Just as significantly, the ocean acts as a massive carbon sink. In recent decades industry and farming have poured enormous amounts of carbon dioxide into the atmosphere. This has caused the gradual warming of our planet. But things would have been so much worse without the ocean's role as our most important carbon sink, storing more than fifty times as much carbon dioxide as the atmosphere[4] (and here again we should tip our hats towards the ocean's plankton). There is only so much carbon the ocean can absorb, however, without setting into train dangerous chemical and biological changes. The more carbon seawater contains, for instance, the more acidic it becomes – and the harder it is for plankton to survive. An ocean without plankton would be a terrifying prospect for all of us.

Compared to the land, our knowledge of the ocean and its web of life remains in many ways rudimentary.[5] But each new scientific advance only reaffirms the centrality of the ocean to all of life on earth. Without our ocean, life might not exist on our planet at all. Without a healthy ocean, the prospects for all life on earth would be bleak.

THE OCEAN AS CORNUCOPIA

For the most part, people live on the land. Much of our food is grown there. We work, play and rest on it. The ocean, by comparison, is often 'out of sight, and out of mind'.[6] In many societies, direct physical interaction with the ocean is actually diminishing.[7] The greater affordability of air travel has reduced our reliance on the sea as a means of getting from place to place. Fishing, in many places, has become a high-tech activity which no longer provides large-scale employment in our coastal communities.

The appearance this seems to give – that the ocean is somehow marginal to our lives – is hugely and dangerously deceptive. Our lives are closely entwined with the ocean whether we appreciate it or not. Roughly half the world's population lives close to the sea, with two-thirds of larger cities lying in the vicinity of estuaries and river deltas.[8] Over time, the ocean is actually becoming more, rather than less, crucial to human wealth and well-being. The Hindu epic *Mahābhārata* described an ocean 'teeming with fish, a mine of pearls, vast resting place of water'.[9] In our own era, the 'Blue Acceleration' is seeing the gravitational centre of our economies shifting steadily seawards. In the first decade of this century, nearly seven-tenths of major oil and gas discoveries happened offshore.[10] Our interest in climate stability means most of these fossil fuel reserves should be left exactly where they are. But even as we make our slow and painful transition away from fossil fuels, we will turn once more to the ocean. Wind power is already capable of meeting 3 per cent of global electricity demand. Most of it is sourced at sea.[11] Wave power too is a great, largely untapped, resource. If we could find a way of tapping into the temperature gradients in the ocean, on the other hand, they might provide ten thousand times more energy than wind and wave power combined.[12]

We also take many minerals from the sea. 'Aggregates' like sand and gravel are the basis of the most important 'extractive' industry in the world after fossil fuels. A large proportion of them are dredged from the ocean floor. Embedded in deep ocean clays are rare-earth elements that are crucial for the manufacture of computer chips, phones and other high-tech products, and which are in increasingly short supply on the land. The deep seabed is also scattered with huge stores of 'polymetallic' resources, which are only now on the cusp of being exploited. The amount of cobalt, thallium, nickel and yttrium contained in the Clarion-Clipperton Zone in the Northeast Pacific alone outstrips all known reserves on the land combined.[13] Accessing them would bring a treasure trove of rare minerals within our reach, many of which are key to the industries of tomorrow.

The Blue Acceleration is also influencing the way we feed ourselves. Before the dawn of civilisation twelve or thirteen thousand years ago, human beings fed themselves in three ways: by foraging for wild plants, by hunting and by fishing. Foraging and hunting have for the most part fallen by the wayside, with industrialised agriculture and livestock farming taking their place. But we still catch wild fish in enormous quantities. In the global South, fish are a key source of valuable protein and micronutrients for hundreds of millions of people.[14] Many of them have few other options, which means that if fish stocks collapse as a result of overfishing or climate change, major waves of nutritional deficiency could follow.[15] Fish is big business too. Though there is some disagreement about the figures, the World Bank estimates that the value of the trade in fish easily exceeds that in other animal-source foods such as meat, cheese or milk.[16]

These are all examples of extractive activity, in which we take things from the sea and consume them. But the ocean is also important as a surface, as a conduit for travel. As anyone who has jumped into the ocean knows, seawater is buoyant – it supports your weight much better than the air around you. This greatly reduces the amount of fuel required to move goods from place to place. Moving a 20-foot container from Shanghai to Frankfurt by ship costs a mere third as much as shifting it by plane.[17] It is no surprise, therefore, that four-fifths of international trade in goods depends on sea freight.[18] The emergence of enormous container ships has meant that fewer and fewer people now work in shipping, but it remains very big business – the biggest ocean industry of all in terms of total income. Every day, huge quantities of goods pass through major bottle-necks like the Panama and Suez Canals – which Laleh Khalili, in her wonderful book on the sea routes that thread their way through the Arabian region, calls the 'sinews of war and trade'.[19] The world was given a stark reminder of the impor-tance of these bottlenecks in March 2021, when one of the world's largest container ships, the *Ever Given*, blocked the Suez Canal for six days, prompting widespread concern about the ramifications for world trade. Elsewhere, however, climate change is now opening up the Northeast and Northwest passages through the Arctic, potentially taking weeks off freight times.

People also move from place to place across the ocean's surface. From the fifteenth century onwards, relatively modest seaborne migrations became epic in scale. The Indian Ocean was the best travelled and most cosmopolitan ocean region, but major movements also took place across the Atlantic and Pacific.[20] Later the Atlantic became a conduit for the brutal forced migration of millions of enslaved Africans, as part of the so-called 'Middle Passage'. For others, the ocean was an escape route on which to flee persecution, prejudice, poverty and slavery.[21] Think of the millions who fled famine in Ireland, for whom the first glimpse of New York represented a second chance. Southampton, the city where I work, was the port of embarkation for many of these voyages to the New World, including the fateful voyage of the *Titanic* (my great-great-grandfather Thomas Utley cast its portholes and ship's bell at his foundry in Liverpool, another historic maritime city). Several decades later, Southampton was also a destination for ships travelling from the West Indies, bringing migrants keen to work in the booming post-war economy as part of the 'Windrush generation'. Nevertheless, as tragic scenes in the Mediterranean and elsewhere continually remind us, the ocean is a place of danger as well as opportunity for those seeking a better life elsewhere.

Many cultures remain intimately connected to the ocean. One vivid example is the regional seafaring culture shared by Pacific Islanders, many of whom call their wider community 'Oceania'. For islanders, this community is not a set of islands surrounded by water, but an ocean dotted with islands. The late Fijian writer and academic Epeli Hau'ofa put it this way: 'Oceania is vast, Oceania is expanding, Oceania is hospitable and generous. Oceania is us. We are the sea, we are the ocean. We must wake up to this ancient truth.'[22] On a planet mainly covered with water, we would all do well to think in these terms. In many other places, political identities have been bound up with a shared experience of living on either side of the Atlantic,[23] the Pacific or other stretches of the ocean. These deep connections with the sea are not quirks of history. Across the globe, millions of people continue to live by the sea, to work in fishing and allied industries and to derive a sense of community and solidarity from their connection to the ocean. For still others, the ocean in its permanence and repetition is a source of comfort in difficult times.

These examples reveal only some of the ways in which human well-being is intertwined with our engagement with the ocean. Though in some respects

1.1 A rower at sunset by Tahiti in the South Pacific.

our direct exposure to it is declining over time, this should not obscure the broader picture, in which our overall dependence on the ocean is steadily growing. The expansion of capitalism across the globe has intensified pressure on the land and its resources. As terrestrial minerals, energy sources and agricultural land come close to exhaustion, we look elsewhere for raw materials for a rapacious global economy. Increasingly, this means our gaze is turning to the sea. We are rapidly developing the technological capacity to exploit resources that had once been considered inaccessible – even down to the very seabed. The so-called 'Blue Economy' is expected to double in value – to over US$3 trillion – by the year 2030. If it does, it will have grown faster than the global economy as a whole.[24] But who will benefit from the new opportunities at sea?

AN OCEAN OF INEQUALITY

Although it is true that we are coming to rely more and more on the ocean for resources and energy, our engagement with it is highly uneven. Wealthy corporations working in fishing, fossil fuels and aggregates take the lion's share of its many treasures, while others are left poor and hungry. In many ways, this is no surprise. Back on dry land, after all, our societies are characterised by profound inequality. But there are signs that the ocean economy is becoming a site of especially stark gulfs between the haves and the have-nots, or between the top 10 per cent and the rest. Three factors help to account for the polarisation of the ocean economy.

The first is connected to geographical variations between states. The most cursory look at the atlas of the world reveals that some countries lack coastlines. 'Landlocked' countries struggle to access ocean resources, and must rely on neighbouring countries to gain access to the world's trading networks. In many cases, their neighbours will take advantage of this situation by charging 'transit fees' merely for allowing goods to be moved across their territory. Even among states that do border the sea, some enjoy greater advantages than others, because not all coastlines are equal. Some, for instance, are long and others short. Think of the narrow ribbon of Chile, running down the west coast of Latin America. Chile has 4,000 miles of coastline, whereas other Latin American countries (even if they have many more mouths to feed) must make do with less. China has a very large population, but a surprisingly modest coastline for its size. Aside from their length, the physical character of some coastlines offers better access to valuable resources. Each country sits on a continental crust. A portion of that crust – called the continental shelf – typically extends out to sea, sitting shallowly under the water, before dropping away into the deep ocean. If you could go shopping for a coastline, you would be well advised to pick one with a broader continental shelf attached. Many of the world's fish live in shallow waters, which trap more heat from the sun and are therefore more ecologically fertile. Having a shallow coastline also makes it easier, and hence cheaper, to access offshore minerals and fossil fuels. States with broad, shallow coastlines (which geographers call 'broad-margin states') include the United States, Canada, Australia, New Zealand and Brazil. By contrast, countries like Mexico, Iraq, Syria and Zaire are 'shelf-locked'. They sit on narrow continental shelves that drop away rapidly to the deep ocean. As a result, they will struggle to access fish and minerals.

Geography, of course, is not necessarily destiny. If we were prepared to be imaginative, rules could be put in place that gave landlocked countries access to the ocean and its resources.[25] But for the most part we have allowed access to ocean resources to track these brute geographical facts. It is international law, and not geography, which dictates that the resources off the coast of a particular state *belong* to that state. In 1994, a new Convention on the Law of the Sea came into force. As we will see in Chapter 3, it gave coastal states the right to 'Exclusive Economic Zones' (EEZs) extending for 200 nautical miles from the shore. Within those zones, resources are subject to the jurisdiction of the coastal state and nobody else. The convention has brought riches to some, while shutting landlocked countries out of the spoils of the sea.

These changes were accompanied by very little in the way of public debate. I was certainly unaware of the likely ramifications of the Convention on the Law of the Sea, and I was a student of politics when it came into force. I don't mean to imply that this was somehow a secret process: those who followed ocean law keenly would have been gripped by the debates leading up to the signing of the convention, intended to be a comprehensive 'Constitution for the Ocean' (in the words of Tommy Koh, the Singaporean diplomat and President of the Convention).[26] But the governance of the ocean has rarely figured prominently in current affairs, and has seldom found its way to the forefront of political debate. Most citizens, I would hazard to guess, could probably not recite the key rules of the oceanic legal order, or tell you what an Exclusive Economic Zone is. This is a great shame: these rules have had consequences for people's opportunities the world over, and decisions about how to govern the ocean are too momentous to be left to lawyers and political elites.

A key starting point is to recognise the impact that these rules have had. Outside of Europe, no landlocked country has ever become wealthy. They are far more likely to be mired in poverty. No fewer than nine of the world's twelve poorest countries are landlocked.[27] Most of them lie in Africa, where being landlocked – left dependent on others for access to world trade, and shut out of the fishing and offshore fossil fuel industries – has left an enduring legacy of

TABLE 1.1. SIZE OF EXCLUSIVE ECONOMIC ZONES, SELECTED COUNTRIES[29]

Country	Area in square kilometres
France	11,691,000
United States	11,351,000
Australia	8,505,348
Russia	7,566,673
United Kingdom	6,805,586
India	2,305,143
China	877,019
South Korea	473,280
Zambia	0
Ethiopia	0

(Figures based on Nolan, 'Imperial Archipelagos'.)

disadvantage.[28] Most of the biggest beneficiaries of the enclosure of the ocean, by contrast, have been large and prosperous economies: in that sense EEZs have heaped still more wealth on the already fortunate. The five largest EEZs in the world belong to the US, the UK, France, Russia and Australia. The 'Big Five' countries now command the resources of more than 45 million square kilometres of the ocean.

Russia's position in the Big Five is easy to explain: it has a huge coastline, though much of it is frozen. Why, though, might modestly sized countries like the United Kingdom or France command such enormous EEZs? The answer harks back to the colonial period, when major powers acquired (or conquered) 'possessions' in many far-flung places, from which they could exercise control over naval or trading routes.[30] Some of these possessions were almost forgotten – until the introduction of EEZs, when they brought about an unexpected resource bonanza. What might look like a tiny pinprick on the atlas of the world may now command an enormous swathe of marine territory for the home state or its dependencies. Take for instance St Helena, Ascension Island and Tristan da Cunha, each of which was acquired by Britain in the colonial era (though very few Britons will ever have had reason to visit them). Between them, they have a total land area of a mere 417 square kilometres – about the size of the city of Vienna. Their combined human population barely exceeds five thousand. But dotted through the ocean, they command more than *one and a half million* square kilometres of marine territory. Or consider the Pitcairn Islands group, a British Overseas Territory in the South Pacific with a population of fewer than seventy people. Its EEZ now ranges over 800,000 square kilometres, which makes it three times the size of Britain's total land area. Strikingly, this section of marine territory is comparable in size to the entire EEZ of China,[31] which must help feed a population approaching one and a half billion people. France, meanwhile, controls nearly seven million square kilometres of territory in the Pacific, which surrounds a variety of small islands.[32] In a world of EEZs, colonial adventure has come to deliver remarkable dividends for those who once ruled the waves. Many of the world's poorest countries, meanwhile, must make do with little or no marine territory at all.

A second reason why we reap such unequal rewards from the ocean economy lies with access to capital. The technology required to access the minerals of the deep seabed is only now being developed, and when it eventually emerges it is likely to require massive investment – of the sort that will be beyond many poor countries. Offshore petrochemical development is hugely expensive, and off the coasts of most countries in the global South it is outsourced to multinational corporations based in the global North (which are content to retain most of the proceeds). Fishing, you might suppose, should be a much cheaper industry to enter – and many poor people do rely on fishing as a source of both employment and sustenance. But even here, the emergence of 'factory ships', super-trawlers, GPS technology, sonar and many other advances has led to a global fishing industry dominated by a few superpowers. Foremost among them are the US, South Korea, China, Taiwan, Spain and France. Within those countries, there has been a trajectory of increasing market dominance by a small number of corporations, with almost half of revenues flowing to just ten companies, and relatively meagre benefits flowing down to local communities.[33]

One major problem – or advantage, if you are an investor – is that the technical capacity to harvest marine resources is developing much faster than the rules that regulate access to them. The exploitation of 'marine biological diversity' is a worrying example. Genetic material from the odder creatures of the ocean might well hold the key to new medical and scientific advances. Many of them are 'extremophiles', which have adapted to live under what to us would be intolerable conditions. Perhaps a cure for some deadly disease might lie in the resilient DNA of a deep-sea squid or mollusc. But who has a right to patent, and benefit from, the secrets of these creatures' genetic codes? When it comes to deep-sea organisms, there is a legal vacuum. A new framework regulating marine biodiversity in the deep sea is now being negotiated within the United Nations. But progress is slow, and it is not clear that the benefits will be fairly shared. In the meantime, the patenting of marine genetic sequences has already begun. A 2018 study found that 98 per cent of the sequences patented so far had been registered in just ten countries, while 165 countries had yet to patent a single one. Again, within these ten countries, we see a similar pattern of dominance by just a few keystone companies.[34]

The final factor that drives oceanic inequality is state capacity: the ability to make, and enforce, effective policies. There is a key difference between possessing an Exclusive Economic Zone in the eyes of the law, and being able to reap the proceeds in practice. Many countries in the global South are simply unable to enforce their legal rights over local marine resources. Around a fifth of all fish landed worldwide are caught illegally, by vessels which cynically exploit local countries' inability to patrol their coasts effectively. Off the coasts of Africa, the figure may be two-fifths.[35] Struggling with the aftermath of colonialism and facing a hostile global economy, governments in the region lack the resources to monitor and prosecute the culprits. Not only does this deprive local citizens of important opportunities and vital nutrition, it also means that effective conservation policies cannot be implemented. Many countries have established Marine Protected Areas – stretches of the ocean in which commercial activities are restricted in order to protect local ecosystems – within their EEZs. The introduction of these MPAs is likely to be key to the sustainability of many fish populations, and to ocean health more broadly. But effectively policing MPAs – which can cover many thousands of square kilometres – can be very difficult. In some cases, there has been no serious political will to do so, leaving many forced to operate as mere 'paper parks'.[36]

The ocean economy is not unique in displaying widespread inequality. Back on dry land, state capacity and access to technology, for example, can make an important difference to people's livelihoods. But these engines of inequality appear to run especially powerfully within the ocean economy. Mining for minerals, or drilling for oil and gas, is a much more complex proposition at sea, and to date this has meant that the rewards have accrued to a relatively small set of actors. Even a simple activity such as fishing is increasingly capital-intensive. Meanwhile individual seafarers, as we will see later in the book, can find it especially difficult to escape from patterns of exploitation and abuse. For this reason, the ocean is, in many ways, a driver of greater and greater inequality within the global economy, enhancing the benefits flowing to the top 10 per cent while leaving most others behind. This sets up an intriguing contrast. In its role in regulating our climate and weather, the ocean is a great equaliser, evening out extremes of temperature or climate that would otherwise make our planet much less hospitable. The ocean *economy*, on the other hand, is far from being a great equaliser. It appears to be driving ever greater inequality. How can we arrive at a fairer ocean economy that would offer more equal opportunities to people the world over? That question will occupy us throughout the rest of this book.

THE FRAGILE OCEAN

The ocean makes indispensable contributions to our living environment, stabilising temperatures, absorbing carbon, cycling oxygen and much else besides. But the ocean now faces serious environmental challenges, which threaten its ability to support life and flourish on our planet.

The most important of them is climate change. Anyone who has ever stepped into a greenhouse on a sunny day will have noticed how hot they can become. The sunlight entering it is no brighter or hotter than anywhere else in the garden. But the glass traps some of the sun's energy, preventing it from leaving again, and the greenhouse slowly warms. Pumped full of greenhouse gases (including carbon dioxide, methane and water vapour), our atmosphere is now acting in the same way, trapping more and more heat from the sun. But where does that energy go? Only around 7 per cent of it remains trapped within the air, the land and the ice caps that top and tail our planet. The vast majority, we now know, is captured by the ocean.[37]

If the ocean hadn't locked away all of this heat, life would already have become intolerable for many of us. But its protection has come at a heavy cost. As the ocean warms, it also inexorably expands. As the ice caps melt, huge quantities of additional water pour into the sea. Both processes point in the same direction: higher sea levels. For many people, this will turn the ocean from a source of life and livelihood into a major threat. Millions of people living in small island states and low-lying coastal areas will be highly vulnerable to rising tides. As we will see in chapter 8, small island states such as Kiribati and Tuvalu could be completely inundated. But the encroaching sea will also see salt leaching into the soil in many places, leaving farmland infertile. People in poor countries probably have the most to fear, since they can least afford to adapt to such dramatic changes. But even in wealthier countries, sea-level rise, along with more extreme weather patterns, will present a major problem.

Our carbon emissions are having a second dramatic impact on the ocean. When carbon dioxide dissolves in seawater, it forms carbonic acid. The ocean has already seen a 30 per cent increase in acidity since 1900.[38] Acidification has huge consequences for the many life forms to which it is home. Oysters, mussels, clams and squid have calcified shells or body parts. But acidification reduces the amount of calcium carbonate minerals in seawater, making it more difficult for these organisms to grow and repair. Some creatures that play keystone roles in the broader ocean ecosystem – including tiny swimming snails called pteropods – will eventually lose their shells and die as a result. Acidification is also causing the systematic erosion of coral reefs, destroying the symbiotic relationship between corals and the algae which give them their colour. The first global mass coral bleaching event occurred in 1998 and affected three-quarters of reefs worldwide. A second followed in 2002. A third, in 2016, affected more than three-fifths of the Great Barrier Reef. The future existence of the Reef, one of the world's greatest natural treasures, will be highly uncertain if our carbon emissions are not rapidly curbed.[39] The slow death of the world's reefs is a terrible tragedy in itself. But it will also have major knock-on effects for the ocean's life, a quarter of which depends upon the reefs' existence.

Pollution poses another massive challenge at sea. In 2010, the *Deepwater Horizon* disaster caused nearly five million barrels of crude oil to spew into the ocean.[40] Though this grabbed the world's attention, a similar amount of oil is spilt into the ocean every year.[41] We continue to treat the ocean as a sink for incredible quantities of waste. Some of the substances that find their way into the ocean – including detergents and pesticides – will be present for many decades, while radioactive isotopes and toxic metals can last for centuries and longer. Sometimes, the resulting problems are localised. When farmers allow nutrients to enter rivers, this can feed a massive growth of bacteria and other microbes around the coast. This can poison shellfish and other creatures, and trigger the emergence of toxic plankton capable of killing fish and marine mammals. We are already seeing the emergence of more and more 'dead zones' in the ocean, where there is not enough oxygen to support marine life.[42]

Other problems are global in scale. Plastic production began in earnest in the mid-twentieth century and has now reached truly epic proportions. Consumption of plastic products in North America now stands at 100 kilograms per person per year.[43] But a tenth of all plastic produced globally ends up in the ocean. Small plastic particles from many products are flushed down the drain and end up in the sea. Plastic bags and other 'disposable' products are thrown into rivers, or blow into them from landfill sites. But the biggest single contribution is made by the global fishing industry, which discards nets and other equipment on a mammoth scale. Either way, an estimated five *trillion* fragments of plastic are now afloat in the ocean.[44] Huge quantities have collected in massive eddies or 'gyres' in the South Pacific. An estimated nine-tenths of seabirds, and many fish, now have plastic in their guts.[45] When fish and birds' stomachs are full of plastic, they can no longer digest food, and slowly starve.

Overfishing is another major problem for the ocean's ecosystems. Fisheries experts have long known that the ocean contains too many boats, chasing too

1.2 A clean-up operation removes 103 tonnes of plastic and other debris from the Pacific.

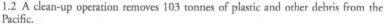

few fish. Nevertheless, many countries continue to invest in new boats, and provide them with subsidised fuel. Total catches from large marine ecosystems are, scientists estimate, double the level that would be sustainable.[46] The Food and Agriculture Organization of the United Nations has suggested that four-fifths of the world's fish populations can now withstand no increase in capture rates.[47] But fishing effort shows no sign of reducing. To the contrary, as our favourite fish become depleted, we are increasingly 'fishing down the food web', by harvesting the smaller organisms upon which larger species depend. This is having knock-on effects for other denizens of the ocean. Take, for instance, blue whales. These were once hunted almost to extinction. Though largely protected now, we are still ravenously outcompeting them for the food they require for survival. These incredible creatures – the largest animals ever to live on our planet – depend for their diet on tiny crustaceans called krill. But krill are being harvested on an industrial scale, and ground up for use in fish farms and as pet food; as a result, blue whale populations have been unable to recover. For every hundred blue whales that lived before the catastrophe of commercial whaling, only one roams the ocean today.[48] An ocean that once resounded with their calls has become a place of ghostly silence.

Finally, consider habitat loss. The ocean, needless to say, is not shrinking. Quite the opposite – it is growing as it warms, and reclaiming land in the process. But many coastal ecosystems are being degraded or destroyed as a result of our relentless drive to free up land for industry, agriculture and housing. The loss of mangrove forests in the tropics and subtropics is a dramatic example. These watery forests support hugely diverse populations of life, but between 1980 and 2000, 35 per cent of the world's mangroves were destroyed.[49] In the final two chapters, we will consider some ways in which this loss of marine habitats could be slowed or even reversed.

RISING TO THE CHALLENGE

It is abundantly clear that we depend upon the ocean in a whole variety of ways, for our lives and our livelihoods. While we may not think of the ocean every day, our reliance on it is only growing. That dependence is matched by the many other species that make the ocean their home, and which help to make our earth's ecosystems diverse and resilient. But the acceleration of our exploitation of the ocean forces us to confront two major challenges. The first is the accelerating degradation of the ocean environment. Left unchecked, this threatens to devastate many ocean ecosystems. Since we rely on the ocean in so many ways – as a source of nutrition, as a carbon sink, as a cycler of oxygen and weather patterns – it also threatens our own livelihoods. The second challenge is the profound inequality of the ocean economy. Our exploitation of the ocean has enriched some and threatens to impoverish others. Given that a growing global population will come to rely more and more on sustainable ocean industries, it is imperative that the ocean economy is a fair one, which brings opportunities to all rather than to the privileged few. In light of these twin challenges, it is hard to resist the conclusion that the ocean politics of the past must have somehow failed us. If so, this prompts several questions. How have we come to this point? What is it about our current modes of law and politics that have allowed such outcomes? And, just as importantly, can we do better? Are a resilient ocean and a just ocean economy within our reach? Showing how we have come to this crisis point, and how we might move beyond it, are the aims of the rest of this book.

2

FREEDOM AT SEA

What kind of ocean politics has brought us to our contemporary situation, in which the twin challenges of environmental destruction and spiralling inequality loom so large? This chapter will provide an important part of the answer to that question. For centuries, our oceanic politics was dominated by the ideal of the 'freedom of the sea'. This freedom guaranteed the right of all to sail the seas but also, just as significantly, to make use of the ocean's resources without constraint. I will show how the ideal of the free sea emerged, and what interests it served. But I will also show how that ideal left us ill-equipped to respond to the major challenges we now face in governing the ocean fairly and sustainably. I will begin by discussing some early attempts to exert control over the ocean, before showing how the pendulum eventually swung towards the idea of the 'free sea'.

THE STRUGGLE FOR CONTROL OVER THE OCEAN

Why would anyone try to control the ocean? One answer is that, for much of history, hardly anybody did. In places like the Indian Ocean, traders plied their trade for many centuries in conditions of relative peace.[1] Indian, Chinese and Islamic civilisations made no attempt to turn the ocean into their own fiefdoms.[2] Though disputes over fishing or mooring spots no doubt took place from time to time, by and large nobody seems to have sought to prevent anyone else from benefiting from the ocean or its many natural treasures.

But efforts to control the sea – or at least portions of it – did emerge in time. The first moves to assert control seem to have occurred, perhaps unsurprisingly, in places where communities were closely packed around relatively small expanses of water. Struggles for dominance broke out in the waters around the Pacific Islands, in the North Sea, and, especially, in the Mediterranean.[3] For the most part, the idea of political control over the ocean was a distinctively European one. In the Mediterranean, local naval powers realised they could use their military might to control, and therefore tax, the flow of commerce. Doing so would produce a valuable source of income. This is not to say, though, that the naval powers of the time believed they could *own* the sea. The ancient Greeks vied to control trading networks in the Mediterranean, but considered the ocean itself to be un-ownable. Later the emperors of Rome would come to consider the Mediterranean as lying within their proper 'sphere of influence'. But they did not claim the sea as Roman property. In the language of the day, Roman leaders argued that they were entitled to exercise *imperium*, or jurisdiction, over the Mediterranean: they claimed, that is, the right to make and enforce rules over how the sea was used. But they did not claim *dominium*, or ownership, over the sea. No one, in their view, could claim that.[4] Whatever else they disagreed about, the Greeks and the Romans shared the view that 'the sea and the sand beneath it belong to no one'.[5]

Claims to exert *imperium* over the sea were also a feature of the medieval period, although those claims tended to remain quite modest in scope. From the late thirteenth century onwards, the powerful city state of Venice asserted supremacy over the Adriatic, and charged a toll to any vessel that wanted to pass through it. Between the thirteenth and fifteenth centuries, kingdoms bordering the North Sea and the Baltic vied for regional control, and those struggles sometimes spiralled into open conflict.[6] Nobody appeared to claim control over the wider ocean, however – over what we would now call the Atlantic or Pacific, for example. It is hard, in fact, to see what purpose any claim along those lines would have served. The idea that anyone *could* control shipping or fishing on the wider ocean would have appeared fanciful.

That was not to change until the advent of colonialism. As European societies grew in military might, domination over new and distant spaces began to
appear attainable. In the 1490s, two momentous voyages were crucial in
stitching together what had previously been thought of as distinct oceans into
a single, interconnected whole. First, Christopher Columbus demonstrated to
his compatriots the existence of the Americas, or what he called an 'Indies' to
the West (though Italian, he sailed in service of the Spanish crown); then the
Portuguese navigator Vasco Da Gama showed that vessels could sail from the
Atlantic to the Indian Ocean by rounding the tip of Africa (perilous though
that journey was). By the end of the sixteenth century, European powers had
taken full advantage, unleashing bloody conquest on a number of far-flung
communities. Once colonial powers managed to wrest control over much of
Asia and the 'New World', power over the wider ocean came to be a much-
cherished prize. Whoever controlled the world's sea routes could determine the
future pattern of colonial conquest. Though maintaining naval supremacy
would be expensive, the riches to be gained from empire were enough to make
supremacy over the ocean an enticing prospect.

European colonial powers were, however, pitted against each other in their
pursuit of empire, and in a world of great power competition rival claims to
naval supremacy soon ran into one another. At times, naval powers took steps
to prevent rivalry spilling into open conflict. Perhaps the most famous attempt
to negotiate oceanic rivalries came with the Treaty of Tordesillas, signed by the
rulers of Spain and Portugal in the year 1494. According to the treaty, a notional
meridian would bisect the Atlantic from North to South. On the western side,
Spain would have the exclusive right to engage in colonial activity. On the
eastern side, Portugal would have free rein. This treaty has sometimes been
called a great division of the world ocean.[7] In reality, the idea that this treaty
achieved – or was even intended to achieve – a great division of the ocean itself
is probably misleading. For all their naval power, there was no way that Spain
and Portugal could actually exert effective control over the Atlantic. Instead,
the treaty seemed designed to ease potential conflict over *land* rather than ocean
spaces. On its own side of the great Atlantic meridian, Spain would have a

monopoly of missionary and colonial activity on whatever land it happened to encounter. On the other side, Portugal would have the same prerogative. But this was not quite the same thing as *imperium* over the wider Atlantic itself.[8]

But even if the Treaty of Tordesillas was not quite the great division of the ocean it is sometimes said to have been, there is no doubt that effective control of open waters did soon come to be crucial to rival colonial strategies. During the sixteenth century, the Portuguese Empire advanced into what we now call India, Sri Lanka and Indonesia, among other places. It would begin to charge fees to non-Portuguese vessels that plied trade routes between its new possessions, even if they had done so for hundreds of years.[9] Spain came to conquer Peru and Argentina, as well as several other places in the New World. But before long Spain and Portugal would have their upstart challengers. Throughout the sixteenth century, France, England and the United Dutch Republic (the forerunner of the modern-day Netherlands) would come to be engaged in a fierce struggle to insinuate themselves into trading relationships in the Indies – East and West – which until that point had been monopolised by the Iberian powers. It was in that context that the Dutch jurist Hugo Grotius came to publish his famous essay.

GROTIUS ON THE FREE SEA

History's most famous philosophical engagement with issues of oceanic governance was delivered in 1609, by the Dutch scholar Hugo Grotius (1583–1645). As a result, Grotius – or de Groot, as he was known to his compatriots – is often called the intellectual godfather of the Law of the Sea.[10] Grotius's intervention sparked what came to be called 'Battle of the Books'. This scholarly battle concerned the question of whether sea routes should be considered 'open' to the trading voyages mounted by *all* nations, or whether they could be 'closed' – that is, controlled by major naval powers such as Portugal and Spain. The larger question that loomed in the background was whether the apparently boundless sea could be *politically* bounded, or occupied, by particular communities.

A lawyer by trade, Grotius had been hired to provide legal advice to the Dutch East India Company, usually known as the VOC (Verenigde Oostindische Compagnie). The VOC was a burgeoning megacorporation with a close relationship with the fledgling Dutch state. In its drive to find profits overseas, the VOC had become locked into a struggle with the Portuguese in Asia. For years, Portugal had managed to blockade the VOC's efforts to join in the lucrative spice trade in places such as Java, Sumatra and the Moluccas. In an act of retaliation, in 1603 VOC ships captured the Portuguese vessel *Santa Catarina*, a ship that happened to be laden with a hugely valuable cargo of silk and musk. From the Portuguese point of view, this looked like a shocking act of piracy. From the Dutch side, it might – perhaps – be considered a just response to the VOC's exclusion from trade in the region. The full title of Grotius's essay – *The Freedom of the Seas, or the Right which belongs to the Dutch to take part in the East Indian trade* – made his own view abundantly clear. Grotius aimed to show, in this essay, that the capture of the *Santa Catarina* was a perfectly just response to Portuguese interference in the VOC's freedom to trade wherever it liked.

On his way to supporting that conclusion, Grotius was to make several new and controversial arguments. One was that acts of war could be a just response to restrictions on the freedom to trade. Another was that such acts could legitimately be carried out by private actors – such as companies, or the captains of ships – in parts of the world where their state's authority did not extend.[11] But most important for our purposes are the essay's wider claims about ownership and jurisdiction at sea. In Grotius's view, portions of the ocean could not be owned by particular merchant powers, or reserved for their exclusive navigation. To the contrary, the ocean should be considered open to all. A basic right to freedom of navigation explained why Portugal's actions were so objectionable. That freedom, after all, was a necessary foundation for the ability to trade effectively; and trade between peoples was a right – and perhaps even a duty. The diverse scattering of resources between continents, Grotius claimed, revealed God's plan for the emergence of commerce between peoples.[12] The industrious Dutch were second to none in heeding this summons to trade.[13] Portugal's actions, by contrast, were an indefensible interference with it.

2.1 A replica of a VOC cargo ship, at harbour in Amsterdam.

Grotius's argument that the sea could not be owned – which explicitly harked back to Greek and Roman arguments to the same effect – was enduringly influential. He presented two main arguments for his conclusion. The first was that the ocean could not be *occupied* and, without occupation, there could be no ownership. This was true of any place or thing we could name. When it came to objects such as stones or apples, it was straightforward to see what 'occupation' might mean: such things could simply be grasped or taken up by whoever wanted to use them. The identity of an object's owner would then hardly be in question. The same could be said of the fish and the wild beasts that inhabited the ocean: these could be turned into our private property by the simple act of capturing them. But claims over *immovable* objects would have to operate differently. Land, for instance, cannot be simply taken up or grasped. Since it cannot, we require some other way of making our possession clear to others. An obvious way of doing so would be to build walls or fences around stretches of land. No one could then plead ignorance when they trespassed upon your property.

The problem when it comes to the ocean, however, is that it cannot realistically be fenced off. No one can drive stakes into the sea; they would simply float away. Neither would a ship sailing across the water leave permanent tracks that might serve as legal boundary markings. For Grotius, this suggested that the wide ocean was *not* the kind of thing that could be occupied.[14] Fish or seashells could become our property; but the ocean itself could not. Instead, it should considered, as the Romans had once said, as the common preserve of all. Nothing humans had done to it thus far appeared to alter that basic moral situation.

A second argument against ownership of the ocean was that its uses – by which Grotius appeared to have in mind navigation as well as fishing – were 'inexhaustible' in nature. If one person removed a netful of fish from the ocean, or sailed across its surface, Grotius claimed, they did not detract from anyone else's ability to do the same. As a result, declarations of ownership of the sea itself would be simply pointless. What useful goal would be advanced by naming owners and non-owners at sea, if the sea could easily meet all of our needs without any resort to the language of ownership? Again, the ocean appeared different in this respect to the land, or even to rivers. Grotius declared that 'it is manifest that if many hunt on the land or fish in a river, the forest will soon be without game and the river without fishes'; but this, he claimed, 'is not so in the sea'.[15] There appeared to be no practical prospect of us ever exhausting the ocean's stores of fish or other resources. The same point applied to the ocean's surface as a plane of navigation: when a ship passed over a stretch of the ocean it did nothing to reduce the ability of later ships to make the same journey. On that basis too, claims to ownership would be at best an irrelevance. The ocean had been 'ordained by nature' so that, whoever happened to use it, it remained in 'the same condition' as it was when humankind first discovered it.[16] The fish of the ocean, and its navigable surface, were fundamentally limitless. As a result the sea should remain as it had always been: free to all.

SELDEN ON THE CLOSED SEA

Grotius's arguments were immediately, and enduringly, influential.[17] Notwithstanding the fact that other traditions – such as the Islamic Law of the Sea – had earlier arrived at strikingly similar conclusions (that all communities should be free to navigate and fish wherever they liked; that the territorialisation of the sea should be limited to narrow coastal waters), it is Grotius who is remembered as the godfather of the Law of the Sea.[18] The United Nations Convention on the Law of the Sea would, in 1982, enshrine a regime of several oceanic freedoms, including freedom of navigation, freedom of scientific research and freedom of fishing (albeit with some constraints on the latter). In fact, within international law the idea that our freedom to consume oceanic resources should be unlimited only really came to be challenged in the late twentieth century, as we will see in the next two chapters. For centuries, the rules governing the global ocean were described as Grotian in spirit.

Grotius's ideas did not, however, go unchallenged at the time. If Grotius had a chief foe in the 'Battle of the Books', it was the Englishman John Selden. In his essay *Mare Clausum*, or 'The Closed Sea' (written in 1619 but eventually published in 1635), Selden defended the right to 'close' off portions of the ocean. The view of England's rulers on whether the oceans should remain 'open' or 'closed' had actually wavered during the late sixteenth and seventeenth centuries, according to the current monarch's conception of the country's self-interest.[19] In 1580 Elizabeth I had declared, in rather Grotian language, that 'the use of the sea and air is common to all; neither can any title to the ocean belong to any people or private man, forasmuch as neither nature nor regard of the public use permitted any possession thereof.'[20] That notion suited England's role at the time as an emerging naval and mercantile power seeking to insert itself into lucrative trading routes. But as its naval capacity grew – and as fishing conflicts in the Channel and the North Sea intensified – its rulers' perspective changed. The desire to exert control over Dutch trade and fishing in those stretches of water became paramount. Selden would provide the justification.

Selden's essay suggested that the English monarch of the time was not only the rightful governor of the island of Great Britain, but also the 'Lord of the sea flowing about' its shores, as an 'inseparable and perpetual appendant of the British Empire'.[21] Far from ownership of the sea being a nonsensical idea, Selden claimed that both history and scripture provided abundant examples of dominion over the ocean. What, though, might justify that dominion? Selden agreed with Grotius that the ocean was *originally* owned in common. But while Grotius had been sceptical that portions of the sea could practically be carved up into the dominion of particular states, Selden maintained that modern navigational instruments made this an entirely practical possibility. Lines of latitude and longitude, and the location of islands, would easily suffice, Selden claimed, for the drawing of effective marine boundaries. Although we might not be able to fence off the ocean, we could at least *know* when we had passed from one community's marine territory to another's. Selden's riposte to Grotius's suggestion that the ocean must always remain in a state of common access was, therefore, that nothing 'can be said or imagined more absurd'.[22] If so, then Grotius's first argument against the occupation of the ocean fell. If marine boundaries could be precisely measured, states *could* hope to control navigation, and also restrict fishing within their exclusive marine territories.

Consider next Grotius's second argument for the freedom of the seas. This argument declared that the resources of the sea were inexhaustible. Selden pointed out, however, that this did not appear to be true. At least *some* of the benefits the ocean provided did appear to diminish in value or abundance when others came to consume them. We often see, he noted, 'that the sea itself, by reason of other men's Fishing, Navigation, and Commerce, becomes the

2.2 A map showing the waters off Western Europe, from Selden's *Mare Clausum.*

worse for him that owns it. . . . So that less profit ariseth, than might otherwise be received thereby.' Giving the example of pearl fishing, Selden noted 'that the abundance either of pearls themselves, or of those shell-fishes, which produce them, may through a promiscuous and common use of the Sea, be diminished in any Sea whatsoever. Where then is that inexhaustible abundance of Commodities in the Sea, which cannot be impaired?'[23] Selden, as it happens, was not alone in making this argument. Others had already pointed out that Grotius's assumption that fish stocks were inexhaustible flew in the face of the contemporary evidence from the North Sea and the Channel.[24]

Taken together, these two arguments suggested, for Selden, that there was nothing at all spurious about England's claims to both jurisdiction and ownership over its immediate coastal waters, and indeed over those surrounding its colonial possessions in North America too.[25] Claims of ownership of oceanic territory were both *feasible* (since they could be demarcated) and *worthwhile* (since the benefits the sea provided us with did diminish when others joined in with their consumption). If Selden was right, the Grotian argument for oceanic freedom appeared to fail.

FREEDOM VERSUS CLOSURE?

One of the most striking things about the Battle of the Books was that Grotius emerged victorious despite the fact that his arguments were so flawed. Selden was surely right that there was nothing especially difficult about setting marine boundaries (though policing them might be challenging). Vessels' ability to chart their positions at sea has only improved since. He was also right that many of the ocean's resources were distinctly limited in supply. This too has become still more obvious in the centuries since the Battle of the Books raged. But while Grotius's arguments for oceanic freedom were surprisingly weak, it is he who is remembered as the godfather of the Law of the Sea. For better or worse, the idea of the freedom of the sea would be the dominant force within ocean politics for centuries to come.

But another striking thing about the argument was that the protagonists appeared to be talking past one another. Received wisdom tells us that there was a great chasm between the perspectives of Grotius and Selden, and between freedom and enclosure at sea.[26] But in many ways this is a misleading verdict. From the point of view of oceanic power politics, there was no deep and permanent division between those who defended the freedom of the sea and those who defended closure. Far from it, the positions of major naval powers turned out to be highly flexible as the balance of power ebbed and flowed. In the years following the publication of *The Free Sea*, the VOC would come to achieve domination in the East Indies. When it did, it would go on to ruthlessly exclude competitors from ports, establish local monopolies in the spice trade and adopt a licensing system for trade which closely paralleled the

Portuguese practices they had been so keen to overthrow.[27] The upstart raging against Portuguese control over the sea would soon replace it as regional bully. The VOC's monopoly over the spice trade would be a powerful spur to the Dutch economic 'miracle', and would soon cement its role as the undoubted leader in world trade.[28]

When the VOC began to exclude other vessels from 'its' marine territory, Grotius is not known to have objected. In fact, by 1613 Grotius was being employed as a negotiator to press the exclusion of English ships from 'Dutch' fishing grounds.[29] So much, it seemed, for the free sea. England also wavered between justifying and rejecting the enclosure of the ocean, depending on its interests at the time. A few decades later, the philosopher John Locke would claim that the ocean could not be owned, and for a time this, instead of Selden's argument for enclosure, appeared to become the official view.[30] Prevailing interests, and the ideals which sought to justify them, were prone to shift with the tide.

Even at the philosophical level, the opposition between Grotius and Selden could easily be overdrawn. Selden's claim in *Mare Clausum* was, after all, that there was a *part* of the sea which could rightly be ruled over by England. He did not appear to be claiming that England – or anyone else – could own the open ocean (or what came to be called the 'High Seas') more broadly.[31] Neither did he object to the principle of innocent passage for which Grotius had argued.[32] For his part, Grotius did not actually reject, in *The Free Sea*, any and all claims to rule over the sea. He appeared to have had no objection, for instance, to the dominion which had been exercised in the Mediterranean by the Venetians. To the contrary, Grotius appeared to believe that merely occupying the waters off a country's coast would be enough to generate an exclusive claim over them, although that claim would lapse if the waters in question ceased to be used.[33] His reticence about grander oceanic claims was in large part grounded on a practical worry about whether they could be marked out and defended. It is not clear that he believed they could never be justified if and when these practical barriers receded. In his later work *De Jure Belli Ac Pacis*, Grotius continued to hold that 'the sea, either in its whole or in its principal divisions, cannot become subject to private ownership'. But he declared that some *parts* of the ocean *were* enclosable, much as rivers were.[34]

Whether Grotius and Selden were really defending incompatible conclusions appears far from certain, then. As ocean politics evolved, it became commonplace to embrace a compromise between *both* coastal jurisdiction *and* 'High-Seas' freedom, and in that sense both Grotius and Selden appear to have been victors.

This compromise between freedom and enclosure came to attract many other illustrious adherents. Later in the seventeenth century, the German philosopher Samuel von Pufendorf also dismissed Grotius's claim that because the sea was not susceptible to demarcation, it could not be occupied and hence possessed.[35] Grotius's first argument, he claimed, added nothing to the case for freedom at sea. If there was a proper objection to dominion over the seas it would have to be based upon the second argument – that the ocean and its resources were inexhaustible. But even on this score Grotius was only partly right. Pufendorf claimed that the resources of the open ocean were, as Grotius had suggested, inexhaustible; and this, in his view, undermined any argument for ownership far out to sea. The same went for the ocean's role as a surface for navigation. But the same did *not* hold for the resources contained in or under coastal waters – such as pearls, amber and coral – which were often in distinctly limited supply.[36] This suggested that there *was* a point to claims made over coastal waters – but not beyond. In the eighteenth century, the Swiss international lawyer Emmerich de Vattel would agree that the use of the High Seas for navigation and fishing was inexhaustible, and that, as a result, 'no Nation has the right to take possession of the high seas, or claim the sole right to use them, to the exclusion of others'.[37] But like Pufendorf and Selden, he argued the same could not be said of coastal resources, which were capable of depletion. Rights over coastal seas could be justified, to the contrary, insofar as control could be effectively maintained.[38] Within the Islamic tradition, too, there was widespread agreement about the freedom to fish and to navigate, while control by coastal communities was held to be limited to narrow territorial waters.[39]

What is striking about these philosophical arguments, then, is just how much consensus they actually displayed. There was certainly some dispute about just which of the ocean's resources should be considered exhaustible. There was also some disagreement about whether the ocean could be effectively occupied, and if so which parts. But there was widespread and enduring agreement on the key claim that coastal seas could legitimately be occupied, whereas the High Seas could not. A clear method of drawing the lines between the two would, of course, have to be supplied. The best-known solution to that puzzle was advanced by the Dutchman Cornelius van Bynkershoek in 1702. Van Bynkershoek gave the rather brutal answer that effective occupation at sea terminated at the maximum range of a cannon-shot. Given continual improvements in ballistic technology, this was actually a rather moveable feast. But by the middle of the eighteenth century it was widely taken to imply that states could claim 'territorial waters' 3 nautical miles wide.[40] The view that states were entitled to rule over these territorial seas, but that a regime of freedom should apply beyond those limits, came to characterise international law until well into the twentieth century.

FROM PLENTY TO PRECARITY

How should we reflect today on these historical arguments? Though they originated in an arcane debate about whether the VOC was within its rights to capture a Portuguese ship, the ideas tossed around during the Battle of the Books resonated for centuries within international law. In particular, the idea of the freedom of the seas would eventually be elaborated and expanded into a broad set of oceanic freedoms. The 1982 United Nations Convention on the Law of the Sea would delineate four of them: freedom of navigation, freedom of fishing, freedom of overflight and the freedom to lay underwater cables. The first two ideas have an obvious heritage in Grotius's work. The latter two would not, of course, have occurred to him. But they appear to be rather straightforward developments of the basic idea that anyone should be free to make use of the ocean's spaces as well as its resources.

How compelling, though, is the argument for such freedoms? The case for freedom of navigation has never been seriously challenged, not least since the dominant naval power of the day has always seen it as being indispensable to its interests. If a country like the United States is going to act as a global hegemon, it will need to be able to sail wherever it likes, including through narrow straits running close to the coasts of other countries. Warships continue to possess a legal right to 'innocent passage' even through the narrow territorial seas of their enemies.

The freedom to exploit oceanic resources, however, is – or ought to be – much more controversial. In our current oceanic predicament of deep inequality and the increasingly unsustainable exploitation of marine resources, the Grotian ideal of unrestrained resource consumption looks like being part of the problem rather than part of the solution. The idea that marine resources could rapidly become depleted seemed to play no role in his discussion of ocean justice. For Grotius, the ocean appeared to be primarily a two-dimensional surface across which naval powers could seek out profit and, potentially, project their military might. The key question was who, if anyone, would get to control that surface. Grotius appeared much less interested in questions about custodianship over the resources to be found within the three-dimensional volume of the ocean. Even Grotius's critics appeared to share his view that the fruits of the ocean were for the most part limitless. Although they pointed out that *coastal* resources could be put under pressure, these scholars assumed that the wider ocean was such a reliable provider of resources that its bounty could be taken for granted indefinitely. Neither Grotius nor Selden, Pufendorf nor Vattel ever suggested that the living resources of the wider ocean were capable of exhaustion. The idea that the wider ocean is in fact home to complex and interdependent ecosystems with many points of vulnerability, and that life in the High Seas can be just as precarious as its coastal counterpart, did not occur to them. During the seventeenth century, questions about the conservation or sustainable management of the ocean were to that extent out of sight, and out of mind.

Within its historical context, the depiction of the wider ocean as a dependable and robust provider of resources may have been understandable. During the seventeenth century a million Dutch people – a fifth of the entire population –

were employed in the vast North Sea herring fishery. Single boats captured hundreds of thousands of fish in a single haul, and regularly turned back only when they ran out of the salt needed to preserve them.[41] Shoals of herring may well have appeared simply limitless (some etymologists believe that the name of the fish actually derives from the German word for 'army', though we cannot be sure). During the 1620s – while the Battle of the Books was raging – propagandists for colonial efforts in the New World were sending back enthusiastic reports suggesting that the sheer volume of cod on the Grand Banks exceeded anything that Europeans had yet seen.[42] The bounty of the North Sea promised to be a mere shadow of that to be found further afield.

The large-scale collapse of fish populations (or, as fisheries economists call them, 'stocks') was still some centuries in the future. Under pressure from overfishing, North Sea herring stocks collapsed precipitously in the 1950s, and again in the 1970s and 1990s. Herring populations are today a mere fraction of what they were in the seventeenth century. The decline of huge fish populations off the eastern coast of North America was even more dramatic. By the twentieth century, overfishing had produced catastrophic falls in the number of Atlantic cod on the Grand Banks, with the population declining to a hundredth of its level before fishing began.[43]

This story of collapse and virtual extinction is also familiar from the brutal trade in marine mammals. Whaling and sealing were lucrative businesses in the seventeenth century, and Basque whalers in this period already found themselves having to travel further and further from shore in order to catch their prey. But the unconstrained freedom to 'harvest' on the ocean had not yet led to the widespread global collapse of whale and seal populations. By the middle of the eighteenth century, however, whalers were experiencing increasing difficulty in locating their quarry in the Atlantic, and instead turned their attention to the much more hazardous Arctic and Antarctic regions. By the mid-twentieth century, the use of faster boats and exploding harpoons had driven many whale species close to extinction, with 1.6 million whales killed in the Antarctic region alone during the twentieth century.[44] Populations of these remarkable, intelligent and long-living animals have still not returned to their former levels. The seal trade – spurred by the demand for fur – was equally cataclysmic. The population of fur seals on South Georgia Island in the Southern Atlantic is the greatest concentration of marine mammals anywhere in the world, but during the late eighteenth century, 1.2 million seals were killed there for their pelts.[45] The advent of steamships in the nineteenth century would facilitate killings in the hundreds of thousands every year, and would drive many populations close to extinction.

During the twentieth century, early portents of collapse began to inspire moves to constrain the whaling, sealing and fishing industries (largely, it should be said, out of concern for the future profits of those industries and the livelihoods of those employed in them). The North Pacific Fur Seal Convention of 1911 – signed by Britain, the United States, Japan and Russia – outlawed open-water seal hunting in the region, and was the first international environmental treaty in history.[46] Moves to protect many fish stocks from complete exhaustion have more recently spurred the establishment of numerous Regional Fisheries Management Organisations on the High Seas, though they have often had only marginal success in conserving fish stocks.[47] In the cases of fishing, sealing and whaling, moves to restrict capture encountered resistance from many in those industries who claimed that they represented an intolerable infringement of their freedom to exploit marine resources.

BEYOND GROTIUS

Insofar as he discussed marine life at all, Grotius's focus was on who ought to be able to exploit it. He appeared to place no moral weight on the interests of the creatures that live in the ocean, and his theory did not take on board the possibility of ecosystem collapse. Indeed, Grotius believed that a 'primitive' right, based on our entitlement to secure our own physical self-preservation, meant that humans' ability to make use of the 'fruits' of the sea should not be limited. In *The Free Sea*, the only constraint Grotius proved willing to impose upon fishing activities was the requirement that fishers should not prevent *other people* from fishing too. To seek to control others' fishing would, he

44

claimed, be an exercise in objectionable greed, depriving others of resources that they too had a right to make use of.[48] Pufendorf, for his part, agreed that there ought to be limits on the carving up of oceanic territory. 'Greedy' seizures of territory out at sea, he suggested, might even constitute proper cause for war on the part of those who were excluded from the ability to make use of the ocean.[49] But like Grotius, Pufendorf did not appear to demand any constraint on the appropriation of marine resources. To the contrary, one reason excessive seizures of marine territory were objectionable was precisely that they stood in the way of unconstrained resource exploitation.

Defenders of Grotius have suggested that we *can* find some basis for constraints on our use of ocean resources elsewhere in his work. In his essay *De Jure Praedae*, Grotius suggested that we each possess the right to consume the fruits of the commons 'up to the limit of our needs'.[50] This has sometimes been interpreted to mean that *beyond* the satisfaction of our needs, we no longer possess such a right.[51] But it is not at all clear that this was Grotius's view. Elsewhere in this essay Grotius appeared ready to extend our primitive right to use the fruits of the commons to cases where that use served not just our needs, but our 'well-being' or 'comfort' more generally.[52] As such this apparently Grotian constraint on the exploitation of the ocean, if it exists at all, remains at best vaguely defined.[53]

Given our current predicament – that we live in a world characterised by rampant inequality and imminent ecosystem collapse – more demanding rules for oceanic exploitation are imperative. In working up more demanding rules, we might still begin with ideas found in Grotius's work. If, as Grotius thought, we all have a right to self-preservation, then for me to use up so many of the ocean's resources that you can no longer survive looks like an obvious act of injustice. We might even say that acting in such a way is simply incompatible with seeing the ocean as a 'commons' available to all. On the back of such a thought, we could work up a kind of basic needs principle. According to such a principle, each of us should stop consuming at or before the point where the ocean can no longer support *everyone's* basic needs.

A principle along those lines would be a good start. If we all have the right to lead decent lives, free from evils such as extreme poverty, then some kinds of ocean exploitation already push too far. Industrial fishing activities, for example, currently threaten both the employment opportunities and the basic nutrition of people in coastal communities throughout the global South. For the wealthy to outcompete the less advantaged, leaving them unable to feed themselves, looks like a clear enough instance of oceanic injustice. A principle guaranteeing that exploitation of the ocean will not prevent us meeting our basic needs would rule out such practices. It would be an important constraint on the idea of free exploitation of the ocean's resources.

But a principle along those lines would not be enough. We should be concerned about more than people's ability to meet their basic needs. We could imagine a world in which everyone had enough to meet their basic needs, but some people were able to become very well off simply because they possessed the technology to gather up the rest of the ocean's resources. The less well off, meanwhile, would hover just above a basic minimum. That world would not be a fair one, because justice is also concerned with how our opportunities *compare* to those of others. The ideal of equality cautions us that a world where a privileged few came to be rich while everyone else was consigned to a basic standard of living would not be a fair one.

A basic needs principle, then, is important, but not sufficient on its own to make the ocean economy a just one. Consider what it would mean for the many pools of resources that are not currently necessary for anyone's basic needs. Nobody currently relies on the extraction of seabed minerals for the protection of their basic needs. If or when the mining of the deep seabed finally comes to pass, it would likely be carried out by wealthy countries or corporations, rather than poor ones. Should they be able to retain all of the proceeds, simply because they managed to get there first? Consider also the fish of the High Seas, hundreds of miles out to sea. Nobody currently relies on these fish for their basic needs either. Fishing on the High Seas is expensive – it takes a lot of fuel and equipment even to get there – and for that reason High Seas fishing is usually highly subsidised, and is overwhelmingly the preserve of high- and middle-income countries.[54] Less well-off communities tend to feed themselves close to the shore, with much more modest technology. If all we cared about was the protection of basic needs, there would be nothing wrong with this scenario. The poor could continue to feed themselves close to the shore, and the rich could scoop up the riches in or under the High Seas, becoming still more wealthy in the process.

There is something deeply troubling about that scenario, however. The ocean economy should not be the place where the dream of greater equality goes to die. It should not be a frontier economy where the lion's share of the spoils go to the top 10 per cent, to the corporations that already possess capital and complex technology. That would make a mockery of the idea that the ocean is in some sense a part of our *common* heritage. In Chapter 4, I will show how leaders from the global South began, in the second half of the twentieth century, to argue that the benefits from exploiting the resources of the wider ocean should be used to narrow global inequalities, rather than widening them.

It is clear, though, that we can find no basis for such ideas in the work of scholars like Grotius. Nowhere in Grotius's work is the unequal *ability* to exploit marine resources recognised as an important issue from the point of view of justice. In one sense this is understandable: the debate in which Grotius was participating was one between European communities, each of which possessed comparable levels of technological capability (to fish and to navigate). In such a context, the inability of some communities to make equal use of the fruits of the ocean did not seem to arise as a moral problem. But problem it is. If the ocean is to be a space of equality rather than inequality, the actual capacity of different communities to take part in, and benefit from, the sustainable exploitation of marine resources must be a central issue. Will the exploitation of the ocean's resources become an engine for catch-up development, rather than a new gold rush which will widen global inequalities still further? In posing that question, we move decisively beyond the terms of the Grotian debate on the freedom of the sea.

The idea that freedom at sea licenses the largely unrestricted appropriation of resources still characterises the fishing regime of the High Seas. Pending a new United Nations agreement on biodiversity in the areas beyond national jurisdiction, it is also the 'rule' in place for genetic resources in the High Seas. But why should we accept this rule of first come, first served? We have seen that those who defended the unrestrained freedom to exploit assumed quite wrongly that the ocean was a limitless treasure trove of resources. Far from it, the ocean's ecosystems are often fragile, its resources limited, and the need for environmental protection will often require us to leave those resources where they are. It is dangerous to hold on to philosophies grounded on the false assumption of plenty. They will not provide us with adequate principles for governing resources which have in fact turned out to be far more precarious. Grotius's suggestion that nothing we have done to the ocean has altered its plenty – that our actions to date have left the sea 'not at all impaired'[55] – is a perilous anachronism.

But where should we look for guiding principles if the ocean is in fact characterised by fragility and precarity? I will argue that our predicament requires us to investigate the possibility of shared international governance, peaceable cooperation, robust environmental protection and the global sharing of both the benefits and the burdens flowing from sustainable ocean industries. But before getting to that point, we must address some fundamental changes to the Law of the Sea which served to bring much greater portions of the ocean under the control of individual states. If Grotius 'won' the debate during the seventeenth century, Selden – with his argument for enclosure and state control – has made a great resurgence in recent decades.

3

ENCLOSING THE OCEAN

For the three centuries following the publication of Grotius's *The Free Sea*, leading maritime powers ensured that the ideal of navigational freedom reigned supreme. Britain – which eventually became the world's naval superpower – held firm to that principle throughout the nineteenth century. By the middle of the twentieth century, the United States had become the world's dominant naval force. It would adhere just as determinedly to the ideal of the freedom of the sea. The smooth operation of capitalism, as well as the projection of military power, would demand that the ocean – and especially key strategic straits – remained open rather than closed (even if local conflicts would occasionally break out). The same was true for the resource politics of the ocean. Beyond each state's narrow territorial seas – reaching 3 miles out from the shore – fish or whales could, for the most part, be caught by whoever had the inclination, and the equipment, to do so.

The second half of the twentieth century, however, brought new challenges and new opportunities. The major powers (which now included the Soviet Union) would continue to insist on navigational freedom. But oceanic politics would come to be marked by increasingly intense struggles to control natural resources. It was by now obvious that many species were coming under serious pressure from industrial fishing, and in response states sought to exert control over (what they called) 'fish stocks' further and further from the shore. Meanwhile new extractive technologies opened up the prospect of a resource bonanza on the

49

seabed. The first offshore oil installations went into production in the 1930s, and by the end of the Second World War their output had soared.[1] Aware that there might be still greater mineral wealth on the sea floor, countries made claims over greater and greater portions of the ocean and the seabed below it.

In the decades after the war, states therefore began to seek clear legal rules determining which oceanic resources belonged to whom. After a somewhat tortuous series of international conferences, a new United Nations Convention on the Law of the Sea (UNCLOS) was completed in 1982. When it finally came into force in 1994, it was said to represent a veritable 'Constitution for the Ocean'. It certainly brought about a fundamental realignment of ocean politics. The convention would see resource sovereignty being extended farther and farther out to sea, in a rapid extension of state territory which was unparalleled in history. Each extension represented a significant defeat for the ideal of free access. If the period between the seventeenth and early twentieth centuries is often presented as Grotian, our own ocean politics is decidedly more Seldenian – or perhaps we should say hyper-Seldenian, because it is not obvious that Selden himself ever imagined states would come to be sovereign over such enormous swathes of the ocean and seabed. Although Grotius is still spoken of fondly as the father of the Law of the Sea, the Canadian representative at the final phase of negotiations for the new convention quipped, revealingly, that the delegates had come to bury Grotius, not to praise him.[2]

Our historical memory can be very short, and ocean politics is often far from the forefront of public debate. As a result, many readers may not realise just how far sovereignty over the ocean now extends, and just how recent a phenomenon states' oceanic sovereignty is. We should begin with a brief overview of this enclosure, which has seen the resources of two-fifths of the ocean being converted into the preserve of states.

SELDEN'S RETURN

The enclosure of the ocean proceeded in a series of momentous steps. The first came with the widening of 'territorial seas'. Following the lead of Cornelius van Bynkershoek, states had eventually settled on the view that their territorial seas would range for 3 nautical miles, measured from the low-water mark. The new convention, however, extended the reach of territorial seas to 12 miles. States enjoy sovereignty over these stretches of water, along with the seabed below them and the airspace above them. Foreign vessels still possess a right of 'innocent passage', meaning they can enter a state's territorial seas so long as they do not fish there, and so long as they do not threaten the state's military security. Otherwise the territorial sea is a part of the state like any other, and domestic laws are assumed to apply there unless the state says otherwise.[3]

A second and far more important act of enclosure was the creation of 'Exclusive Economic Zones' (or EEZs) extending 200 nautical miles out from the shore. Their role is quite specific. A coastal state does not have general legal authority over people sailing within its EEZ, and cannot determine who can enter it (that would interfere with the right of innocent passage).[4] But the coastal state does have authority over natural resources. A state with an EEZ possesses the legal right to harvest all living and non-living resources found within it, and to retain the proceeds.[5] UNCLOS does not explicitly declare that states *own* these resources, but they can certainly exercise rights typical of ownership. They can consume or conserve their EEZ's resources, if they choose; they can exclude others from access to these resources, or allow them access; and if they do allow outsiders to access their EEZ's resources, they can charge them for the privilege.

In allowing for the declaration of EEZs, UNCLOS followed in the trail of earlier, rather more unilateral moves by some states. As early as 1945, the Truman administration had issued a Proclamation declaring its right to govern fish stocks off the US coast. In 1976, it passed the Magnuson-Stevens Fishery Conservation and Management Act, which attempted to extend US sovereignty over fish stocks up to 200 nautical miles away. A number of countries in the global South, and especially in Latin America, were soon to make similar moves;[6] by 1994, when UNCLOS eventually came into legal force, over a hundred EEZs had been proclaimed. The declaration of these EEZs has been called, with some justification, 'the largest enclosures in human history'.[7] The

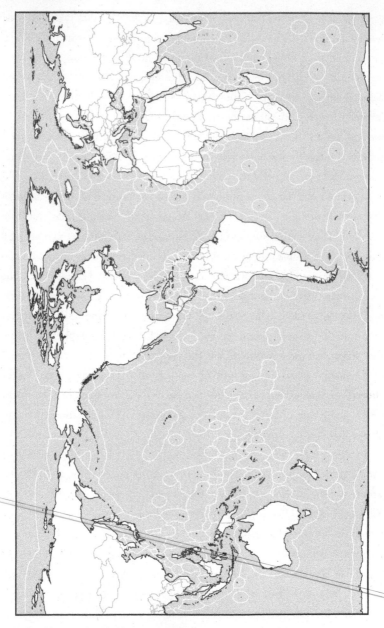

3.1 World map of Exclusive Economic Zones.

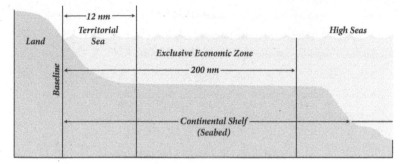

3.2 Key legal zones in the ocean.

consequences have certainly been momentous. Resource rights within almost two-fifths of the world's ocean space – containing close to nine-tenths of the world's fish catch[8] – have become the preserve of individual states.

But UNCLOS was not finished yet. EEZs only apply to the resources contained within the water of the ocean. In a third act of enclosure, UNCLOS granted states jurisdiction over all non-living resources on or under the sea floor, as well as the 'sedentary' living resources to be found there. (This move also followed in the path of more unilateral declarations of intent made by some states. The 1945 Truman Proclamation on Coastal Fisheries was accompanied by a twin Proclamation insisting that the 'continental shelf' abutting the United States was 'subject to its jurisdiction and control'.) Up to 200 miles from shore, UNCLOS gives states the right to determine whether seabed resources are exploited, and to retain the proceeds if they are. In that sense, the 'continental shelf regime' complements the EEZ, with one reserving resource rights over the seabed and the other the water column itself.

But the two regimes are not identical, because continental shelves can range even further than EEZs. States gain resource rights up to 200 nautical miles automatically, but UNCLOS allows them to claim 'extended continental shelves' which can range far beyond. 'Extended' shelves can range up to 350 nautical miles from the coast, *or* for 100 nautical miles beyond the point where the continental shelf drops to 2,500 metres below the ocean surface. In practice, this means that some extended shelf claims range for considerably more than 350 miles. Russia has famously staked claims to an extended continental shelf reaching all the way to the North Pole; but it is not alone in its territorial ambitions. The states ranged around the Arctic have now made claims over the vast majority of the Arctic region, which mainly consists of relatively shallow continental shelf.[9]

JUSTIFYING OCEANIC ENCLOSURE?

The enclosure of the ocean has had a profound impact upon people's opportunities the world over, not least since some countries have coastlines and some do not. As a result, the enclosure of large swathes of the ocean requires some kind of moral justification. That justification cannot simply declare that control over the ocean is useful to coastal states. It has to provide everyone with reasons why a regime of coastal state control is desirable. Contemporary philosophers have had relatively little to say about this issue, apart from noting that the enclosure of the ocean looks like being very difficult to justify.[10] In this section I will sketch some arguments we *could* turn to in order to justify enclosure, and see how far they might take us.

Effective Occupation

Perhaps the simple fact that a state is 'occupying' a piece of marine territory means we should respect its claim to rule over it. The idea of occupation, though, can be interpreted in different ways. On one interpretation, 'occupation' means something like control: when we can impose our own rules over a place, we occupy it. The idea that rights over the ocean could be grounded on occupation-as-control played a significant role in the seventeenth-century Battle of the Books. Selden's position in *Mare Clausum* was that parts of the ocean could be turned into a state's territory, and that all a state needed to do in order to achieve this was to exercise enduring control.[11] His opponent Grotius *also* appeared to believe that countries could gain rights over coastal waters through this kind of occupation.[12] The argument between Selden and

Grotius was not about whether effective occupation was possible, but about how far into the ocean it could realistically stretch. Perhaps states are now capable of exercising effective occupation over much greater stretches of the ocean than either Grotius or Selden imagined.

The idea that occupation-as-control can justify territorial holdings has been highly influential within both philosophy and the law, and served as a prominent justification of colonialism.[13] But it is an argument that should be consigned to history. One reason is that it is circular, or very close to it: it tells us that the reason I should be allowed to control a given bit of territory is simply because I *do* control it. That takes us dangerously close to the idea that might makes right. In contrast to Selden and Grotius, we no longer tend to think – or no longer *ought* to think – that mere control is enough to ground rights over territory. Especially in a world of ecological limits, we should be seeking an argument as to why communities *should* be governing particular spaces and resources, rather than taking their control to be self-justifying.

But there are other ways in which we can occupy territory, which might be more significant from a moral point of view. In her discussion of territorial rights, the philosopher Anna Stilz notes that as individuals we all need to live somewhere on the earth. And once we come to inhabit one place rather than another – once we are occupying it – we may have a powerful (if not always decisive) claim not to be removed from it. When we occupy a place, we put down roots, build connections and make plans that depend on our ability to remain there.[14] *That* kind of occupation – in which the shape of our lives is comprehensively bound up with being in a place – should count for something.

I agree that this kind of occupation can be important. Imagine there was some global authority that issued people with rights to live upon the earth. We would want such an authority to pay attention to where people already *are*, rather than shuffling them around randomly. Perhaps there is, as Stilz suggests, a right to continue to live where you have already made plans and built up connections. All I want to note is that, if we attempted to use the argument to justify resource rights at sea (which is not Stilz's aim), we would immediately run into serious problems. The most obvious is that we simply do not occupy the ocean in the same way that we occupy the land. If the ocean is 'occupied' by anyone, it is by the other species that make the ocean their home, and as a result it is plausible that ocean-dwelling creatures do have rights of occupancy. By contrast, very few humans ever spend sustained periods of time at sea. Even those who do tend not to be 'fixed' to particular parts of the ocean in the way that people inhabit particular tracts of land. Humans do not, by and large, build fixed settlements at sea (not, at least, outside of the territorial seas of any particular country). The same is obviously true of the seabed. Although science fiction writers and military planners have conjured up visions of people living happily on the sea floor, they have not yet come to pass.[15] Technological advances in seabed mining have certainly increased the attractiveness of sovereignty over the seabed many miles from shore. But while we remain for the most part land-dwelling creatures, it is not obvious that we can be said to 'occupy' the ocean or the seabed in Stilz's sense.

Even if we did, we would face a second major problem. The right to *be* at sea, even to live one's life at sea, is not what is at stake in the debate about EEZs and continental shelves. Anyone can live at sea, whether an EEZ exists or not, and whether a state possesses rights over the continental shelf or not. We do not need enclosure to protect that right. EEZs and continental shelves are not *about* the right to live in a particular place. They provide a state with rights over the natural resources of the ocean, not the right to determine who can visit it or even live there. EEZs and continental shelves allow local states to exclude outsiders from exploiting the natural resources within those areas, and to retain the profits if they decide to exploit them. We need a more closely tailored argument to support that conclusion, and the reference to occupation does not fit the bill.

Geographical Contiguity

In Article 77(3) on the continental shelf, UNCLOS actually declares that coastal states' rights 'do not depend on occupation, effective or notional'. To the extent that it reaches out for a justification for enclosure at all, UNCLOS draws on an equally problematic idea – that of 'geographical contiguity'. It is because the continental shelf is a *natural extension* of the land on which a community lives that such a community can come to exercise rights over it. The International Court of Justice has since reaffirmed that a state's rights over the continental shelf exist 'by virtue of its sovereignty over the land' adjacent to it.[16]

This claim is surprising, because international lawyers had long expressed scorn for the idea that mere contiguity was capable of grounding rights to territory. In 1928, a famous tribunal judgement had even declared that 'contiguity, understood as a basis of territorial sovereignty, has no foundation in international law'.[17] One worry was that the idea of contiguity promised to open up many disputes over borders, both at sea and on dry land. If a state could annex a portion of the ocean because it was 'contiguous' with its territory, then why not part of a neighbouring state? This is far from being an idle question, since contiguity has been 'one of the banners under which nationalist expansion has frequently sought to justify itself'.[18] A second worry was that the idea of contiguity is 'wholly lacking in precision' and likely to 'lead to arbitrary results'.[19] If states can claim territory 'contiguous' with their own, how will we know where to draw the line? Might the whole of the ocean be annexed by whichever states are closest?

UNCLOS seemed to give a reassuringly scientific response to this worry, by describing the continental shelf as a 'natural extension' of the continental crust that a country sits on. But the connection between *scientific* definitions of the continental shelf and the *legal* one to be found in UNCLOS is surprisingly loose. On average, the geological continental crust extends for no more than 50 nautical miles before dropping away into the deep sea. But UNCLOS is unconcerned with that fact. It declares that states have a right to a 200-nautical mile 'continental shelf', whether the continental crust actually extends far out to sea or not. Some states are therefore granted, by UNCLOS, legal rights over long stretches of the deep seabed, which cannot in any meaningful sense be called a 'natural extension' of the land. As a result, as Surabhi Ranganathan has argued, the 'continental shelf' under international law looks like a legal fiction designed to facilitate territorial claims regardless of the physical features of the surrounding ocean.[20]

Improvement

One potential justification of states' claims over territory points to the fact that communities often 'improve' land or resources. This idea, it should be noted, also has a troubling historical association with colonialism. Colonisers often claimed that the land they were seizing from 'natives' was not *really* occupied, because locals had done nothing to improve it. Colonisers, by contrast, would clear forests, drain swamps and convert 'wilderness' into productive territory. We should certainly resist the idea that there can be no rights to territory *unless* the land is transformed in such a way; in an age of environmental crisis, we will often do much better to leave the wilderness intact. Nevertheless, the general idea that improvement has *some* moral weight is very widespread. Imagine that I 'improve' a stretch of wild land, converting it into productive farmland. If someone else then comes along and starts planting their own crops on it, I might well object that since *I* had already improved that land, I have the right to decide what happens to it, or to reap the benefits it now provides.

Whatever we think of that general argument, it seems highly unlikely that we could use it to justify claims over oceanic territory. There is no doubt that individual resources can be taken from the sea and then improved. When people do that, they presumably generate some kind of claim over them. But why would we think that the *ocean itself* could be improved? As Grotius pointed out, the ocean, unlike the land, 'needs no cultivation to bear fruit'.[21] Ploughing or fertilising the land might increase its bounty. But activities such as mining or fishing do nothing to increase the bountifulness of the sea. (This is not to say that the argument has not been pressed: during the nineteenth century, defenders of deep-sea fishing sometimes argued that dredging the seabed was just as vital as ploughing the soil, because it would enhance its fertility. But those defenders were wrong: on the whole, activities such as dredging or bottom trawling are highly destructive of marine environments.[22])

On this point, John Locke – the philosopher most commonly associated with the idea that improvement is the foundation of ownership – was in perfect agreement with Grotius. His account of land ownership has sometimes been called an 'agricultural' one, since it emphasises the way in which the farmer (in his view) greatly magnifies the value of the land by means of improvements such as draining, ploughing and fertilising. For Locke, there were two kinds of reason why we might want to grant people ownership over tracts of land. First, if people labour over specific plots – if they 'mix' their labour with them, in Locke's intriguing phrase – it would seem wrong to allow others to then make use of them. Second, allowing people to become the owners of specific plots can be economically useful, because private ownership encourages care and investment. But Locke was clear that the ocean was not susceptible to this kind of improvement, and as a result the argument leading from improvement to ownership was of no use there. Instead the ocean should be seen, as Locke put it in chapter V of his *Second Treatise of Government*, as a 'great and still remaining Common of Mankind'.[23]

Attachment

Another argument for rights over territory builds on what we can call 'attachment'. Sometimes places or resources mean a great deal to people. They can even be said to build their lives around them, in some cases. For the coast-dweller, the ability to visit the shore might be a major source of fulfilment and well-being, without which their life would be robbed of meaning. Likewise, the ability to catch fish might be crucial to the very identity of a fisherman or fisherwoman. Treating people with due respect can mean recognising that they are wedded to various projects, plans and places.

It is undoubtedly the case that many people are attached to particular stretches of the ocean. This is a fact that any account of oceanic justice must take proper account of. Our question, though, is whether patterns of attachment are capable of justifying the acts of enclosure endorsed by UNCLOS. There are several reasons for doubting that they are. First, acts of enclosure do not simply advance the interests of those who are attached to the ocean or its resources; in some cases, they threaten those interests. In the years leading up to UNCLOS, the United States had suggested that states which were unable to fully harvest the sustainable catch within their EEZs should allow 'States that have normally fished for a resource' in that zone to carry on instead. But that proposal failed.[24] In declaring an EEZ, a coastal state gains the right to exclude or include fishers according to their whim. In discussions about the relationship between Britain and Europe post-Brexit, leaders from France and Spain argued that their fishers should be allowed to continue fishing in places they have fished for generations. Britain pointed out that this is not what possessing an EEZ means. It is key to the concept of an *exclusive* economic zone that countries are not required to pay attention to facts about past usage or attachment. In practice, states with newly declared EEZs have often excluded fishers from areas they had fished for generations.[25]

Second, whereas attachment often matters, it is not obvious that giving states resource sovereignty is the right response. In many cases, what will matter to people is simply the ability to continue to visit particular places in the ocean. That ability is already protected by the right to innocent passage. In other cases, what will matter to people is the ability to harvest natural resources in a sustainable way. Think, for instance, of the millions of small-scale or 'artisanal' fishers who are engaged in subsistence fishing worldwide. Those fishers largely operate relatively close to shore, and as such the establishment of EEZs means little to them. The real threat they face is that of being outcompeted by technologically advanced industrial fishing fleets. If we care about the interests of artisanal fishers, we might want to exclude or limit the activities of industrial fishers. But it would be a mistake to assume that giving each coastal state an EEZ is the only way to achieve that end. The philosopher Margaret Moore has also noted the close relationship that some coastal communities have developed with local fisheries. Even if this relationship is worthy of respect, she notes, it could surely be protected at an international level by some suitable global agency.[26]

Finally, if we care about attachments, then we ought to care about sustainability. If fishing destroys a given fish population, then so much the worse for those attached to fishing as a pursuit.[27] But it is far from obvious that those who care about sustainability should endorse a world of Exclusive Economic Zones. In fact, I will argue in the next section that the record of EEZs has been mixed at best, and often very poor, when it comes to advancing sustainability.

In short, although attachment to the ocean will often be normatively significant, it is far from obvious why the right response to it is to endorse the territorialisation of the ocean.

Subsistence Needs

We should consider one final argument for giving coastal states sovereignty over EEZs and the continental shelf. It might be that coast-dwellers need a degree of resource sovereignty in order to protect their most basic interests, including their interests in nutrition and secure employment. The Truman Proclamation on Coastal Fisheries gestured towards some such idea, observing that 'fishery resources have a special importance to coastal communities as a source of livelihood'.[28] It *is* vital that people are not prevented from using the ocean's natural resources when doing so is key to meeting their basic rights. But taking people's basic rights seriously is likely to justify at best rather limited claims to oceanic resources. It is hard to see how access to the resources of the seabed, for instance, is vital to meeting anyone's basic interests. Seabed minerals are typically very expensive to access, and as a result their extraction is overwhelmingly the preserve of the wealthy. If anything, the expansion of sovereignty over the seabed is now *jeopardising* people's basic rights the world over, given that it has extended the global supply of fossil fuels still further beyond safe limits.

The argument from subsistence interests looks much more plausible when applied to resources which are key to people's basic nutrition. Many people depend on salt harvested from the sea, or saltwater which they then desalinate. Millions of people worldwide are highly dependent on fish for their nutrition, and possess few alternative sources of vital micronutrients. That may mean they have a continued right to fish, at least as long as alternative sources of basic nutrition are not available. But it is not obvious that the best response is to grant sovereignty over fish to local states. For one thing, *any* authority governing the ocean could reserve fishing permits for small-scale, sustainable fishing operations. For another thing, subsistence fishing typically operates over a very limited geographical range. It is usually confined to territorial waters (within which a boat can go out to sea, and return, within a single day), with fishing in the EEZ beyond for the most part remaining the preserve of industrial fishing operations. Even if an argument could be made for reserving fishing rights within territorial waters for subsistence fishers, it is not likely to justify exclusive rights over resources 200 nautical miles from the shore.

Though some of the justifications discussed above have merit, none of them are capable of defending the momentous acts of enclosure ushered in by UNCLOS. If we care about attachment and about subsistence rights, then we have good reason to protect the right of coast-dwellers to make sustainable use of coastal resources. But it is not obvious that these require sovereignty over marine territory, and even if they do, it seems likely that granting coastal states sovereignty over 12-mile territorial seas would be enough. Most subsistence fishing, and most traditional maritime pursuits, take place in those relatively narrow strips of water. But it is hard to see what due care for attachment and for subsistence interests can add to the defence of EEZs and continental shelves. We are left with the uncomfortable possibility that the most extensive single acts of enclosure our world has ever seen have occurred without any good defence at all.

GOOD GOVERNANCE OF THE OCEAN AND ITS RESOURCES

The arguments I have considered so far concentrate on the relationship between coastal states and the sea. But perhaps that is the wrong place to look. Perhaps the real reason we should embrace state sovereignty over EEZs and the continental shelf is that this sovereignty has desirable *effects*. Perhaps enclosure is vital in securing just, effective or sustainable governance of the ocean. An argument roughly along those lines is suggested by the Truman Proclamation on the Continental Shelf. It declares that 'recognized jurisdiction over these resources is required in the interest of their conservation and prudent utilization'.[29] We can also find this type of argument in the work of philosophers like Locke. Locke's view was that allowing individuals to become owners of the land will incentivise them to become good stewards. Perhaps we can say something similar about state control over the ocean. Locke was not sure that people do anything to improve the ocean. But perhaps making coastal states owners of the ocean or the seabed encourages them to make efficient and sustainable use of them? Alternatively, could it be that extending state sovereignty over the ocean will serve to achieve greater equality?

Sustainability

One of the most familiar arguments for the enclosure of land is based on the importance of avoiding what is called the 'tragedy of the commons'. Imagine a stretch of common pasture on which individual farmers are allowed to graze their livestock. If any farmer can graze as many animals as they like, we might expect this pasture to become exhausted over time. This is because individual farmers reap the immediate *benefits* of grazing, and so will be tempted to put more and more animals out to pasture. If this leads to the collapse of the pasture, the eventual *costs* of over-grazing will be shared by everyone. But knowing that only makes things worse. If every farmer knows that one day the pasture will be exhausted, they may *increase* his grazing before that happens. In a famous 1968 article, the ecologist Garrett Hardin therefore claimed that 'Freedom in a commons brings ruin to all.'[30] The only way to prevent such a tragedy, Hardin argued, was to introduce some kind of enclosure in which individual farmers come to own particular tracts of what had once been the commons. Individual owners would then reap the benefits *and the costs* of their own decisions, rather than being left at the mercy of other people's actions. They would have ample incentive to use their own land wisely, because their own livelihoods would depend on it.

Hardin's argument sounds perfectly plausible, and as an argument for enclosure it has been enormously influential. But it misrepresents the actual history of the commons. In fact, commons – including common pastureland – have often been governed in highly sustainable, and equitable, ways. Practices of common management *did* limit what each individual could do, and succeeded for generations in preventing the commons from being exhausted. In medieval and early modern England (one of Hardin's key examples) the real tragedy for individual 'commoners' was enclosure itself, which saw them being evicted from the land by wealthy landowners.[31] Why then did Hardin make such a major mistake? Because he seemed to believe that the fact that a place *was* a 'commons' – a place, that is, from which people could not practically be excluded – meant there must be a complete absence of effective rules constraining their consumption. But that is far from being true. A few miles away from where I write, the New Forest is a commons, on which long-standing rules ensure that commoners have the right to graze *limited* numbers of livestock (including the famous New Forest ponies) anywhere they choose. Nearly a thousand years have passed under this system, and the New Forest continues to be one of the most diverse ecosystems in the United Kingdom, and a haven for many endangered species. In fact we have abundant examples of common resources and places being cooperatively, equitably and sustainably managed without recourse to enclosure.[32] As a result, our choice does not have to be one between perfect freedom on the one hand and enclosure on the other. As we will see in the next chapter, varieties of inclusive and collective co-management also deserve our attention.

The flaws of Hardin's argument have not prevented the notion of a tragedy of the commons from being deeply influential in practice, though (and neither have his dubious views on race and population control).[33] What is less well known is that the arguments Hardin sketched had already been presented in much greater detail in the case of fisheries. In 1954, the economist H. Scott Gordon had argued that overexploitation was inevitable in fisheries, so long as fish were treated as an 'open-access' resource. The problem in such a scenario was that 'the fish in the sea are valueless to the fisherman, because there is no assurance that they will be there for him tomorrow if they are left behind today'.[34] The fisher's incentive therefore is to harvest as many fish as possible, before others can. This, Gordon argued, has two entirely predictable consequences. First, fish 'stocks' will eventually be depleted or destroyed. Second, the fishing industry will become highly inefficient, as more and more boats enter the industry in order to catch fish while stocks survive. The 'overcapitalisation' of the fishing industry will then cause its profitability to fall.

Like Hardin, Gordon believed that the solution to these problems lay with the creation of property rights over fish stocks. If fishers came to *own* the right to fish particular stocks – or at least to fish in particular times and places – they would have an incentive to go about their business in an efficient and sustainable way. This is the rationale behind the widespread use of Individual Transferable Quotas, under which individual fishers or fishing companies are given (and can later sell) the right to fish certain quantities of fish at specified times. The proper objective of fisheries management – which was not the maximisation of fish catch, but the maximisation of *profit* from fishing – would be secured by an enclosure along these lines.

As a diagnosis of the fate of the fishing industry, Scott's narrative contains a good deal of truth. Worldwide, many fishing industries are busily destroying their own futures in much the same way he suggested they would. The important question for our purposes, however, is whether the enclosure of the ocean represents the only, or the best, remedy. Strikingly, Scott's argument did not make any reference to the enclosure of the ocean by *states*. His claim was that the activities of individual fishers should be rationed. Fishing effort should be licensed by a public authority capable of making impartial decisions about the maximum sustainable catch. Fish could either become private *or* public property, he claimed, so long as catches were set by a 'unified directing power'.[35] In the same way, the Truman Proclamations of 1945 suggested that some form of 'recognized jurisdiction' over oceanic resources was necessary if they were to be used sustainably and efficiently. But the claim that a stable form of jurisdiction is necessary somewhere does not establish that it should be exercised by individual states over their neighbouring waters. We can imagine alternatives, in which an international organisation allocated fishing rights on a global basis, for instance. A successful argument for state enclosure would need to establish that state-by-state governance of fish stocks was the optimal, or at least the only feasible, solution.

In any case, if the proof of the pudding is in the eating, the history of EEZs has been a rather sour one. Far from reducing the over-exploitation of fish populations, their introduction coincided with a major intensification of fishing activity. Global fishing effort grew *ninefold* between 1970 and 2008.[36] As a result, the proportion of fish populations considered over-exploited increased from 10 per cent to 32 per cent (with a further 53 per cent of populations considered fully exploited).[37] The result, remarkable as it sounds, is that despite a massive increase in fishing effort, overall catches have gradually declined.[38] Enormous sums of money, and ever-improved technology, are being pushed into an industry which is chasing fewer and fewer fish, and gradually destroying its own future.

It might be true, of course, that fishing effort would have intensified even without the introduction of EEZs. But there are reasons to believe that the introduction of EEZs played a key role in stimulating increasing fishing effort. For years, 'Distant Water Fleets' from countries like the United States and Spain had fished off the coasts of West Africa and Latin America. When countries there declared EEZs and shut them out, these fleets did not cut back their fishing effort. Instead, fishing corporations lobbied successfully for a massive expansion of fishing subsidies so that they could continue their operations elsewhere. In practice, this meant more and more fishing on the High Seas, and more and more intensive fishing within the EEZs of countries that did continue to accommodate them. But High Seas fishing is basically unprofitable. Too many vessels expend too much fuel to get to the High Seas, and when they get there, they chase too few fish.[39] Half of all High Seas fishing revenue is now earned by four countries which highly subsidise their fleets: the US, Japan, South Korea and Taiwan,[40] with the bulk of these revenues flowing to relatively few corporations.[41] Without the subsidies they continue to attract, fishing on the High Seas would make no economic sense at all. Why voters would willingly pay so much money to sustain these destructive activities – especially when most subsidies are reaped by a few wealthy companies, which employ fewer and fewer people – is a curious political question to say the least.

In principle, individual states could act differently. They could reduce or remove subsidies, especially on the High Seas, impose stricter limits on fishing within their own EEZs, and reduce destructive practices such as bottom trawling, the use of drift nets or the throwing of 'bycatch' dead into the water. But it is not clear that individual states have the solutions at their fingertips, because a world of Exclusive Economic Zones exhibits major systemic problems. First of all, many states simply lack the capacity to enforce regulations on fishing, or to drive out illegal, unreported and unregulated (IUU) fishing. This has been a particular problem off the west coast of Africa, where foreign vessels have exploited the weakness or fragmentation of governance in the region. IUU fishing there is the worst in the world,[42] and it is not obvious that states *can* enforce serious restrictions on fishing.

Second, there is a poor 'fit' between EEZs and individual fish 'stocks'. Environmental policy-makers have often defended what they call the 'matching principle'. This suggests that decision-making about resources should correspond with the boundaries of resource pools or ecosystems.[43] Decisions about a river should be made by people who live in the river's catchment, and decisions about a forest should be made by people who live in or near that forest. Who, then, should make decisions about particular fish stocks? Presumably people in whose waters those fish live. But fish are mobile (although some species move far more than others). They pay no attention to the legal-political boundaries of individual EEZs. They regularly migrate across the borders of different EEZs. In such cases, it is not obvious that effective decisions about conservation can be made by one state alone. The United Nations has addressed this problem to a degree. The 1995 Fish Stocks Agreement aimed to define the duties of states in governing so-called 'straddling stocks', which span more than one EEZ. But it is an opt-in agreement, and although it does have a dispute-settlement process, its decisions are not compulsory. As a result, if states choose not to cooperate with one another in managing fish stocks, they cannot be forced to do so.

UNCLOS actually gives rather conflicting guidance to coastal states in any case. Article 61 of UNCLOS declares that states have a duty to avoid the over-exploitation of living resources within their EEZs, and makes clear that they should put in place effective conservation policies. But it also declares that it is up to individual states to determine the 'total allowable catch'. The duty to conserve fish stocks therefore remains highly discretionary in nature.[44] UNCLOS's conservation provisions are very general in tone, to the extent that it is not obvious when a state can be said to have violated them. No mechanisms exist for compulsory international arbitration or adjudication in cases where states appear not to have fulfilled their conservation obligations. At the same time, other elements of UNCLOS suggest that its practical focus falls not so much upon conserving fish stocks anyway, so much as ensuring that they are fully exploited. Article 62 declares that 'The coastal State shall promote the objective of optimum utilization of the living resources in the exclusive economic zone.' In cases where the coastal state cannot consume fish up to the maximum sustainable yield, it should 'give other States access to the surplus' instead.

So far in this section we have concentrated on fish stocks, where enclosure has often failed to secure sustainability. There are other cases besides in which enclosure appears to have made environmental protection a more distant possibility. One thing that enclosure has brought to coastal states is control over huge new supplies of fossil fuels. In the first decade of this century, almost seven out of ten major discoveries of oil and gas happened offshore.[45] Humanity has a collective interest in ensuring that the majority of the world's fossil fuels remain where they are, buried in the ground and under the seabed. While we used to worry that the oil would one day run out, we must now worry that there is too much of it to safely use, and too many countries capable of extracting it. Aware that at some point our economies will have to radically decarbonise, many states are racing to extract and sell what they can before that happens. As I write, only one country is bucking that trend: the Danish government has just voted not to explore for any more oil and gas supplies in the North Sea (though it will continue to exploit existing wells).[46] In a rapidly warming world, we must hope that other countries place offshore fossil fuels beyond use. But the Law of the Sea leaves that choice to each nation-state, and too often the result has been a game of 'after you, sir'. Since it is a choice for each state, it can be hard for governments to explain to their voters why their country is going to take the lead when others are dragging their feet. Sustainability in a time of climate emergency demands that these resources are not exploited, and it is hard to resist the conclusion that climate stability will ultimately require limits on states' resource sovereignty in the ocean.

Equality

The introduction of EEZs does not appear to have advanced the goal of sustainability. But perhaps it has advanced the goal of promoting greater equality. In the 1960s and '70s, many countries newly emerged from colonialism faced what they saw as a form of neocolonial behaviour at sea. By 1970, wealthy states representing one-third of the world's population were landing three-fifths of the world's fish catch.[47] Distant Water Fleets from countries including Britain, Germany and the Soviet Union increasingly targeted fish stocks in the southern hemisphere, right up to the shores of poor countries in the global South. Their right to do so was protected by the principle of the freedom of the sea. But the leaders of many newly independent countries were no longer prepared to see the fish off their coasts as part of an open commons available for all the world to fish. Latin American states with rich fishing grounds were at the forefront of the movement towards enclosure, though they eventually succeeded in bringing other countries in the South along with them. This suggests another possible defence of enclosure, then. Perhaps extending resource sovereignty to local states is necessary in order to prevent the spoils of fishing being monopolised by a privileged few. Although they would provide no consolation for poor states without coastlines, EEZs might at least ensure that poor coastal states could enjoy a fairer share of the global fish catch.

In practice, the introduction of EEZs has not pushed us in the direction of greater equality. One reason is already familiar from Chapter 1. The world's largest EEZs have been claimed by the UK, the US, France and Australia, because they happen to possess many overseas dependencies (alongside Russia, which simply has an enormous coastline). European societies used their dominance over the ocean to conquer many small islands, and colonial adventure has now reaped a quite unforeseen dividend in the form of control over lucrative fishing grounds.

For countries in the global South, the consequences of the introduction of EEZs were decidedly mixed. The total catch of countries in the South did increase somewhat after the introduction of EEZs. The gains, however, overwhelmingly accrued to ten such countries which, by 1990, accounted for 83 per cent of developing-country catch.[48] The majority of southern countries did not have the capacity to scale up their own fishing operations. For the most part, these countries instead signed access agreements with Distant Water Fishing Nations (as Article 62 of UNCLOS suggested they should), which would see distant water nations paying a fee in return for the right to fish. These agreements were often signed, however, on hugely unfavourable terms. Distant Water Fishing Nations played individual coastal states off against each other in their effort to secure the cheapest access possible. In many cases they successfully leveraged their political and economic power, including by tying foreign aid to fisheries access.[49] On average, distant water nations pay poor countries no more than 5 per cent of the value of the fish they catch. More than nine-tenths of the profits of the fishing industry are associated with processes higher up the supply chain (including canning, smoking and packing) which typically take place elsewhere,[50] with the profits mainly flowing to large corporations rather than local communities.

The most notorious example of inegalitarian resource politics has occurred in West Africa. This region contains one of the most fertile (or, as fisheries economists put it, 'productive') marine ecosystems in the world.[51] But local states lack the capacity to exploit these fish populations fully. Instead, they have typically signed access agreements with wealthier countries. The money received has often been vital in order to service international loans. But access agreements have sometimes been exceptionally permissive. They tend not to directly limit the quantity of fish which can be caught, but instead regulate the size of fishing vessels that can be used in local waters. In return for a single access payment, fleets from the European Union, for instance, have been able to land essentially unlimited quantities of fish.[52]

These agreements with distant water nations have been described as a form of 'ocean grabbing'.[53] This metaphor may be overdone, because the EEZ itself remains the sovereign territory of the local state. But the result is that fish populations have been left severely depleted,[54] and local people outcompeted in the search for fish, or for employment in fishing. The combined effect of subsidised EU fishing off the coast of West Africa has been 'to destroy any possibility of the African fishing community competing effectively – or at all – in international markets'.[55] At the same time, coastal communities have lost access to a vital source of nutrition, a problem compounded by rampant illegal fishing in the area.[56]

Within countries, meanwhile, enclosure has not led to greater equality. In wealthy Western countries, the most common approach to fisheries management has been a neoliberal one. The right to draw on particular fish 'stocks' has been converted into a tradeable resource, to be bought and sold on the open market. 'Tradeable quotas' for fishing were initially given away to existing users (a curious decision, if these fish purportedly belong to the community as a whole). Over time, these quotas have been bought and sold, and have ultimately been concentrated in fewer and fewer hands (with fishing corporations known in some places as the new 'Lords of the Sea'). Many countries romanticise their fishing industries, which might explain why they continue to attract such enormous subsidies despite the destructive effects of industrial fishing. They have certainly become highly profitable in many places, though whether they can continue to be is very uncertain. But the case for tradeable quotas appears to place total profits above all other potential priorities. Oligarchic fishing industries have progressively squeezed small-scale and indigenous fishers from the seas,[57] reduced overall employment, undermined economic independence and the sense of personal achievement that comes with it, and left many coastal communities as economic husks. Small-scale fishing has been seen as economically inefficient, despite the crucial role it can play in sustaining livelihoods and identities. If fishing can be a crucial economic and nutritional safety net in many disadvantaged communities, then it is not obvious why the neoliberal concentration of economic power represents progress at all.[58]

It is worth considering, finally, the position of landlocked states. Articles 69 and 70 of UNCLOS stipulate that, where a surplus of fish stocks exists which the local state does not have the capacity to exploit, landlocked and geographically disadvantaged states should be allowed access instead. In principle, this provision should ensure that the benefits flowing from EEZs are shared more equitably. But the effects of this provision are rather regressive in nature. It is states that cannot fish to full capacity – perhaps because they lack the equipment – which are required to share stocks with geographically disadvantaged societies, rather than states with high capacity. Although Article 71 of UNCLOS clarifies that states which are 'overwhelmingly dependent' on fish stocks are not required to share those stocks with geographically disadvantaged states, it remains the case that states with greater capacity will not be asked to make any sacrifices, whereas (some) states with diminished capacity will. In any case, these provisions are highly discretionary in practice.[59] In a study of one hundred bilateral treaties granting outside states access to EEZs, *none* of them were found to involve geographically disadvantaged or landlocked states. The latter have too little to offer, and have simply been left out of the hunt for the spoils of the sea.[60] While UNCLOS envisions 'geographically disadvantaged communities' being given the freedom to fish in other states' EEZs, no provision is made for states which lack the finances or technology to make use of that freedom. It is unsurprising, then, that no landlocked country has ever developed a significant fishing industry.

MOVING FORWARD

In one sense, the enclosure of the oceans might look like progress – if the only alternative is the untrammelled freedom of the sea. There is a kind of formal equality at the heart of Exclusive Economic Zones and the continental shelf regime. Instead of a free for all on the wider ocean, each state (or, at least, every coastal state) is given authority over its own pool of marine resources. Rather than rich states scooping up all the ocean's resources, even poor states have the chance to join in the oceanic bonanza. But this formal equality has not translated into anything like equal outcomes. The gains to countries in the global South have been very mixed, but in most cases distinctly limited. In many cases they have simply sold access to wealthy countries at knock-down rates, which have then passed fishing rights on free of charge to corporations (and subsidised their fuel to boot). Geographically disadvantaged states, meanwhile, do not possess even formal equality under the system of enclosure.

We can tell a similar story about sustainability. In one sense, making each state responsible for conserving local marine resources is better than a free-for-all in which no one has such a responsibility. But this general responsibility has not been matched by firm legal duties, and many states lack either the capacity or the inclination to conserve coastal ecosystems. Many wealthy states – and some in the global South – continue to subsidise destructive fishing practices, even if this means paying for fleets to access other countries' EEZs or travel to the High Seas. EEZs have failed, meanwhile, to arrest the rapid depletion of fish populations. The territorialisation of coastal waters has not altered the basic structure of a global fishing industry in which, despite the reliance of many people in the global South on fish for basic nutrients, fish as a commodity overwhelmingly flows from South to North.[61]

But perhaps another way is possible. Perhaps freedom at sea or the enclosure of the ocean are not our only options. In the next chapter, we will return to the original debates leading up to the Convention on the Law of the Sea, in order to identify the emergence of an egalitarian alternative to both freedom and enclosure, which its advocates believed could deliver ocean justice for all.

4

REMAKING THE WORLD ORDER AT SEA

Reading the seventeenth-century Battle of the Books could leave us with the impression that the choice we face is one between freedom and enclosure. Should the sea remain open to all, so that anyone can harvest its resources without limits? Or can much of the ocean or the seabed be converted into state territory, with individual countries monopolising its resource wealth? What is troubling about this choice is that neither freedom *nor* enclosure appear to be attractive models. On the High Seas, the exercise of freedom has produced a fishing industry which is both highly unequal and completely unsustainable. But the model of state enclosure also appears badly suited to resolving large-scale environmental problems, since these problems do not neatly coincide with each country's marine territory. It has, meanwhile, brought riches to some but not to others.

Fortunately, freedom and enclosure are not our only options. In the last chapter we noted the waves of enclosure heralded by the 1982 Convention on the Law of the Sea. While enclosure was the most important result of that convention, buried in this long legal document, and barely noticed by most of us, was another, rather different, thread. It represents a radical alternative to both freedom *and* enclosure. This alternative thread depicted an 'internation-alised' future for the ocean – or at least part of it – which would see it being governed collectively, in the interests of all of humankind. In this vision, the exploitation of the ocean's resources would have to serve *everyone's* interests, wherever in the world they happened to be. Breaking out of the dialectic of freedom and enclosure, the ripples of this great experiment in oceanic governance would, its advocates hoped, be felt far more widely. Rather than a crucible of ever-growing inequality, the ocean would become the seedbed for a more egalitarian world order. Ultimately, the dream of an egalitarian ocean politics ended for the most part in disappointment. Nevertheless, it offers us a powerful vision of ocean justice that is well worth reviving.

DECOLONISING THE OCEAN

The debates leading up to the 1982 Convention on the Law of the Sea were not arcane squabbles waged by lawyers over dry legal principles – even if at times they looked like it. These debates had a political backdrop which it is vital to recognise. Traditional principles of international law had been formed in a world dominated by Europe – a world characterised by imperialism, slavery and the often-violent imposition of a capitalist economic system across vast swathes of the planet. As these legal principles were created in Europe, it is no surprise that they often reflected the interests of Europeans. Centuries later, the United States had become the world superpower, but by and large it also found these legal principles amenable to its global interests.

In the years leading up to the signing of the convention, however, world politics was in the process of being transformed. Empires had recently crumbled, and some were tumbling still. Between the 1940s and 1970s, scores of new states burst onto the international scene. Having been governed for generations by Britain, France, Portugal or Belgium, a remarkable and hard-won wave of decolonisation had seen dozens of communities take their political destinies into their own hands. But having struggled to liberate themselves from colonial rule, the leaders of these newly independent countries (NICs) still faced a global economy in which the odds were stacked against them. This left their leaders highly suspicious of the existing international legal order. That order had been created during the colonial era, and had been complicit in their subjugation. In their (entirely reasonable) view, it continued to serve the interests of the major world powers.

What these new countries in the global South demanded, therefore, went far beyond independent statehood. Sovereignty in a world whose rules had been designed by the rich in their own interests would not be worth its salt. Newly independent countries wanted *both* sovereignty *and* a transformed legal, political and economic order capable of narrowing the gap between the rich North and the global South. As Adom Getachew puts it in her illuminating book on the postcolonial period, newly independent countries on either side of the Atlantic saw themselves engaged not only in a struggle for independence, but also in a project of 'worldmaking'. They wanted, that is, to bring about the kind of egalitarian and democratic world order in which their independence would be truly meaningful, in which their political *and* economic destinies would be in their own hands.[1] Though there were competing worldmaking visions, the most ambitious version set its sights on what came to be called a New International Economic Order (NIEO), in which the South would be full participants in redrawing the rules of the world economy. Only with radical changes would the economic stranglehold of the North over the South be thrown off. Only then would formal sovereignty mean effective independence and the freedom to plot their own destinies.

This context would exert a powerful influence on discussions leading up to the new constitution for the ocean. Issa Diallo, Guinea's representative during the debates leading up to the adoption of UNCLOS, summed up the attitude of many leaders of NICs when he asserted that existing doctrines of oceanic law were 'nothing other than a manifestation of the right of the strongest and a vestige of colonialism', and that to carry them over into the postcolonial era 'would be a grave injustice to the young States which were struggling not only for political but also for economic independence'.[2]

The main worry, in the 1960s and '70s, was that the traditional principle of freedom at sea simply protected the ability of rich states to harvest precious ocean resources which the global South did not have the technology to access. Frank Njenga, the Kenyan representative at the negotiations, claimed in 1972 that the doctrine of the freedom of the sea 'has been designed specifically to favour the strong countries over the weak countries, the industrialized countries over the poor, and the developed over the developing'.[3] For Joseph Warioba – later prime minister of Tanzania – freedom of the sea had become 'a catch word and an excuse for a few countries to exploit ruthlessly the resources of the sea' in a way that poorer states could not.[4] This basic background was, from time to time, recognised by representatives from rich countries too. Keith Brennan, the Australian representative at the negotiations for the new convention, pointed to the 'inherent inequity' of 'the old law of the sea', which meant that 'Beyond three miles, it was "first come, first served," and wealthy countries could sail thousands of miles after a resource, while poorer countries could not – though they were just as free to [. . .] Peru was as free to fish off Russia as Russia was to fish off Peru, but somehow it never did.'[5]

The emergence of dozens of new states across Africa, Asia and Latin America introduced a significant political force determined to transform the old law. The negotiations to draft a new convention provided them with an early opportunity to make their collective voices heard. But their leaders wanted the consequences to resonate far beyond the ocean. The remaking of the Law of the Sea should, in their view, be a central plank in the NIEO. For advocates of the new Order, the negotiations over the new convention represented, as Emmanuel Bello put it at the time, 'a rare and perhaps unexpected opportunity to play a full participatory role in shaping the rules of international law'.[6] In achieving that goal, the sheer number of NICs looked likely to be crucial. In 1945, the United Nations had been founded by a mere fifty-one states. Most of them had also been present at the founding of the League of Nations in 1919.[7] By the time UNCLOS came to be finalised, however, 164 member states were involved. For the first time, the countries of the global North were in a minority.[8] Their new-found numerical strength gave NICs confidence that the traditional Law of the Sea really could be remade in light of the needs of a postcolonial world.

In the last chapter we examined one central plank of the new convention: states would turn significant swathes of the ocean into their own territory. NICs greeted this move with approval: coastal resource sovereignty would protect them, they hoped, from predation by rich countries and their Distant Water

Fleets, and help them achieve a greater degree of economic independence. As we have seen, that dream was not really borne out: enclosure has brought relatively modest benefits to most countries in the global South. But enclosure was not the only matter up for discussion in the convention. Beyond state territory, under the High Seas, lay the promise of great mineral wealth. And if this mineral wealth was governed in the right way – or so NICs hoped – it would help spur catch-up development for the global South. It might even enable them to throw off the economic shackles of colonialism, and take their destinies into their own hands.

NEW GOLD RUSH, OR NEW INTERNATIONAL ORDER?

Scattered across the deep seabed are minerals of potentially vast economic value. They come in many types. Foremost among them are ferromanganese crusts, manganese nodules, and the sulphide deposits that collect near hydrothermal vents. Knowledge of these deposits was by no means new to science at the time of the debates leading up to UNCLOS. In its famous scientific survey of the ocean, the Royal Navy vessel HMS *Challenger* had discovered the existence of manganese nodules as early as the 1870s.[9] But for many years they remained a scientific curiosity, because they lay 4 to 6 kilometres below the ocean's surface, and no ready means of 'harvesting' them existed. As late as 1956, the International Law Commission had decided that legal rules governing the exploitation of these minerals were not needed, because 'the technology for such exploitation did not yet exist and was not likely to be operational for a considerable time'.[10]

This assumption was to be rapidly revisited. The very next year, the University of California carried out a feasibility study into the mining of nodules which confirmed their potential value.[11] A further catalyst to public – and corporate – interest was the publication of John Mero's book *Mineral Resources of the Sea*. Mero, a mining engineer, suggested that if a mere tenth of the minerals of the seabed could be mined, they would meet the needs of humanity for a millennium. And their commercial production would be a reality, he predicted, by the 1980s.[12]

4.1 Manganese nodules at a depth of 5,526 metres in the mid-Atlantic Ocean.

In this context, the question of how these minerals would be accessed, and by whom, came to be far more significant. Mero's view was simple: access should be open to all, under the principle of the freedom of the sea. In practice, that would mean the old rule of first come, first served, and commiserations to less technologically advanced societies. Alternatively, in a more Seldenian solution, individual states might extend their jurisdiction out into the seabed so as to gain control over these minerals. The 1945 Truman Proclamation had already suggested that the USA was entitled to extend its resource sovereignty out over the seabed 'contiguous' to the United States.[13] The 1958 Geneva Convention on the Continental Shelf gave further legitimacy to this view. It declared that a state could harvest resources within its 'continental shelf', or even beyond it, up to a point 'where the superadjacent waters admits of the exploitation of the natural resources of the said areas'.[14] As a statement of legal principle, this was remarkably ambiguous. On a creative interpretation, it might actually allow coastal states to turn the whole of the world's seabed into their own exclusive mineral sectors.[15]

Whether that interpretation was faithful or fanciful, the fear was stoked that states with advanced technology would soon be the major beneficiaries of a new gold rush. A study by the Massachusetts Institute of Technology estimated the start-up costs for seabed mining at approximately US$560 million.[16] This was far beyond the reach of any country from the global South. But it might not be beyond the wealthier countries of the world. And the proceeds, for those who could get there first, might be enormous. As a result, the apparently imminent exploitation of seabed minerals threatened to widen existing international inequalities, rather than narrowing them (as advocates of a New International Economic Order hoped). This outcome appeared likely whether these resources fell under the remit of the freedom of the sea *or* of enclosure. A regime of freedom would lead to a new scramble for resources in which the countries of the global South could not expect to be the winners. Enclosure, by contrast, would grant the right to exploit these resources to coastal states, but would do nothing to address the fact that countries in the South lacked the capacity to exercise it. In all likelihood, they would end up leasing that right to foreign corporations, who could be expected to drive hard bargains.

A radical alternative vision emerged in the late 1960s. It drew on an idea which had been slowly emerging within international law over the previous decade. In 1959, a new treaty had been created to govern Antarctica. It declared – and still does – that the icy continent should be a place of peace and international cooperation, and that any territorial claims over it should be 'frozen'. In 1967, a number of countries signed the Outer Space Treaty, which declared that bodies like the moon could not be turned into the territory of individual countries, because 'mankind' had a 'common interest' in their governance.[17] These ideas would be given their fullest expression in the oceanic arena. In August 1967 a think-tank calling itself the Commission to Study the Organization of Peace had submitted a draft resolution to the UN secretary-general which 'declared both the high seas and the seabed beyond national jurisdiction the common heritage of mankind', and called for 'the establishment of an international authority within the UN framework to regulate the use of these areas'.[18] Its plan did not attract much attention, but a famous speech to the General

Assembly later that year, by the Maltese diplomat Arvid Pardo, would bring such ideas to the forefront of oceanic politics. Pardo's interest was at first rather opportunistic: he wanted to put Malta more firmly on the map within international politics, and believed that a grand proposal along these lines would attract considerable attention (a hope that was amply borne out). But over time Pardo became deeply committed to the idea. Convinced that a massive treasure trove existed on the seabed, he came to believe that it would be highly iniquitous if this treasure was monopolised by technologically advanced countries.

Instead these resources, Pardo declared, should be considered the 'common heritage' of humanity.[19] What was radical about this proposal was that it explicitly rejected the idea that everywhere should be considered the domain of either sovereignty or freedom, *mare clausum* or *mare liberum*. What came to be known as the 'common heritage principle' introduced a new, third category, which takes us beyond the seventeenth-century language of the 'Battle of the Books'. As the concept eventually came to be understood, there are several core characteristics of a 'common heritage' resource regime. First, places that are part of our common heritage must be used solely for peaceful purposes. Second, those places cannot be privately owned. Third, their resources must be managed in common by all of humankind, since everyone – including future people – possesses a stake in what happens to them. As a result, whether the exploitation of resources contained in common heritage areas was allowed or not would be down to the international community as a whole. Fourth, if exploitation was allowed, the benefits from exploitation should be shared. This would reflect our common stake in their future. Any sharing would have to be to the benefit of *all* of humankind, and special consideration should be given to the interests of people in the 'least developed' countries, as well as land-locked countries. Finally, common heritage resources came to be closely associated with proposals for the transfer of technology, which would help countries from the South to engage actively in the exploitation of these resources, instead of being passive recipients of benefit-sharing mechanisms.[20]

These ideas are sometimes said to be Grotian in spirit, but that view is seriously misleading. Grotius *might* have agreed that the seabed cannot become the property of particular communities (though, as we have seen, he was not entirely opposed to enclosure). But ideas of common management, benefit-sharing or technology transfer have no pedigree whatsoever in his writings. In that sense the common heritage principle represents a significant break with his defence of the freedom of the sea. For Grotius, to defend the ocean's status as a *res communis* was to declare that we all individually have the right to support ourselves by drawing on its resources, and navigating its spaces. But his conception of the ocean as our common preserve was not 'community oriented' in nature.[21] The common heritage principle, by contrast, involved essential reference to our common stake in managing the seabed *collectively*.

As he had hoped, Pardo's speech caused an international sensation. By 1969, the UN General Assembly had announced a moratorium on the exploitation of seabed minerals while a new international regime could be worked out. That regime would eventually come to be governed by a new institution called the International Seabed Authority (ISA). In securing this moratorium, NICs had outvoted the global North, and overcome strong opposition from both the US and the Soviet Union.[22]

The potential consequences were momentous. According to Pardo, a new seabed regime could provide a vital source of income for the United Nations, liberating it from financial dependence on – and hence manipulation by – rich countries, and enabling it to spend US$5 billion on development aid each year.[23] Elisabeth Mann Borgese, a colleague of Pardo who came to be another influential voice in the final conference leading up to UNCLOS, argued that revenues from seabed mining would provide NICs with an independent financial basis and remove their reliance on fickle – and often conditional – foreign aid.[24]

In this context, countries from the global South gradually became convinced of the vital importance of a just and effective form of seabed governance. A common heritage regime under the ISA would establish, in the words of the Filipino legal scholar Peter Payoyo, 'a model regime for global governance exemplifying a mini-paradigm, as it were, of an alternative mode of existence for the international community as a whole'.[25] Its potential significance would be both negative and positive. Negatively, Borgese suggested that it would be 'impossible to build an NIEO without including the oceans'.[26] The ocean economy was too important to be left wholly to the whims of the free market. Positively, the common heritage concept supplied a set of ideas which could in principle be applied to a whole range of other cases. According to Borgese, a UN Trusteeship Council could apply the common heritage principle to the ocean more generally (including the High Seas), to the Antarctic region and even to outer space.[27] It might in principle be extended still further: to world food resources, tropical forests and even cultural heritage across the globe. If so, the common heritage principle would come to underpin nothing less than 'a change in the structure of international relations'.[28] Ocean governance, then, would be a crucial test for the project for a New International Economic Order. Given the numerical strength of the NICs, 'Failure here would indeed imply rough going for the NIEO elsewhere.'[29]

Crucially, the suggestion was not merely that some of the profits from seabed mining should be sent in the direction of poorer countries: the emerging plan would involve NICs in mining directly. The key innovation would be an international public corporation called the UN 'Enterprise'. The Enterprise would carry out any mining on behalf of humankind in general, and involve countries from both North and South. The proceeds would then be sent to the International Seabed Authority. As such the Enterprise would embody 'a new form of active, participatory cooperation among industrialized and developing countries'.[30] For its supporters in the global South, it represented 'a real opportunity to gain experience in controlling, and perhaps eliminating dependence upon, multinational corporations'.[31]

It is hard to overstate how radical an idea this was. In plans for the Enterprise, we have a vision for a fully international agency managing what has been designated as the common heritage of *all* people (present and future), using the revenues to ease global inequality, and seizing the opportunity to enable countries from the South to leap the technological chasm separating them from the West. It is a highly innovative vision, but also an inspiring one. Though the dream for a NIEO was soon to experience rough weather, it is a vision which is well worth holding onto.

SEABED RESOURCES IN UNCLOS

In 1982 Tommy Koh, the Singaporean president of the final debates leading up to UNCLOS, declared that the new Law of the Sea Convention was 'a monumental achievement of the international community, second only to the Charter of the United Nations'. Against all odds, he claimed, 'It has successfully accommodated the competing interests of all nations.'[32] Notably, the Preamble to the Convention echoed the language of the NIEO by declaring a hope that its provisions would 'contribute to the realization of a just and equitable international economic order which takes into account the interests and needs of mankind as a whole and, in particular, the special interests and needs of developing countries'.

The final convention was certainly a hugely important, and in many ways innovative, treaty. One major development was the introduction of Exclusive Economic Zones. We saw in the last chapter that this development did not produce the gains for countries in the global South that many of their representatives had hoped for. But the introduction of the International Seabed Authority, and the unambiguous recognition that the seabed was part of the common heritage of humankind, looked like major advances. The portions of the seabed lying beyond the jurisdiction of any state – in what came to be known as 'the Area' – can no longer be appropriated by any state or private actor. Any exploitation of the mineral resources of the seabed, meanwhile, would have to abide by the dictates of the new international seabed mining regime. The emergence of the ISA, charged with representing the interests of all humankind, including future generations, was a remarkable move. It and it alone has authority over seabed resources. 'Any attempt by any State to mine the resources of the deep sea-bed outside the Convention,' Koh warned, will from now on 'earn the universal condemnation of the international community and will incur grave political and legal consequences.'[33] As and when seabed minerals were mined, the ISA would retain a portion of the benefits and employ them to promote the development of the least advantaged and geographically disadvantaged states.

But it is also undeniable that the eventual provisions for seabed mining reflected a series of compromises which, ultimately, dashed most of the aspirations of countries from the South. During the late 1970s, US representatives had voiced dissatisfaction with a number of aspects of the proposed seabed regime. Failure to modify them would, they warned, threaten their country's engagement with the convention as a whole. Throughout negotiations, the fear that the US would walk away from the new convention, and declare that it had the right to access seabed resources unilaterally (as an expression of the freedom of the sea) enabled its representatives to gain a number of crucial concessions.[34]

One highly divisive issue was the question of production controls. The prospect that unlimited quantities of seabed minerals might be mined under the sea was seen as a threat by some countries in the South. A number of them relied heavily on the export of metals such as copper, nickel, cobalt and manganese. For Chile, copper sales made up 78.3 per cent of the value of all exports during this period. For Zambia it was 94.6 per cent, and for Zaire 83 per cent.[35] As a result, they were deeply concerned that seabed mining would produce a glut of minerals and cause world prices to plummet.[36] If so, the hit to their own economies would be severe. To stave off that possibility, they insisted that the ISA should impose a strict limit on the quantity of minerals that could be mined from the seabed each year. But that idea was anathema to the representatives of the US and other leading economies. John Mero had already noted in 1965 that 'Nationalism, which has unfortunately taken hold to an excessive degree in many of the newer nations of the world and not a few of the older ones, can cut [importing societies] off from vital mineral commodities.' One of the advantages of seabed resources, by contrast, was that they would be freely available without any 'political' complications.[37] If countries from the global South achieved their goal of placing caps on seabed mining, that goal would be thwarted.

The oil crises of the 1970s also cast a deep shadow over the latter stages of negotiations. In 1973, Middle Eastern oil-exporting countries had coordinated to cut off supply to several Western countries, in protest against their support for Israel's invasion of Egypt. The ensuing oil shortage caused their economies to grind to a virtual halt. As they scrambled for other sources of fuel, the global price of oil quadrupled. Other resource-exporting countries drew the obvious conclusion: coordinated control over resource supply was one of their best prospects if they wanted to fundamentally change their position in the global economy. But this also helps explain the United States' worry that the global South would use their numerical superiority in the ISA to control the quantity of seabed minerals that could be mined. The countries of the South easily possessed the numbers to force the issue in drafting the new treaty. But if they did so, it seemed likely that many rich states would walk away from the convention as a whole.[38]

These debates about the minutiae of seabed governance were informed, then, by nothing less than opposing visions of the future of the global economy. Mining promised either to lay the foundations for a broader egalitarian movement within the global economy, or to further weaken the position of countries in the South by undercutting their (albeit unenviable) role as providers of raw materials. For the US, the proposals many poor countries were advancing were troublingly redolent of international socialism. Henry Kissinger had argued in 1976 that 'Countries which have no technological capacity for mining the seabed in the foreseeable future should not seek to impose a doctrine of total internationalization on nations which alone have this capacity.'[39] The idea of the Enterprise in particular ran afoul of 'a basic ideological disapproval of the establishment of an international public corporation' on the part of many wealthy countries.[40] US representatives strongly objected, moreover, to the proposal for compulsory technology transfer which, they claimed, would violate the intellectual property rights of US corporations. Despite the socialist flavour of the NICs' position, the Soviet attitude was also deeply cautious. It consistently expressed a preference for unfettered access to seabed minerals. In the end, it was not greatly attached to proposals for international socialism which it could not control, and rather keen to exploit its own potential technological advantages in the mining industry. NICs were therefore in a bind. They undoubtedly possessed the numbers to decide these issues in their preferred direction. But exercising that power 'might have forced out the dozen or so industrial states whose cooperation would be essential to make an International Seabed Enterprise a real-world success'.[41]

When a draft treaty finally emerged, the convention incorporated a number of crucial concessions to wealthy countries. The US saw the ISA's role as a simple one: it would receive and register applications to mine the seabed, and no more.[42] In the view of countries in the South, that would rob the ISA of its political purpose, and leave it a 'weak, pro forma entity'.[43] By way of compromise, UNCLOS ended up sketching a curious 'parallel' system of exploitation. Private parties could apply for a licence to prospect for seabed minerals, but they would be required to explore *two* tracts of the seabed. The ISA would then be empowered to choose one of those tracts for exclusive exploitation by the Enterprise, on behalf of humanity as a whole; the other would be mined by the private party.[44] The parallel system was a major concession by countries of the South, since they had argued that the Enterprise should be the *sole* exploiter of seabed resources. Allowing private actors to exploit our common heritage was a painful step. But it appeared necessary to shift UNCLOS from idea into reality.

In the end, though, these and other compromises were to no avail. By the time UNCLOS was finalised, the Reagan administration had come to power in the United States, and in July 1982 the new president announced that the US would not sign the new convention after all. As Reagan's assistant secretary of state for oceans made clear to Congress, the administration strongly objected to the designation of seabed minerals as part of humanity's 'common heritage'; to US corporations having to compete with an 'international' Enterprise; to the requirement to make royalty payments which would be shared with the South; to obligations to share technology; and to production controls (in short, to all of the radical elements of NICs' proposals). The Soviet Union, for its part, also objected to the Common Heritage designation for seabed resources, insisting that the principle of the freedom of the sea was not in need of any amendment.[45]

The USA and USSR were not alone in expressing doubt about the new regime for seabed mining. Although UNCLOS was finalised in 1982, it could not enter into legal force until it had been ratified by sixty countries. Five years later, it had only attracted thirty-four signatures. Apart from Iceland (which was keen to achieve sovereignty over local fish stocks), all of them were from the global South. The prospect that UNCLOS would become one more failed treaty began to loom large. In the meantime, it appeared more and more likely that rich countries would start to mine minerals of their own accord. To prevent that happening, and to ensure that UNCLOS gained the required ratifications, it was decided that a new legal instrument would be added to UNCLOS, in order to make it more palatable to the global North. The 1994 'Implementing Agreement' – incorporating what would come to be known as the New York Amendments – would mark several further profound compromises which, in combination, have made the just governance of seabed mining a much more distant prospect.

The Implementing Agreement eliminated mandatory technology transfers, and weakened production controls. It also placed serious limits on the Enterprise's operations, not least restricting its ability to borrow money to finance its activities. In addition, the Council of the ISA – within which key industrialised states have a virtual veto – must now explicitly authorise any activity by the Enterprise. Taken together, these effectively rendered the Enterprise 'an inoperable entity',[46] and made the active sharing of benefits from mining much less likely ever to occur.[47] The functions envisioned for the ISA gradually fell away, to the extent that its sole remaining goal now appears to be that of ensuring 'orderly access to minerals for industrialized countries'.[48] In the words of one critic, 'The ISA originally contemplated . . . was stillborn – the cost of universal (or non-universal) participation in a "new" Convention on the Law of the Sea.'[49]

In one last irony, the US has still not ratified the convention on the Law of the Sea that it played such a role in shaping. As so often in global politics, it has played a key role in shaping international rules that it refuses to be bound by. But its reticence, alongside that of many other rich countries, ensured that this pioneering attempt to engineer the common management of an area outside of national jurisdiction ended largely in failure. The Austrian representative at UNCLOS declared, with some approval, that the idea of the Common Heritage of Humankind had been given 'a first-class burial' by the Implementing Agreement.[50] For the global South, the amended seabed regime represented 'the ultimate incarceration of the Third World's New International Economic Order'.[51]

EQUALITY AT SEA

The predictions made during the 1960s and '70s that the mineral wealth of the deep seabed would soon be exploited have not yet been borne out. In retrospect they look wildly optimistic, animated by a short-lived technological utopianism. Even today, technical obstacles – which were arguably apparent even at the time of Pardo's speech[52] – have prevented any commercial mining from taking place. But technology is constantly evolving, and a number of corporations have now contracted with the ISA to explore the deep seabed. Whether or not mining comes to pass in the coming years, the apparently arcane debate over seabed minerals was hugely significant. It revealed radically opposed visions for the future of the ocean – and it saw the birth of a new oceanic perspective. The common heritage ideal broke away from the freedom/enclosure dichotomy, and opened up conceptual space for a new, international and egalitarian model of oceanic governance. Although the precise form the common heritage regime eventually took was desperately disappointing in so many respects, the underlying ideal remains hugely valuable. It could still play an important role in the ocean politics of the future.

The question of how the resources of the open ocean ought to be governed, and in whose interests, continues to be at the forefront of legal and political developments at sea. Negotiations on a new international instrument regulating the exploitation of Biodiversity Beyond National Jurisdiction began in 2015, and are ongoing within the United Nations as I write. Biotech companies are already exploiting unique life forms found in the Area Beyond National Jurisdiction, and several marine-based drugs have found their way onto the market – including Retrovir (AZT), the first drug licensed for treating HIV; and Ziconotide, used to treat chronic pain in cancer sufferers.[53] Nevertheless, bioprospecting in the High Seas remains virtually unregulated. Corporations involved in analysing marine genetic material, and formulating treatments, do so under the principle of the freedom of the sea – which, they point out, safeguards free scientific research. But there is a major difference between engaging in scientific research and claiming *ownership* over the genetic information of marine creatures. There are, moreover, major barriers to entry into the industry which have so far ensured that participation in marine biotech has remained the preserve of a few wealthy countries. Debates are currently taking place, therefore, on whether any instrument which emerges will incorporate a robust form of benefit-sharing, as well as meaningful mechanisms of technology transfer to the global South. Whereas China and the 'Group of 77' developing countries have argued that the living resources of the deep sea should also be considered part of the common heritage of humankind, a number of rich states maintain that they should fall under the principle of the freedom of the sea.[54] At stake still, therefore, is the question whether the ocean can help to promote a more egalitarian world order more broadly, or whether it will be a site in which existing inequalities are intensified.

Joint International Governance

In this section I want to emphasise what precisely is so valuable about the common heritage ideal. Perhaps the most fundamental point is the simple recognition that we all possess a stake in the future of the deep seabed, and its resources. The vision defended by countries in the South saw the whole international community being involved in the governance (and, if appropriate, the mining) of the seabed.[55] It understood international 'community' in quite a wide sense. The common heritage principle was relatively unusual within international law at the time in identifying individuals, rather than states, as the actors who bear the relevant rights and duties. It was also explicitly transgenerational: common heritage resources and places are the heritage of both present *and future* people, and their governance ought to take into account the interests of the latter, as well as the former.[56]

This is not to say that human beings *own* the ocean. Both Pardo and Borgese were clear that the common heritage ideal was not committed to that.[57] The idea of common human ownership of the seabed – or of other oceanic spaces – would be deeply 'anthropocentric' in nature. It would assume, that is, that humans hold a rightful place as rulers over the earth and its ecosystems. But we should resist that idea. The ocean, after all, is not even the place where humans live, by and large; it is, however, a complex and diverse set of ecosystems which are home to many other forms of life. Fortunately, the notion of common heritage does not imply that we own the ocean, or that human interests are the only ones that ought to count in oceanic politics. It simply states that we possess a common stake in the ocean's future. It would be better, I believe, to say that the seabed is part of the common heritage of *all* life on earth, rather than humanity in particular. This is an adjustment that the notion of common heritage seems capable of making. For something to be part of our heritage does not logically preclude it, after all, from being part of the heritage of other species too.[58] But it is less clear that we could say the same thing about ownership. If humanity are the ocean's owners, then presumably no one else is – and that is an idea we should reject. The crucial insight of the common heritage idea is simply that we all have an irreducible *interest* in the future of certain spaces and resources, alongside the members of many other species besides.

Fair Benefit-Sharing

The principle of the freedom of the sea has, for centuries, come closest to being the official ideology of the ocean. Outside of narrow territorial seas, the idea that fish, seals or whales could be 'harvested' by whoever wished to endured well into the twentieth century. That principle, as we have seen, is compatible with sweeping inequality. It could be satisfied in a world in which all oceanic resources were appropriated by the fastest or the strongest, and woe betide the slow and the weak. The political vision of the NICs was a reaction to just such a possibility. Faced with a world in which wealthy states possessed vastly superior technological capacity to make use of the ocean's resources – and were often geographically advantaged too – they argued that resource exploitation must be to the benefit of all, and that special consideration must be given, in designing a framework for seabed governance, to the interests of the least advantaged.

One way in which this could happen would be for the exploitation of seabed resources to be taxed, with the resulting funds being sent in the direction of poor and landlocked countries. That idea played an important role in the vision of NICs and is worth emphasising in contemporary debates on marine biodiversity. Though fair benefit-sharing should be a core requirement, however, it would not be enough to achieve a just ocean economy. Many of those who saw the ISA as a vehicle for achieving a New International Economic Order wanted to ensure that countries from the South were *active participants* in seabed exploitation, rather than being passive recipients of some of the benefits. The ill-fated Enterprise, in particular, opened up a new model of international economic organisation which could over time progressively displace the dominant position currently enjoyed on the world stage by multinational corporations. Ideas about the participatory management of community assets are currently receiving renewed attention in the national and local context.[59] The NICs' original vision for the seabed encourages us to open up such questions in the international context too.

From Benefit-Sharing to Conservation

As it emerged in the 1970s, the common heritage ideal was strongly focused on this question about the fair sharing of benefits. If seabed minerals are going to be exploited, how should we share the proceeds? And how could that spur a greater role for poor countries in determining the future of the global economy? This challenge was a significant one, but it also crowded out important questions about conservation and environmental protection on the sea floor. In some ways this neglect of the problem of sustainability was unsurprising. At the time of Pardo's famous speech, humanity remained ignorant of the existence of any form of life upon the deep seabed. Pardo and his contemporaries saw the sea floor as a barren plain littered with minerals ready to be scooped up once the requisite technology emerged. But that vision is highly misleading. In fact the deep seabed sustains a complex ecosystem. It is home to specialised corals, tubeworms and much else besides. The organisms on the sea floor largely rely on chemicals for their existence, rather than sunlight. They are typically very slow-growing, and as a result they struggle to recover from any significant environmental damage. In that context, our emphasis needs to change. The approach we should take to the deep seabed is one of stewardship and protection. I will suggest in the final chapter that economic activities in and under the High Seas should be radically curtailed. We should move from seeing those places as a store of resources to be plundered to a reserve to be protected – in the interests of both humankind and the other species we share the planet with.

The flip side to the common heritage idea, then, is the possession of duties. If somewhere is part of our common heritage, we ought to cooperate together in order to protect it. One implication is that we have a duty to cooperate internationally to secure the future of sites and resources beyond national jurisdiction. If some spaces or resources are part of our common heritage – and if our interests are unavoidably bound up with what happens to them – then we surely have a duty to put our interactions at sea on a stable institutional footing. Only then will our common and individual interests be respected, and this shared foundation for our lives on earth adequately protected. This idea of a duty of global cooperation is central to the common heritage ideal.[60] It suggests we must continue to search for ways in which the ocean could be governed better, and the lives and livelihoods of all those who depend on it more effectively secured. We must also recognise that protection can come at a cost. In the next chapter, one of the key principles of ocean justice which I will argue for is the principle that the costs of conserving the ocean must be fairly shared. Until they are, effective conservation policies are much less likely to emerge.

If we take our duties of environmental protection seriously, this will also require us to be imaginative about the kinds of institutions that could play a role in oceanic politics. The common heritage ideal is an inherently transgenerational one, and this suggests we must explore ways in which we can better protect the interests of future people. It also mandates a concern with the interests of members of other species. So far, serious attention to ways in which the interests of other animals might be better protected has been somewhat lacking in debates on the future of the ocean. I believe they ought to be central to our thinking about the ocean.

FROM SHARED EXPLOITATION TO SHARED PROTECTION

I have suggested that the vision of the NICs should not be consigned to history. It contains many ideas that are worth revisiting, and which continue to provide a valuable model for a more egalitarian and participatory form of resource governance. But our focus should shift from orderly exploitation to robust environmental protection. The deep sea floor is not a treasure trove of resources ready to be exploited. The interests of the many organisms that live there suggest it ought to be a haven from extraction and the despoliation of the environment.

If we can recover the radical kernel to the common heritage ideal, we can also see that it has implications beyond the deep seabed. For largely pragmatic reasons, Pardo applied the common heritage idea to the minerals on the deep seabed but not to the High Seas above them. This political separation of the ocean from the sea floor is highly problematic, however. For one thing, the common heritage principle clearly has salience in the case of the High Seas too. As we have seen, the debates that are now taking place about the marine biodiversity contained on the seabed and within the water column itself centre around the very same issues concerning benefit-sharing, and technology transfer, which dominated the debate on seabed minerals. In addition, there are complex ecological interactions between the ocean and the seabed which mean that attempts to govern them separately are likely to be ineffective. In place of this political separation between the ocean and the seabed, the governance of living and non-living resources within the ocean, both on the seabed *and* above, should be brought together in a more coherent way.[61] At the end of this book I will explore possibilities for more egalitarian and democratic governance of the wider ocean.

5

SEVEN PRINCIPLES OF OCEAN JUSTICE

Our institutions of ocean governance are failing us. The patchwork of ocean governance established under the Convention on the Law of the Sea – which divided the ocean into a plethora of regions, including Exclusive Economic Zones, the High Seas and others – was always flawed. It failed to treat the ocean as an interdependent web of ecosystems in which destructive activities in one place could generate impacts everywhere. Writing in 1982, its drafters did not anticipate some of the biggest challenges we face today. They had but a glimpse of the fragile and complex forms of life on the deep seabed, and had not yet confronted the full scale of problems such as climate change, acidification and plastic pollution.

The harsh reality we must now face is that the ocean is in a period of massive and multifaceted ecological crisis. The quantity of carbon it has absorbed in recent decades is unprecedented within our current geological epoch. This is triggering rapid alterations of its chemical balance of the type which, in the past, have been associated with truly massive losses of marine life. These changes are already wreaking havoc on the coral reefs, and on the plankton populations that support the marine food web. The effects of climate change are also dynamically interacting with other human impacts, including overfishing, pollution and the destruction of coastal habitats. At the same time as ocean warming is causing major shifts in fish populations, for instance, those populations are being pummelled by destructive fishing practices.

Fortunately, the international community has recognised that something needs to change. In 2015, the United Nations adopted a series of Sustainable Development Goals, aimed at tackling poverty, inequality and host of global environmental problems. Each Goal incorporated a series of more specific targets, to be achieved in full by the year 2030. One of the Sustainable Development Goals refers specifically to the ocean – the first time the world's governments had come together to commit to clear targets for restoring ocean health. SDG 14, as it is called, aims to reduce plastic pollution and illegal fishing, to increase the coverage of Marine Protected Areas to 10 per cent of the ocean, and much else besides. The approach taken by SDG 14 is, however, inadequate to the scale of the challenges we face. It is largely compatible with 'business as usual' in the ocean economy, and it studiously avoids challenging the institutions and rules that have brought us to our current precarious position. Its targets, even if met, would not arrest growing inequality in the ocean economy, or the looming environmental crisis.[1] Early indications, however, suggest that even its modest targets will for the most part be missed.[2]

In light of the scale and the interlocking nature of the challenges we face, we must be prepared to go further. This will involve admitting that the rules and institutions enshrined in the Convention on the Law of the Sea are not fit for purpose. Within its Exclusive Economic Zone, each state has a duty to manage its coastal resources sustainably. But the relevant rules are vague, and there are no sanctions for states which degrade ocean ecosystems. Under pressure from a fishing lobby dominated by big business, as well as a fossil fuel industry eager to extract still greater supplies of unburnable carbon, our governments have too often set environmental standards that are woefully inadequate. A few countries, certainly, have shown that another way is possible. Norway has embraced cautious principles of fisheries management and has seen many fish populations recover impressively; Denmark has signalled that it will no longer explore for offshore oil and gas. But examples of good environmental governance are far outnumbered by cases where the management of coastal resources has been profligate, and also by cases where states simply lack the capacity to enforce sound rules even if they wanted to. Meanwhile, the convention provides coastal states with very mixed signals, emphasising the importance of conservation at the same time as affirming their duty to ensure that local resources are 'fully utilized'.

Whereas EEZs represent the logic of enclosure, on the High Seas the ideal of freedom still reigns supreme. States are in principle obliged to regulate the activities of vessels sailing under their flags, and to cooperate with other states in managing and conserving High Seas resources. A series of Regional Fisheries Management Organisations (RFMOs) have brought countries together to agree catch limits on the High Seas. Their coverage is uneven – some govern specific species (especially tuna), whereas others govern specific ocean regions. But membership of those organisations is optional. Any country that wants to fish a given stock to extinction can simply refuse to join the relevant RFMO. Any country that *does* join can put pressure on decision-makers to allow higher and higher catches, by threatening to leave and fish to its heart's content if its demands are not met. To compound the problem, individual vessels can easily change the nationality under which they are registered. If a ship's 'flag state' joins an RFMO and tries to crack down on excessive fishing, its captain can easily 'swap flag' to a country which is not a member.[3] In some cases, the failure of RFMOs to improve the sustainability of fish stocks has been almost comical. A distinguished professor of ocean law confided to me that the International Commission for the Conservation of Atlantic Tunas (ICCAT) is known in the industry by the nickname 'International Conspiracy to Catch All the Tuna'. It has certainly failed to reverse a dramatic collapse in tuna populations. According to one recent book on the topic, the trajectory of bluefin tuna 'conservation' is better described as a policy of 'managed extinction'.[4]

Even if they *were* determined to achieve the sustainability of fish populations, it is not clear that RFMOs really possess the tools needed to do so. After all, the prospects of a particular population of fish will depend not only on how much it is fished, but on what happens to *other* species in a complex food web. Tuna, for instance, are fast-swimming carnivores, eating large quantities of smaller fish. For an RFMO to agree to catch fewer tuna will not guarantee a rebound in population sizes if other RFMOs fail to protect the fish that tuna eat. Those fish in turn will not be protected if plankton populations are depleted in increasingly acidic seas. High Seas governance has operated on a 'silo' basis, with distinct bodies making decisions on distinct species or distinct regions, as if they were ecologically independent.[5] Effective institutions of ocean governance would begin with the recognition that the ocean's ecosystems are interdependent, and that in many cases they are highly vulnerable.

The same problem of state discretion and institutional fragmentation has also doomed many attempts to establish conservation zones such as Marine Reserves and Marine Protected Areas (MPAs). Reserves prohibit all extractive and destructive activities, whereas MPAs are more modest, placing limits on some activities (though not banning them entirely), and allowing others to continue unchallenged. Although reserves offer much better protection, MPAs can still offer enormous benefits to marine ecosystems. Once established, these zones act as oases of life in the ocean: after a surprisingly short period of time, fish will begin to flood into the surrounding seas.[6] Within their own EEZs, states are free to establish such zones, and to police them if they choose. In practice, however, these zones have often operated as mere 'paper parks', protected in theory but in reality exploited by a variety of destructive industries. One recent study found that 97 per cent of the UK's Marine Protected Areas were visited by dredgers and supertrawlers, making a mockery of their protected status.[7] In general, states have been much too reticent about taking on the industrial fishing lobby, and too slow to spend the resources necessary to properly monitor and enforce environmental protections.

On the High Seas, we face a deeper problem: in the absence of any global-level accountability or enforcement, environmental protection here takes the form of self-regulation.[8] Marine Protected Areas do exist on the High Seas, but they are only binding on states that *agree* to abide by them, and again, vessels can quickly and cheaply switch flag to a country which refuses to recognise them. To date, the most impressive attempt to achieve an MPA on the High Seas has occurred in the ecologically fertile waters surrounding Antarctica.[9] But in response to pressure from recalcitrant fishing states such as Russia, the Ross Sea MPA covers barely a third of the area originally envisaged. While some parts of it are classed as highly protected Marine Reserves, the total quantity of fish which can be caught in the area as a whole has not actually been reduced. Meanwhile, any member state that wishes to can cancel the agreement at any time.[10] That is no basis on which to protect our ocean. As I write, proposals for a further set of MPAs surrounding Antarctica have just been vetoed.[11] Elsewhere, for the most part, protected areas remain even smaller, highly fragmented and inadequately policed. Some ocean scientists have argued that in order to achieve a healthy ocean, a third or more of its total area would need to be fully protected (in the final chapter of this book, I will argue for a still more ambitious target).[12] The United Nations Sustainable Development Goal for the ocean adopted a much more modest target, aiming at the protection of 10 per cent of the ocean by 2020.[13] That would not be enough to reverse the slide towards the depletion of marine life.[14] But even that target has been missed: by 2020 a mere 2.5 per cent of the ocean was fully or highly protected.[15]

The Law of the Sea has also allowed some issues (including the protection of marine biodiversity) to fall between the cracks.[16] A system that focuses on particular resources, often in particular places, does not serve us well. On the contrary, the scale of environmental challenges at sea puts a premium on comprehensive and synoptic approaches to ocean governance, capable of addressing the complex interplays between various environmental challenges.[17] Successful ocean governance institutions would need to be proactive, identifying and heading off threats, rather than being merely reactive in nature.[18] 'Agenda 21', developed at the Rio Earth Summit in 1992, called for approaches to ocean management 'that are integrated in content and are precautionary and anticipatory in ambit'.[19] Three decades later, we are still waiting.

Consider also our second major challenge, that of arresting and reversing major inequities in the ocean economy. Politicians have shown great enthusiasm for the potential of the emerging 'Blue Economy', but they have hardly begun to address important questions about who will benefit from it. If there are significant ecological constraints on our exploitation of the ocean, however, a serious engagement with these questions is unavoidable. The 'Blue Acceleration' will produce many winners as well as many losers. The contemporary governance architecture for the ocean, however, offers little prospect of arresting the prevailing pattern of growing inequality. The enclosure movement behind EEZs and continental shelves has offered benefits to some but not others. While some countries in the South have undoubtedly profited, the major beneficiaries have been those who were already relatively well off.

On the High Seas, meanwhile, more than 70 per cent of fish taken from the sea are caught by ten countries,[20] with relatively few corporations taking the lion's share. Here a regime of freedom has turned out to mean precisely what advocates of a New International Economic Order feared it would: a further widening of global inequalities. The hope that the International Seabed Authority would act as midwife to a new egalitarian and participatory global economy was disappointed. More recently, 'bioprospecting' at sea has offered a new bonanza for those best placed to exercise their oceanic freedom. As of 2017, nearly 13,000 patents incorporating marine genetic sequences had been registered. As I noted in the Introduction to this book, nearly half of them belong to a single German company.[21] Though a new legal instrument on Biodiversity Beyond National Jurisdiction is currently being negotiated, it remains to be seen whether it will implement meaningful benefit-sharing mechanisms (we will discuss its prospects in Chapter 10). The High Seas have been a space of hyper-capitalism, where highly inequitable accumulation has taken place without any semblance of democratic debate or control.

In the remainder of this chapter, I will sketch seven principles aimed at tackling inequality and environmental destruction in the ocean. My goal is not to describe the precise policies and institutions that would be necessary to put such ideas into practice: the remaining chapters of this book take up that challenge. My aim here is to provide some clarity about the basic principles that ought to inform changes to the architecture of ocean governance, to help us reverse the tide of inequality and ecosystem destruction.

1. Our common stake in the ocean

The ocean's future is *our* future. Human exploration of, and interaction with, the ocean is intensifying. Population growth and the struggle to escape from poverty will see us come to rely on it more and more for food and resources. At the same time, we are ever more aware of the many ways in which the ocean sustains life on our planet. This suggests that we all have a stake in ocean governance. If the ocean is governed badly, people the world over will suffer. If it is governed well – if it is nursed back to health, and if ocean industries become sustainable rather than destructive – then we could all benefit.

In the last chapter, we introduced the idea that the ocean is part of the common heritage of humankind. The idea is a radical one. It speaks against *both* the balkanisation of the ocean (its division into a set of fiefdoms, each governed by a coastal state) and the privatisation of its resources (in which corporate interests can grab the lion's share of those resources, under the principle of the freedom of the sea). It suggests that the ocean should be governed in *all* of our interests, including the interests of the least well off in our world, and those living in landlocked countries. At present, the legal scope of the common heritage idea is limited to the seabed under the High Seas (which international law calls 'The Area'). But once conjured up, the idea of common heritage cannot be so easily contained. The core ideas of the common heritage principle – that we should all be involved in ocean governance; that we should all share in the benefits flowing from sustainable ocean industries; that we all have a duty to protect the marine environment; that the ocean should be a place of peace and international cooperation – should not be restricted to the seabed 200 miles or more from the shore. They should guide ocean governance much more broadly, and for that reason ocean justice demands that we explore ways of more fairly sharing the benefits and burdens of our interaction with the ocean, and ensuring that the privilege and responsibility of engaging in the governance of the ocean is a genuinely shared one.

A second way in which the common heritage principle turns out to be a radical one is that there is really no good reason to restrict it to human beings. The arguments that point in favour of our common stake in the ocean count at least as strongly in the case of the other creatures we share the planet with – including, most obviously, the animals that actually inhabit the ocean. Unlike the idea of common ownership, the idea of common heritage – or,

101

more broadly, the idea of a common stake – is flexible enough to take account of the interests non-human life forms have in a healthy and bountiful ocean. As a result we must explore ways of making our ocean governance institutions genuinely responsive to those interests. It is worth pausing here to note a remarkable fact: the United Nations Convention on the Law of the Sea makes no explicit reference at all, throughout its many Articles, to the interests of the animals that actually inhabit the ocean. When marine animals are mentioned at all, they are discussed as resources to be divided up among nations or harvested by corporations. This offers an impoverished view of ocean justice. It is a vision which must be replaced by one that sees the ocean as key to all of life on earth, and the home to a complex web of life worthy of protection in its own right.

2. Democratic inclusion

If we all have a stake in the future of the ocean, then the way is clear for us to argue that we all ought to be involved in decision-making about that future. What philosophers call the 'all affected principle' suggests that those whose significant interests will be impacted by political decisions have a right to participate in making those decisions. Otherwise, decision-makers will not be obliged to give equal consideration to the various interests at stake, and may neglect entirely to protect some of us from harm.[22] When it comes to ocean governance, that principle has potentially radical implications. The rules that regulate the ocean economy and ocean environment will have an impact on all of us. That impact will not be confined to those who live along the coast, or those who are already deeply engaged in the ocean economy. Given its major ecosystem roles, for instance, the all affected principle suggests that *all* of us have a right to participate in decision-making about the future of the ocean.

That would represent a significant shift, because in practice ordinary citizens are very rarely consulted about the future of the ocean. Even in countries which proudly call themselves democracies, leaders hardly bother to campaign on ocean-related issues, and parties seldom give them any prominence in their manifestos. For the most part we have left decision-making about the ocean to our politicians, and to lawyers in the various tribunals set up under the contemporary Law of the Sea. A number of non-governmental organisations do campaign on ocean-related issues, and they have done sterling work in raising the visibility of issues like overfishing and plastic pollution.[23] But they must compete for governments' attention with powerful vested interests, including the fishing and fossil-fuel lobbies. Ocean justice demands that ordinary citizens can make their voices heard. If the ocean's future is our future, we ought to be involved in making decisions about it. This is one reason why the failure of the global South's radical vision for ocean politics was so regrettable. Leaders representing the majority of the world's population attempted to rewrite the old principles of the Law of the Sea, so as to place principles of equality and active participation at the heart of ocean governance. That they were thwarted at every turn – that we still have institutions of ocean governance so thoroughly tamed by dominant world powers, which are in turn beholden to corporate interests – is an injustice in itself. The exclusion of ordinary citizens from decision-making about the ocean is especially regrettable in the case of indigenous communities and other groups of people highly dependent on a healthy and sustainable ocean. Shutting them out of decision-making on the ocean is unjust, and also robs our governments of their wisdom about how coastal environments might be sustainably managed.

Some of those who will be affected by our decisions about ocean governance *cannot*, with the very best of will, participate in those decisions. But even so, we can try to ensure that our institutions adequately *represent* them and their interests. In Chapter 7, I will argue that other animals can possess a right to the equal consideration of their interests in decision-making about the ocean. Even if they are unable to participate directly in our political institutions, we still have a duty to represent those interests as best we can when we make decisions.[24] Think also of the interests of future people. People yet to be born may very well be affected in years to come by the decisions we take now.[25] Representing the interests of future people is certainly fraught with difficulties. Future people cannot vote for their contemporary 'representatives', and neither can they hold them accountable for their successes and failures.[26]

But that does not rule out any possibility of representing future people. Though we do not know their *views*, we can make informed judgements about their likely *interests*.[27] Safeguarding the interests of future people will likely demand the preservation of many critical natural resources; respecting their autonomy, furthermore, will likely also add weight to the argument against destroying irreplaceable resources (see below). Even if neither animals nor future people can be active participants in contemporary decision-making processes, there are good reasons for seeking to institutionalise mechanisms that protect their interests.

3. The ocean as a space of rights

Our political principles, our constitutions and our moral values have typically been formed on a terrestrial footing. Humans are primarily creatures of the land, and we spend the vast majority of our time in political communities that are literally 'grounded'. Perhaps this explains why so little attention has been given to the rights of those who find themselves at sea. Migrants adrift in the middle of the Mediterranean are seen as 'nobody's problem'. The main aim of coastal states seems to be to prevent them from reaching land, at which point they might claim political asylum. As I will show in the next chapter, people working at sea are often especially vulnerable to exploitation and abuse. Their home states do possess some legal responsibilities towards them, but in practice may do very little to protect their rights. The state under which their vessels are flagged will also bear some responsibilities. But so-called 'flag of convenience' countries are associated with a callous indifference about workers' rights at sea.

A British charity called Human Rights At Sea is working to combat this indifference to people's fates on the open ocean. Its mission is to get states to recognise that human rights *continue to exist* at sea.[28] In some ways, that might seem like a strange goal – after all, who would think that someone's human rights suddenly cease to apply once they have sailed off into the ocean? But our rights at sea are not always at the top of the political agenda, and institutional protections are often surprisingly weak. One major step towards ocean justice would simply be to take seriously the fact that our rights do not end at the state's borders. If we *are* serious about people's rights at sea, we surely have a duty to investigate ways of protecting them more effectively. As I will suggest in the next chapter, this might require us to revisit some traditional legal principles, like the notion that it is 'flag states' only which have the right to police what happens on board ships on the open ocean. Morally, others ought to have that right too, and indeed a duty to help ensure that the ocean is not a safe haven for abuse.

Though human rights are very important, we should also remember that other creatures may have rights too. The terrain of human rights is by now well worn, whereas working out exactly which rights are possessed by members of which species would be an unfamiliar and laborious task. But that is not a good reason for failing to take the project seriously. In Chapter 7, I will begin that work by sketching a list of rights plausibly held by whales and dolphins. But this represents only the beginning of an investigation into the rights of marine animals, and not the end by any means.

4. Sustainability and the precautionary principle

The idea that ocean governance should aim at sustainability seems obvious. But the idea of sustainability has been interpreted in different, and sometimes quite contradictory, ways – which means we still have work to do in fleshing out what sustainable ocean governance would look like. One view would be that what needs 'sustaining' is the economic basis of our societies. People will continue to need food, shelter and energy, and an economy is sustainable, we might say, if it can continue to supply those goods indefinitely into the future. That, however, offers an impoverished conception of what sustainability should mean. It is compatible with widespread environmental destruction, so long as the proceeds of that destruction are invested in such a way as to promote further economic growth (for example, by replacing nature with new technology). It places no store in preserving the natural world, unless parts of the natural world turn out to be crucial to the stable functioning of our economies.

Rather than that 'weak' conception of sustainability, we should favour what I would call a moderately strong version. This reading of sustainability incorporates several key ideas. First, the natural world has value in its own right, above and beyond what it provides for human beings. That will often mean that we have a duty to refrain from exploiting it, or even to protect it, not because of what it does for us but simply because a world with a rich natural environment is a better one in general. Second, we are not the only creatures with interests in the health of the natural world, or rights that need protecting. If members of other species also have rights, then we will sometimes have to sacrifice our own economic interests in order to secure *their* interests in flourishing lives. Third, even if we concentrate for a moment on human interests, a flourishing life may involve the ability to interact with a rich and diverse natural world. If a severely depleted natural environment is bad for human flourishing, then that gives us a reason to protect the environment – even if it is far from the only reason. Finally, and to concentrate still on human interests, recall that the common heritage idea is explicitly intergenerational – it suggests that the ocean is part of our common heritage, but also of people yet to be born. We do not know, of course, what future generations of people will come to value. They *might* be satisfied with a world of material comfort, in which the natural world has been reduced to a few scattered oases of biodiversity. But we cannot know that. They might, in fact, deeply regret that they are unable to interact with a rich and diverse natural environment. There is a monumental arrogance, it seems to me, in making that decision for them. The only safe option is to pass a healthy and diverse natural environment on to them, and hope they pass that favour forwards to their own descendants.

These arguments suggest that our policies of environmental protection should be strong, and cautious in nature. We should certainly protect ecosystems and resources that we understand play an important role in sustaining life in the ocean, and on earth more broadly (a test that we are currently failing). But often we do not *know* the likely effects of our actions. If our understanding of ocean ecosystems is still developing, so is our knowledge of their fragility, and the impacts that our actions might have on them. It might be that there will be 'threshold effects', where beyond a certain level resource exploitation causes irreversible environmental damage. Or it might be that there are 'feedback effects',

5.1 The Lodestone Reef, Queensland, Australia.

where one form of environmental damage causes still more profound effects, and potentially spins out of control. But often we do not know – or do not fully know, at any rate. How, then, should we proceed? In this context of uncertainty, many environmental scientists have suggested we embrace a 'precautionary principle'.[29] The precautionary principle requires us to avoid environmentally destructive activities unless we are reasonably confident that their effects will be manageable. It puts the burden of proof on the shoulders of those who propose new or untried forms of exploitation at sea, to establish that their activities will be safe. If they cannot, they ought not to proceed. Given the unintended (though often reckless) damage we have already done to the ocean, we have ample grounds to err on the side of caution and hence to protect parts of the ocean that *may* have critical ecosystem roles to play.[30]

5. Fair benefit-sharing

The ocean bestows many riches. Even if our consumption of those riches ought to be constrained in the interests of sustainability, we face an important question about who ought to gain from whatever goods we can legitimately take from the ocean. Like the defenders of the New International Economic Order, my suggestion is that when we design rules for ocean governance, we should try to advance the goal of greater global equality. All too often the rules of the game in the global economy have provided greater benefits to the top 10 per cent, rather than the majority. But we are not doomed to perpetuate these inequalities, and sometimes opportunities arise to narrow them. The challenge is to recognise them when they arrive. I have argued that our current institutions of ocean governance are now being overwhelmed by the challenges they face. When we come to design new institutions and new rules, as we must, we should ensure that they promote the active participation of the world's worst off in the sustainable ocean industries of the future, rather than leaving them ever further behind in a race to consume scarce resources.

That idea leans on a wider view about the nature and importance of equality. In my view, when we advance the goal of equality, what we ought to care about is people's ability to lead flourishing lives. What we should be interested in, from the point of view of justice, is what people are able to *do* or *be* in their lives. A good life will be one in which people are able to enjoy, for instance, good health; friendship and meaningful personal relationships; pleasure; a degree of personal autonomy; the ability to come together with others in order to determine the shape of our common life; the ability to live within a secure and diverse environment; and the aesthetic experience of beauty.[31] If someone is able to do or be those things, then we can say with confidence that their lives are going better rather than worse.[32] If we have equal moral worth, the goods or relationships that make flourishing possible should, unless a powerful reason can be given for acting otherwise, be arranged so as to give each of us an equal prospect of living a flourishing life.

When we come to allocate access to the ocean's resources, this view has important implications. For instance, it means that we should reject the view that people should always have access to strictly equal amounts of resources. One reason for this is that some people might require more than others in order to enjoy equally good health, for instance. A second reason concerns the background context in which we make our decisions about resource use. Whether we like it or not, our world displays staggering inequalities, in which place of birth is much the most important determinant of one's overall prospects in life, while class, gender and ethnicity also exert a powerful influence.[33] In that context, to insist that our access to the ocean's natural resources ought to be strictly equal would be perverse. Instead, when we design rules for (sustainable) access to marine resources we should make it possible for the worst off to *close* the gap, even if this means giving them access to greater-than-equal shares of resources. That is the right kind of policy for someone who cares about equality to pursue, since it is not our access to resources that matters fundamentally, but our ability to lead equally flourishing lives.[34] I believe this also resonates with a central idea within the vision of the newly independent countries whose leaders argued powerfully – if unsuccessfully – for a New International Economic Order in the immediate postcolonial period. Those advocates for global reform believed that when we come to draw up rules for the exploitation of the minerals of the seabed, we should take the opportunity to offset broader global inequalities, and to promote especially the position of the least advantaged. That is also the clear meaning of Elisabeth Mann Borgese's claim that the seabed could be rendered 'a great equalizer', 'mitigating the harshness of the land-based inequalities among nations'.[35] Such an idea should inform our governance of the ocean as a whole, rather than the deep seabed alone.

A concern with well-being means, however, that this cannot simply be a discussion about financial revenues. All too often – and especially in the narratives of the 'Blue Economy' and the 'Blue Acceleration' – a concern with monetary gains is allowed to crowd out other ways in which our connection with the ocean is good for our wellbeing. Exposure to vibrant ocean environments can be important to us emotionally and spiritually. A recent study of the emerging field of 'Blue Care' has emphasised the way in which a connection with the ocean can help with our physical and mental well-being.[36] In many places in the world, people derive a sense of peace and security from the sea, and even place it centre-stage within their cultures. And of course, the ocean supports millions of jobs worldwide. In this respect subsistence fishing has gained the most attention, but 'gleaning' – the gathering of marine organisms from tidal zones – is also a hugely important activity. It is an activity overwhelmingly performed by women and children (which might explain why it has been relatively neglected in academic studies), and appears to be valued by the individuals involved not only because it supports nutritional subsistence but also because of the personal relationships, sense of empowerment and connection to nature that the activity sustains.[37] The focus on the economic bottom line too often distracts our attention from the ways in which healthy and vibrant ocean ecosystems can drive well-being more broadly. Taking what some social scientists are beginning to call 'blue well-being' seriously will lead us to re-evaluate many claims about the benefits that the ocean can provide.[38] It may well mean, for instance, that building a busy port might not be an advance at all, notwithstanding the returns it provides for the Blue Economy, if it destroys the connection many people have to a part of the coast. And it will likely mean that a more profitable, industrialised and globalised fishing industry should not be seen as a boon at all if it undermines the food security of the local poor, and destroys the employment prospects of millions.

6. Fair burden-sharing

Protecting the ocean, and restoring it to vibrant good health, will involve costs. These will include the costs of protecting precious resources from various threats, such as plastic pollution, where removing the abandoned 'ghost nets' that litter the ocean, killing thousands upon thousands of marine animals, will be an expensive business. They will also include the costs of restoring ecosystems which have been degraded, as when ecologists reintroduce corals harmed by fishing activities, or transport them to cooler or less disturbed sections of the ocean in which they might survive the threat of climate change. Often the most pressing quandary revolves around what economists call 'opportunity costs', which include the costs involved when we *refrain* from harmful activities like overfishing. Conservation projects can hinder people's ability to secure their livelihoods, and this is also an important cost we must reckon with.[39]

An important question of justice is where these costs should fall. In my work on conservation justice, I have suggested that we must employ a two-step procedure in order to find an answer.[40] In the first step, we assess whether any actors bear special responsibilities that would justify laying burdens at their door. What philosophers call the 'contribution principle' ties burdens to our moral responsibility for various harms. When actors are aware (or ought to be aware) of the likely consequences of their actions, and possess reasonable alternatives to acting in the way they do, then it can be appropriate to ask them to pay for any harms they cause. This principle will tell us that it is those who produce plastic, or allow it to be swept into the ocean, who should pay for clean-up. If coral reefs are damaged as a result of anthropogenic climate change, by contrast, it should be high-emitters who bear the costs of restoration.

The contribution principle cannot be the whole story, however. I have already implied it may not be applied in cases where people did not know the likely results of their actions, or did not have alternatives. The lack of alternatives explains why it will usually be wrong to ask very badly off people to bear conservation burdens, even if they are playing a role in damaging the environment. We will also see cases where it is unclear who is causing environmental degradation, or where it has been caused by people who are no longer with us. In cases like that, we must turn to our second step. When we have conservation burdens that we cannot allocate according to the contribution principle, we must turn to the 'capacity principle' instead. That principle tells us that those who have the *ability* to make sacrifices without incurring excessive setbacks to their well-being ought to do so. The better off we are, the more we should contribute, and below some minimum level of well-being people should not be asked to make sacrifices at all. The capacity principle is familiar enough in the national context, where we ask the better off to pay higher taxes, for example. I am suggesting that we can apply the same principle at the global level, when it comes to allocating the burdens of ocean conservation. The capacity principle is attractive inasmuch as it dovetails with the goal of reducing inequality. Those who can afford more should pay more, and those who cannot make sacrifices will not be asked to.

There is one final idea that can be relevant when we take this second step. As well as capacity, facts about the *benefits* flowing from successful conservation efforts can also be relevant when we allocate costs. Often, the protection of vital ecosystems means that people can continue to enjoy important benefits, such as protection from storms, or food security. When this is true, it seems appropriate that those who benefit more should pay more towards conservation efforts. This principle is especially persuasive in cases where people *need* the benefits in question, and have the ability to contribute to their upkeep without being pushed into disadvantage.[41]

The questions I have focused on here are by no means the only important questions of conservation justice. It is also important that local people are involved in formulating conservation priorities, and do not see conservation policies as an imposition from outside. Conservation policies that are imposed on people are less likely to be successful, and this helps explain why democratic participation in ocean governance is so important. This includes participation in forming conservation priorities. This is just as important as ensuring that the costs of conservation are fairly shared, and do not make existing inequalities in flourishing still worse.

7. Fair transitions

The need to protect the ocean environment will require many people to moderate the demands they place on its ecosystems. These changes will in turn involve disruptions to jobs and livelihoods. Consider the example of reforms to the fishing industry. Some ecologists suggest that achieving sustainability in fish populations would require an overall reduction in global fishing effort roughly to the level of the 1990s.[42] A sustainable future for the fishing industry would also likely involve the phasing out of many damaging fishing practices, including certain forms of bottom trawling, the use of longlines associated with the death of many seabirds, and the use of poisons and explosives. The transition to less damaging methods would in itself be costly. But more significantly still, an overall reduction in fishing effort along the lines suggested could mean the loss of very many jobs. In many places in the global

South, coastal communities possess little in the way of social safety nets which might help cushion the blow to the livelihoods of those affected. The consequences for many people could include major losses to income, as well as to social networks, self-respect and a sense of personal efficacy.

Some of these losses would be long term in character. But even short-term adjustments can be costly and difficult. Consider, for example, proposals for an extensive set of Marine Protected Areas, which some ecologists have suggested should cover upwards of a third of the entire ocean.[43] In the long term, the establishment of effective MPAs can be highly beneficial to fishing communities. When protected from fishing, more individual fish are able to reach full maturity and hence spawn many more eggs, which can then disperse over long distances. As such MPAs act as 'centres of production that radiate outward to surrounding fishing grounds'.[44] In the short term, however, prohibitions on fishing can be very costly for individual fishers, especially in communities where alternative sources of employment, and meaningful government support, are thin on the ground.

It is important that these 'transitional' costs are not borne by the worst off. That would be unfair, and it would also trigger resistance to vital reforms to the ocean economy. This means that various forms of transitional assistance will be required. A similar idea has been clearly recognised – if not always put into practice – in the case of climate change. The Paris Agreement on climate change explicitly notes the effect that 'climate change responses' can have on 'sustainable development' and the 'eradication of poverty'.[45] The Agreement accordingly pledges to 'take into consideration . . . the concerns of Parties with economies most affected by the impacts' of those responses.[46] If the need to combat climate change must not make it harder for disadvantaged communities to escape poverty, then those countries will require international assistance. The same point should also apply to vital transitions towards sustainability in ocean governance. Although moves away from environmentally destructive practices are morally necessary, the *costs* of those transitions should not be borne by the poor. Just transitions will therefore be accompanied by policies designed to ensure that less well-off communities have adequate opportunities available to them. I will provide a number of examples of such policies in Chapter 9, which examines the prospects for a Blue New Deal.

The scale of the challenges we face in achieving a just and sustainable ocean requires new thinking about the future of ocean politics. That new thinking must in turn be guided by clear principles, which do justice to the various ways in which we and members of other species depend on our single world ocean. Taken together, the seven principles outlined in this chapter provide an important moral compass capable of guiding ocean politics as it evolves to meet the challenges of the future. If it is to be just and sustainable, ocean governance will have to embody each of these principles. At present, ocean governance has too many blind spots – for the complex, interlocking nature of the ocean ecosystem, for the interests of non-human animals, for human rights at sea, for the many serious environmental challenges we now face, and much else besides. Putting these principles into action would make ocean governance more just and sustainable. They would also make it more participatory, bringing ordinary citizens into processes of ocean governance for the first time. In the remaining chapters of this book, we will investigate a number of concrete policies that would bring these principles closer to reality.

6

PROTECTING WORKERS AT SEA

In 2013, the Bangladeshi media reported that at least forty fishermen had been bound hand and foot and thrown into the sea to drown. Despite the existence of video evidence, no prosecutions followed.[1] In a survey of Cambodian men and boys sold to Thai fishing boats the following year, many of them reported having witnessed officers killing workers.[2] These shocking abuses are extreme examples of a much broader pattern. Some sectors of the fishing industry remain heavily dependent on trafficked and forced labour, and regularly expose workers to violence and mistreatment, as well as to dangerous and unsanitary working conditions.[3] Many of the fish these workers catch eventually find their way onto the plates of consumers in wealthy economies. The Gulf of Thailand, for instance – the epicentre of forced labour in the fishing industry – is also the biggest source of shrimp and prawns for the US market,[4] as well as being a major supplier of raw materials for the pet-food, dietary-supplement and aquaculture industries.

For many readers, these facts will be horrifying. For the most part, the exploitation and abuse of workers at sea takes place out of sight and out of mind. One of our key principles of ocean justice is that people's rights should not go unprotected simply because they find themselves at sea – but there is a great deal of work to do in delivering on that principle. In this chapter I will consider who is morally responsible for the plight of these workers, and how we might better safeguard their rights. The examples I discuss will all focus on people who work in the fishing industry, because the evidence suggests that this is where the greatest problems of abuse and exploitation are to be found.[5] But people who work in shipping, or on oil rigs, can be vulnerable too, in their own ways, and many of the proposals I make for reform would also help to improve their position. With that in mind, the first step towards pushing fishers' protection higher up the political agenda is to recognise just how, and why, they are so vulnerable.

WHAT MAKES FISHERS SO VULNERABLE?

The exploitation and abuse of workers on the margins of the global economy is depressingly widespread. Millions of migrant workers, for example, are made vulnerable to exploitation by the conditions placed upon their entry visas, or by their lack of them. Knowing they can be deported at any point, they may have no choice but to accept abject treatment from employers. Too often, host countries show little concern for their rights. It is not the case, therefore, that fishers are alone in their vulnerability to abuse. On the contrary, in many ways the conditions they can face – working in confined spaces, performing exhausting work, often in extremes of temperature, supervised by people who do not speak their language and who may be dismissive of their culture or religion – are typical of the migrant worker experience. But it is true that the sources of fishers' vulnerability are in some respects distinctive. Responding adequately to them may therefore require distinctive remedies.

One factor that can leave fishers vulnerable to abuse is their sheer physical isolation. On board ship, fishers are cut off from their fellow citizens, from access to lawyers, and often from all but the most basic medical care. In recent decades, visits to the world's ports – where coastal states could, if they chose, punish any abuses of workers' rights – have become less regular and shorter in duration. The emergence of large 'mother ships' capable of processing hundreds of thousands of tonnes of fish out at sea means that many fishing boats now visit those vessels to unload rather than going into port themselves. For workers on fishing boats, periods spent at sea can turn into months or even years.

Going in to port can be very challenging in any case, in an era where border control has become highly politicised and even criminalised. The United States, for example, requires a seafarer to secure a visa, costing $160 and requiring an interview, *before* they can leave their vessel.[6] This geographical isolation marks out a clear difference to other migrant workers, and plays a major role in explaining their vulnerability.

A second factor that can weaken protection is the patchy coverage of relevant laws and conventions. The contemporary Law of the Sea has surprisingly little to say about the human rights of those who find themselves at sea, and UNCLOS included no sustained discussion of workers' rights. Some conventions that seek to protect the rights of workers at sea explicitly exclude fishers from protection.[7] For the most part they must rely on the 2007 Work in Fishing Convention, which guarantees them free food and water, sets minimum standards for accommodation and medical care, specifies rest periods and makes clear that eventual repatriation for workers should occur at the vessel owner's expense. But states are allowed to exclude fishers working on small boats from many of its provisions, meaning in practice that many of the poorest fishers go unprotected.[8]

Many migrants, of course, live and work in states that are not serious about protecting their rights. But a third factor that makes the fulfilment of fishers' rights much less straightforward (and also helps explain how their plight is so distinctive) is their peculiar legal position. Within territorial seas, which extend for 12 nautical miles from a country's coast, the coastal state can, if it chooses, apply the full gamut of local legal protections to foreign fishers. Fishers plying the waters 10 miles from the Norwegian coast, for instance, should in principle benefit from the same rules as workers on Norwegian soil, including health and safety or minimum-wage legislation. But outside of those territorial seas, things are less certain. Each boat is required to sail under the flag of one country or another (which need not be the country the boat is owned in, or indeed the boat where its crew hail from). The boat is then subject (and only subject) to the jurisdiction of the country under which it is 'flagged', as if it were a tiny extension of that state's legal territory. When workers are in trouble they must first find out which country their vessel is flagged under (its 'flag state'), and then appeal to that state for help. But many flag states have not signed key conventions protecting fishers' rights in the first place. To date, only eighteen countries have ratified the Work in Fishing Convention.[9]

Their geographical isolation, and their distinctive legal situation, help to explain why fishers are so vulnerable to mistreatment by unscrupulous employers. At sea, the fisher will often be far from possible sources of assistance. Moreover, the legal ground beneath his or her feet is subject to sudden shifts. A fisher could find himself under the jurisdiction of two or more different states on the same day, without leaving his boat, since vessels will often 'flag out' to another jurisdiction in order to avoid difficulties with the law. Changing flag is quick, and relatively inexpensive, for boat owners. But for individual fishers, the consequences can be bewildering. They may not even *know* which state they should appeal to when experiencing difficulties.

Flag states are supposed to enforce relevant national laws, as well as international agreements on workers' rights to which they have signed up. But, in practice, flag states are often chosen by vessel owners precisely because they will not offer effective protection for employees. Countries that are prepared to rent their flags to vessel owners without insisting on even basic respect for workers' rights – so-called 'Flag of Convenience' (FOC) countries – operate as mobile exploitation havens, selling their flags while turning a blind eye to abuses. Panama's Law Decree 8/98 of 2005, for instance, abolished protections of the right to strike, the minimum wage and compensation for injuries, and the country is not a signatory to any treaty limiting working hours.[10] Liberia, Honduras and Equatorial Guinea are also key FOC states. These countries charge a one-off fee to register a boat, and explicitly advertise their services on the basis that they will minimise the risk of legal liability. Seafarers themselves do not come from FOC countries in any significant numbers, and very few ships are owned there. In fact vessels will typically never have any reason to visit the ports of their FOC states, making it very difficult for a seafarer with a grievance to initiate legal proceedings, even if flag states *were* serious about upholding their rights. This distinctive legal situation places fishers in an unenviable position on the frontier of the contemporary capitalist economy, with jurisdiction – and therefore notional responsibility for the protection of their rights – potentially subject to rapid shifts, and effective legal protection often far out of reach. By contrast, it offers significant cover to predatory employers wishing to avoid any consequences for violating workers' rights.

PATTERNS OF ABUSE AT SEA

Exploitation and abuse at sea are probably as old as sailing itself. Out of sight of their home turf, seafarers have long complained of short rations, long hours and inhospitable working conditions. But the sheer scale of these problems – and their ethnic and gender-based subcurrents – grew as shipping and fishing became truly industrial in scale. The emergence of steamships in the nineteenth century was particularly important. It spurred a great intensification of global trade, and it also accelerated the 'internationalization' of the ocean-going labour force. In the past, training the crew for a sailing ship might have taken several years, as workers graduated from landsman to ordinary and then able seaman. But labourers could be turned to stoking furnaces on the new steamships immediately, with minimal training. This led to a depression of wages across the shipping and fishing industries, and the emergence of truly miserable working conditions. Traditional maritime countries recruited larger and larger proportions of their crews from Asia, paid them far less than their European counterparts and gave them inferior living quarters. That, combined with awful conditions stoking furnaces, meant Asian crews were far more susceptible to diseases like tuberculosis and pneumonia.[11]

These Asian workers – sometimes called 'lascars' – played an often invisible role, literally 'below water', and unseen by fellow crew members. The novelist and former sailor Joseph Conrad provided a telling description of his own fleeting encounters with Chinese 'firemen', who were charged with stoking furnaces below-decks. While working on a steamship, he reported, 'I had my only sight of Chinese firemen. Sight is the exact word. One didn't speak to them. . . . They never looked at anybody, and one never saw them direct

Their appearances in the light of day were very regular, and yet somewhat ghostlike.'[12] Their invisibility may have made a 'triumphant tale of European seafarers heroically globalizing the world' easier to sell, but they were vital to the globalisation of fishing and commerce nonetheless.[13] Far from being an accident, the invisibility of these 'alien' seafarers was often coercively enforced even back on dry land. The Special Restriction (Coloured Alien Seamen) Order of 1925, for instance, banned Asian seafarers from entering British ports, albeit apparently with limited success.[14]

The internationalisation of crews was given further impetus by the oil crisis of the 1970s, which caused the price of fuel to spike dramatically. The introduction of new fishing technologies also drove up operating costs, and sent many small-scale operators out of business. How could owners restore profits, and keep their boats afloat? One response was to cut back on the maintenance of boats and equipment, often with tragic consequences.[15] Another was to cut labour costs, by employing seafarers from the global South. The oil crisis also accelerated the process of 'flagging out', which made it easier to impose miserable conditions on workers. By 2014, over 70 per cent of the world's vessels by weight were flagged under states other than their home states.[16] As far as we can tell, the ultimate ownership of vessels went largely unchanged during this period.[17]

At the extreme, the contemporary fishing industry has now become a major global site for forced labour. In the Indian Ocean and the South China Sea, the fishing and aquaculture industries rely extensively on trafficked workers,[18] defined as workers who have not offered themselves voluntarily for work, and who work under the threat of penalties.[19] But the Gulf of Thailand is probably the epicentre of abuse within the fishing industry.[20] An estimated 200,000 migrant fishers work in the seas around Thailand, mostly recruited from Cambodia, Myanmar, Laos, Indonesia and the Philippines. A survey by the International Labour Organization found that at least one-sixth of workers on long-haul boats had been either coerced or deceived into working against their will.[21] Far from dealing effectively with the problem of trafficking, the Thai authorities have themselves, it is claimed, been complicit in selling Rohingya Muslim refugees into forced labour.[22]

6.1 Indonesia, 2015: Workers rescued from slavery in the fishing industry gather in a temporary shelter.

Even in cases where workers have actively sought out employment on fishing boats, their position can be characterised by deep vulnerability. Many workers, driven by poverty, pawn their families' assets in order to pay fees to the agents who will assign them to vessels. These assets can then be seized if the fisher breaks his or her contract.[23] Thet Phyo Lin, a Burmese worker trafficked onto a Thai fishing boat, described his situation thus: 'If I want to quit working here I need to request permission from the employer. Some employers allow us to leave but some will claim we must pay off debts first.'[24] Unexpected costs are often added to the 'debts' of fishers, resulting in a form of bonded labour.[25] As a result, contracts give considerable leverage to employers – but they may do little or nothing to protect the rights of workers. In his study of fishing workers in Thailand, Philip Robertson reported that he 'was unable to identify a single fisher who had ever received a written contract'.[26] The International Labour Organization's Conventions outlaw deductions from pay to cover food accommodation, and insist that travel to and from a vessel should be pa by employers, rather than employees. But workers are frequently unaware of their legal rights, and in reality deductions are commonplace. So too are excessive working hours. Myint Hein Htay, another Burmese trafficking survivor, reported that employers 'don't care how much you are working. Even if you die, they'll just throw your body in the water.'[27] Fishers who defend their rights face the threat of abandonment in foreign ports. Given that fishers are often asked to surrender their identification documents upon boarding a vessel, the consequence of abandonment is often arrest for illegal entry into the port state.[28] For others, the consequences of protest may be still worse.

It might be expected that workers plying the waters off the coasts of wealthy liberal democracies would achieve more consistent protection of their rights. Within their 200-nautical mile Exclusive Economic Zones, states can in theory determine who can fish and who cannot. But to date they have shown remarkably little interest in the protection of foreign fishers. Conditions of modern slavery have been observed in the fisheries of wealthy countries such as New Zealand, with an estimated two-fifths of the squid shipped from New Zealand caught using coerced labour.[29] Even where foreign workers are employed legally, they may not be protected as well as local fishers. The thousand Filipino fishers who work off the coast of Scotland, for instance, are employed by British companies but earn considerably less than British fishers would for the same work, and often face inferior working conditions.[30] As a result of these working conditions (on older boats, with equipment that may be in need of repair), they are three times more likely to die at sea than their British counterparts.[31] The scallop fisheries off the British coast have also been found to be the site of forced labour.[32]

MORAL RESPONSIBILITY FOR ABUSE AND EXPLOITATION

We have seen that the contemporary fishing industry is home to distressing patterns of abuse and exploitation. Though definitions of abuse and exploitation will vary, on any reasonable definition the industry is the site for considerable injustice. Parts of the industry are abusive, in the sense that employers violate widely recognised labour rights, and indeed the human rights of fishers more generally. They are also exploitative, in the sense that employers take advantage of workers' vulnerability in order to deprive them of a fair return on their labour.[33] Though some regions are hotspots of abuse and exploitation, these problems have been witnessed throughout the ocean, including within the marine territories of wealthy liberal democracies. This situation is partly explained by the deep vulnerability of fishers, a vulnerability which is exacerbated by their physical isolation on board fishing boats, far away from possible sources of help.

The question I want to pursue now is who, if anyone, is morally responsible for these abuses. Such questions are complex and difficult, because the contemporary capitalist economy spins an intricate web, with ownership, production and consumption dispersed over a bewildering variety of locations. The result is that many of us may be 'connected' to abuses in some way, whether we realise it or not. When are those connections morally blameworthy, and when do they give us reason to change our behaviour? These are questions that philosophers have thought about deeply. They have provided us with vital tools for unpicking questions about moral responsibility, allowing us to distinguish between different kinds of connection to abuses and different degrees of responsibility for them.

The most immediate culprits are undoubtedly those who employ, and then abuse, vulnerable workers. In practice, this means the owners and skippers of individual fishing boats. Using forced labour, and making people work for long hours or in dangerous conditions under the threat of violence, are clear-cut cases of abuse. Relationships with workers are often exploitative too, when they involve owners and skippers taking unfair advantage of workers' vulnerability in order to deprive them of a fair wage.

Owners and skippers are the principal wrongdoers, then, because they are the people who actually commit acts of exploitation and abuse. But people traffickers who supply fishing vessels with unwilling workers also act immorally. Like owners, they knowingly violate the rights of vulnerable workers in order to gain material rewards. We might say the same thing about seemingly legitimate employment agents too, if they have reasonable grounds to suspect that the workers they supply will go on to be abused.

This much is perhaps straightforward. But a number of other actors can potentially be considered *complicit* in wrongdoing within the fishing industry, even if they do not commit abuses themselves. We can say that someone is complicit in abuse when they knowingly play a role in sustaining it, and when they could act otherwise but nevertheless choose not to.[34] Identifying people who are complicit in abuses is important to give us a full moral picture. This will in turn help us understand better who ought to bear the burdens of eradicating injustice within the fishing industry.

First, consider corporations further down the supply chain – the major fish companies that buy fish from smaller operators and then sell it on to restaurants, supermarkets and the manufacturers of pet food or nutritional supplements. These firms may not *intend* for abuses to happen. They may even believe these abuses are terrible. But if they continue to buy fish which they know to be sourced in abusive or exploitative ways, and if they understand that they are thereby sustaining abuse and exploitation, they can be considered complicit in wrongdoing. Significantly, the global fish industry is dominated by just a handful of corporations.[35] These corporations have considerable power, for good or ill. If they chose to exert pressure for reform in the fishing industry, the results could be dramatic. But so long as they continue to buy fish without asking difficult questions, abuse will continue to be a lucrative option for unscrupulous employers and people traffickers.

It is harder to argue that individual consumers are complicit. Whereas large corporations have a huge impact on what happens in the industry, each individual does not. If you or I stop eating fish, this is not likely to make any difference to the scale of abuse. If we are not individually *sustaining* abuses in that sense, the charge of complicity is out of place. But this does not mean that consumers are wholly blameless. We may still bear some moral blame if we choose to continue buying fish even in the knowledge that those fish are sourced in unethical ways. This point about choice is important. There are many people in the global South who have very few alternatives to eating fish, if they are to secure vital protein and micronutrients in their diet. People in that situation can hardly be expected to change their purchasing habits. For them, eating fish is not blameworthy, even if that fish is sourced in unethical ways. But if we have plenty of alternative, and non-costly, sources of protein and micronutrients – as people in wealthy countries typically do – then it is much more plausible to argue that we have a moral duty to avoiding buying unethically sourced fish.

So far in this section I have dealt with highly familiar categories of employers, agents, corporations and consumers. But in the fishing case, there are two somewhat less familiar sets of actors that can still bear significant moral responsibility for wrongdoing. First, consider policy-makers in *flag of convenience states*. When the authorities in a flag state agree to sell their flags to boat owners without making good faith efforts to ensure that even the most basic labour standards are adhered to, they help to sustain the abuses that result. If flags of convenience did not exist, it would be much harder for owners and skippers to get away with abuse and exploitation. By definition, flag of convenience countries make no significant effort to ensure compliance with even minimal labour standards. Instead they operate as mobile exploitation havens, facilitating a race to the bottom in labour standards – and they are entirely aware of that fact. They even make it easier for vessel owners to evade legal scrutiny, putting obstacles in the way of outsiders who wish to trace the ultimate ownership of boats. Allowing each vessel on their books to be registered under a different company name, for instance, makes it more difficult for victims of injustice to establish ownership, and to pursue remedies under the law.[36]

It's possible that an *individual* flag of convenience country could claim not to be complicit in labour abuse. It might declare that nothing would be achieved if it alone decided to clean up its practices. After all, unscrupulous owners would simply register with another flag of convenience country instead. In that sense, it might say, it is *not* playing a crucial role in sustaining abuses. In my view, this response does not hold up to scrutiny. To see why, imagine the following, slightly fanciful, case. A factory owner declares that his employees are not working hard enough, and that he is going to buy a gun to force the to work until their tasks are complete – even if they drop dead in the process. There are twenty people who could sell him a gun. Fifteen of them will do the right thing and refuse to do so. Five of them – including me – will agree. As it happens, the factory owner randomly knocks on *my* door and I do indeed sell him the gun, and he goes on to use it to exploit and abuse his workers. Here it seems to me that I am still complicit in his wrongdoing. I have facilitated that wrongdoing by supplying a vital tool. Sometimes complicity involves acting alone, being the one bad apple who makes abuse possible. Sometimes it simply means *agreeing to be the one* who makes abuse possible, even if others are prepared to act in the same way too. The presence of other flag of convenience countries does not get each flag of convenience country off the moral hook for complicity in abuse.

Finally, I will argue that *coastal states* can bear significant moral responsibility for exploitation and abuse. They can help sustain wrongdoing in two ways. One relates to their role as 'port states', where fish catches are unloaded and sold. In principle, the countries where fish are unloaded could play a vital role in defending workers' rights. Along their own shorelines, they are authorised to board ships and assess the conditions in which fishers live and work. Anyone guilty of abuse can be punished under domestic law, regardless of their nationality or the flag state of their vessel. Unfortunately, some countries have proven disinclined to exercise this power. So-called 'port of convenience' countries compete for business by being lax about inspections. Their desire to attract more trade outweighs any interest in protecting the rights of workers. These countries must bear some responsibility: if vessels engaged in abuse could not unload their catch, their incentive to engage in abuse would be radically curtailed.

Another way coastal states can bear responsibility lies in their role as decision-makers over Exclusive Economic Zones, where nine-tenths of the world's fish are caught. States that allow fishing boats to ply their EEZs can share in moral responsibility for exploitation and abuse that takes place on those vessels. A foreign seafarer working within a country's EEZ occupies a peculiar role: contributing to that country's economy, but not benefiting from the labour or safety or environmental protections that a visiting worker would normally expect. If coastal states are aware of the abuse and exploitation of workers in their EEZs, but fail to take available steps to prevent it, they are complicit in that abuse.

This claim requires some explanation, though. Coastal states enjoy full legal authority over people within their ports and territorial seas. But they do *not* enjoy the same authority over people sailing or fishing within their EEZs. A coastal state enjoys rights over the resources within its EEZ, including the fish that swim in and out of it. But it does not, in general, have the authority to enforce labour rights. Its warships are entitled to board ships suspected of being engaged in the slave trade, though countries have rarely exercised that power.[37] But the coastal state's powers certainly do not extend to the routine protection of labour rights. How, then, can they be considered morally responsible for any abuses that happen there?

In fact, coastal states are far from powerless when it comes to preventing exploitation and abuse within their EEZs. After all, states have the legal right to determine who can fish in their EEZs and who cannot. A boat fishing in Canada's or Vietnam's EEZ requires that country's permission to do so. There is no reason why coastal states should not *leverage* their authority, by demanding that all fishing vessels in their EEZs extend basic protections to workers. If they refuse to do so, then the coastal state can deny access. Likewise, coastal states can refuse to allow access to vessels sailing under flags of convenience. Regrettably, they have not made this move very often. But some have. I noted earlier that boats in New Zealand's waters have historically been associated with some dreadful abuses. But in 2014, a coalition of NGOs, lawyers and organised labour brought about a significant change in government policy. Fishing permits are now only issued to ships that agree to implement the very same protections that New Zealand would apply to its own workers.[38] The policy has not been perfectly implemented, but this still represents real progress. It shows that effective coastal-state control over labour practices is possible within EEZs, and this fact serves as a condemnation of other states which possess but refuse to deploy that potential control.

Things may be different, of course, in cases where coastal states simply lack the *practical* capacity to determine who fishes in their waters and who does not. Off the coast of West Africa, for instance, illegal fishing is rife, but local states' ability to do anything about it is limited. But this is not typically the case in the global North. When the capacity to monitor and control abuses exists, it would be wrong for coastal states to wash their hands of the problems faced by fishers in their EEZs. If they refuse to exercise this capacity, they are complicit in exploitation.

PROTECTING WORKERS

The abuse and exploitation of fishers is a deep, structural problem, which is sustained by the actions of a wide variety of actors. Tackling it will therefore require complex, multifaceted solutions, in which many actors will have to play a part. In some cases, individual citizens can make a difference, in their capacity as consumers or activists. On other occasions, organisations such as Trade Unions may make a significant difference to working conditions, as they have in many cases in the shipping industry. Most workers on small fishing boats are not unionised, however, and employers may be highly resistant to employing union members. In this situation, we must try to address the structural context in which workers become vulnerable in the first place; this is likely to involve large-scale legal and political reforms.[39] This section sketches four sets of reforms which can help to reduce fishers' vulnerability to exploitation and abuse. They range from the relatively modest to the more radical and transformative, but I do not see them as competing with each other. Each of them will be important if the rights of vulnerable workers within the global fishing industry are going to be better protected.

Transparency. Sometimes, the first step in dealing with a problem is to recognise it, and to bring it home to the people who can do something about it. In that sense, knowledge is power. A good first step would be to establish a global registry of fishing vessels, making clear who the ultimate owners are. That could be invaluable in helping seafarers to pursue legal remedy against abusive employers,[40] and in helping concerned coastal states to hold owners accountable.

We should also aim to provide much better information to individual consumers about labour practices within the fishing industry. Despite some horrifying stories in the press, and notwithstanding the excellent work of charities like Human Rights At Sea, the public are often unaware of human rights abuses within the fishing industry. In some ways this is surprising, because people are often aware of ethical issues in fishing. But for the most part, their attention is captured by (albeit very important) concerns about the sustainability of fish stocks, or the need to cut back on cruel and destructive fishing practices like the use of drift nets, or bottom trawling. There are some very prominent certification schemes for fish, which are intended to allow people to shop with greater ethical confidence. The best known of them is run by the Marine Stewardship Council (MSC), which offers a 'blue tick' for fish caught in sustainable ways. But workers' rights matter too, and to date the MSC has not shown sufficient concern with the issue. Recently, it has begun to refuse certification to any company prosecuted for using forced labour in the previous two years.[41] This is a positive step, but it sets the bar too low. Respect for a much wider set of labour rights should become one of the core standards which define a 'well-managed' fishery. Otherwise, consumers will not be in a position to make informed decisions.

Sometimes, fish are one ingredient among others in the manufacture of products such as pet food or nutritional supplements. Here, it is less obvious that consumer-oriented campaigns like the blue tick scheme are going to be the most effective policy. When this is the case, it makes more sense to place the onus on the corporations that process fish products. They should be required by national law to ensure their supply chains are free from abuse. At present, few companies systematically track the origins of the fish they use in their products. This is not because the necessary technology is unavailable.[42] The political challenge is to make them use it. In 2012, California took an important step in passing the Business Transparency Law, which requires large corporations to document exactly how they can be sure that their imports are trafficking-free.[43] In Britain, the Modern Slavery Act of 2015 obliges all large companies to report on the risk of slavery and forced labour within their supply chains. This example should be reproduced much more broadly, wherever countries have the capacity to enforce these or similar rules.

Leveraging coastal state resource sovereignty. We have noted that the possession of Exclusive Economic Zones gives states jurisdiction over natural resources, but does not by and large give them jurisdiction over people (other than when that is necessary to defend their resource rights). Coastal states cannot therefore *directly* promote workers' rights within their marine territories. This has led most states to wash their hands of the problem of abuse there. But this is indefensible, because coastal states can *leverage* their resource sovereignty to insist that abuses are not tolerated. It is worth pointing out that this would not require the creation of new laws or institutions. It would simply involve states exercising their existing resource sovereignty in a more ethical way. States should only sell access to fish when companies are willing to guarantee the protection of workers' rights, and agree to periodic checks on their working conditions. New Zealand has shown that such an approach is possible; concerned citizens should lobby their leaders to adopt such a policy more widely. Doing so could make a major difference to working conditions.

This policy would shift industry incentives from the 'supply' end, making access to stocks conditional on respect for labour rights. But port states could also exert a stronger influence from the 'demand' end of the fishing industry. If boats that abused workers were unable to unload fish, this would significantly reduce the incentive to engage in bad practices. This would require port states to show a more consistent determination to board and inspect vessels. Under the 2016 Port State Measures Agreement, port states agree to robustly monitor and inspect fishing vessels. Its focus is on driving out illegal fishing, rather than labour abuses. But a more robust and consistent approach to inspecting vessels could also pay dividends for workers. To date, only a third of states have signed up to the Agreement.[44] Encouraging wider uptake should be a priority if we are to reduce the extreme vulnerability of many fishing workers.

The 'genuine link'. In many ways the practice of exclusive flag state jurisdiction lies at the heart of the difficulties faced by fishers. Workers have to turn to flag states for help when they are in difficulties – but what if the flag state is not interested? The problem of flags of convenience – where flag states may simply be uninterested in defending workers' rights – has focused attention on the way in which the link between boat and flag state is forged. Many international legal instruments, including the Law of the Sea Convention, declare that there should be a 'genuine link' between a state and any boat sailing under its flag. Unfortunately, there has been no legal consensus on what a 'genuine link' means. One view – which was put forward in the 1986 Convention on Conditions for Registration of Ships – is that a genuine link only exists if a significant equity stake is owned within the flag state, if the identity of owners is readily discernible, *and* if the flag state provides a significant portion of a vessel's crew.[45] If we went down that line, it would be easier for victims of abuse to achieve effective legal remedy in cases of abuse. Unfortunately, the 1986 Convention has not attracted sufficient ratifications to come into legal force. Until it does, the only 'link' that is legally required between a vessel and a flag state consists in the very act of registering a ship. That situation continues to smooth the path for those who would abuse and exploit workers.

Ending exclusive flag state jurisdiction. The reforms discussed so far could make a significant positive difference to the prospects of people working in the global fishing industry. But they would not eradicate bad practices. Take the proposal that coastal states should exercise the leverage they possess over foreign fishing fleets plying their Exclusive Economic Zones in order to demand compliance with basic labour standards. This could only represent a partial solution to the problems of exploitation and abuse. First of all, even within Exclusive Economic Zones, some states lack the practical capacity to enforce compliance with labour rights. And second, some fishing takes place on the High Seas, where there is no coastal-state resource sovereignty in the first place. On the High Seas, fishers are even more dependent upon the scruples of their employers, and the flag states their boats are registered with.

I have also suggested that greater information-sharing, as well as reforming the 'genuine link' clause, can help build political, legal and consumer pressure on owners to curtail their participation in instances of exploitation and abuse. But these reforms would not be a total solution either. The ocean economy possesses many grey zones, where working practices are murky at best. In some cases, fish caught illegally, and/or using slave labour, are transferred to boats otherwise operating legally before landing (a practice called 'trans-shipment'). This represents a major problem for anyone concerned to drive out exploitation and abuse. It seriously clouds the legal picture and makes it much harder to drive abusive owners out of business.

In this context, it is difficult to escape a more radical conclusion. In my view, fully protecting the most basic rights of workers will demand direct action by authorities which do *not* come from the flag state. Flag states have proven themselves, in all too many cases, to be unable or unwilling to tackle the problem of abuse. Solutions must therefore involve other bodies that *are* willing and able. States must be prepared – and authorised – to board vessels which are *not* sailing under their own flag, when they have good grounds to believe that basic labour rights are at stake. Only then will wrongdoers encounter a genuine deterrent.

This proposal sets a clear collision course with the practice of exclusive flag state jurisdiction (EFSJ). But this collision is unavoidable if the rights of some of the most vulnerable workers in the world are to be protected. The practice of EFSJ may once have made moral sense. For the bulk of maritime history, switching flag was a relatively rare event. The nationality of seafarers, owners and flag states typically overlapped, meaning crew could, in theory, rely on the country in which they, and their vessels, possessed nationality to protect their rights. But the globalisation of the fishing industry changed that background fundamentally. Most fishers now work on vessels registered in countries other than their own, which are owned in yet other countries. In this context the practice of EFSJ has acted as a lubricant to a race to the bottom in labour standards, and has seriously weakened the protection afforded to workers.

How might we move beyond the practice of EFSJ? The ideal solution would probably be to establish an international body which was legally entitled to police labour rights at sea. Such a body – call it an Ocean Police – would need the legal right to board vessels suspected of infringing workers' rights. Skippers found to be involved in abuse would then be liable to prosecution under a suitable international court. This itself would be a radical move, since it would involve either expanding the remit of the International Criminal Court, or creating a new court dedicated to protecting rights at sea. To be effective, such a court would need the power to pursue claims for damages against boat owners, and even, in serious cases, to seek their extradition. The Ocean Police, and the court that accompanied it, would need to exercise authority within both the High Seas and states' Exclusive Economic Zones. But that would not actually infringe upon the sovereignty of coastal states – because outside of their 12-mile territorial seas, they possess no general jurisdiction over people in the first place. As such it would fill an important enforcement gap, remedying the problem of systematic non-compliance with key labour standards on the part of many flag states.

While this would be the optimal solution, it might be too much to hope for, at least in the short term. But there is an alternative, which would not require the establishment of new institutions. The Law of the Sea could be reformed so as to give third parties – including other concerned states – the right to enforce minimal labour standards. Within a given country's EEZ, that country might be given permission to board vessels, and arrest and prosecute offenders. What, though, about cases where the coastal state does not have the capacity or resources to enforce the law? In principle, that state might authorise another state to do so in its place. We could also extend this model to the High Seas: any state encountering a boat engaged in labour abuses could be granted the permission to board, arrest and prosecute offenders.

These suggestions are radical, but they are not entirely without precedent. Warships operating anywhere in the world already possess the legal right to board vessels suspected of engagement in slavery, regardless of the flag those vessels happen to be sailing under. This right is defended within the 1926 Slavery Convention, and again within the 1956 Supplementary Convention on Slavery. As their names suggest, however, the right to board is restricted to cases of slavery, where one human being is treated as the property of another. Policing 'forced' or 'compulsory' labour remains a matter for the flag state alone.[46] This is not good enough. Slavery is a gross affront to morality, but it is part of a broader continuum of practices – including bonded labour, the refusal to issue written contracts, the use of physical threats, the confiscation of passports and the threat of abandonment in foreign ports – which are employed in order to infringe on the rights of many vulnerable workers. While the Supplementary Convention shows an interest in controlling 'bonded labour', it does not extend the right to board vessels beyond cases of slavery proper.

There are two problems here. First, it is not obvious why slavery alone can justify constraints on the freedom of vessels to escape scrutiny by third parties. Slavery is certainly a terrible practice – but so are forced and bonded labour. If forced and bonded labour are an affront to international legal norms too, then they should also provide the basis for a right to board fishing boats anywhere. Second, the rights granted to those seeking to prevent slavery or other forms of abuse are too limited. The two conventions mentioned above give foreign vessels the right to *board and inspect* any vessel suspected of engagement in the slave trade, and to report infractions to the flag state. But they do not grant any power to make arrests, or even to free those found to be held in conditions of slavery – even if the flag state proves not to be interested.[47] If we are serious about protecting even the most basic workers' rights, third parties must be given power to free workers, and preferably to make arrests too. That power should extend to cases of forced and bonded labour, as well as to classic forms of slavery. The claim to exclusive jurisdiction over vessels at sea is ripe for revolution in light of the basic interest of workers in freedom from coercion, exploitation and physical abuse.

The evolving Law of the Sea has displayed a consistent blind spot on the topic of the human rights of those who live and work at sea, and not least those workers who decide – or are pressed – to join one of the most dangerous of all professions. I have suggested that actors in distant states are often complicit – in ways that ordinary citizens, and our leaders, may never have taken time to reflect upon – in the global problem of the mistreatment of fishers. But we can also do much to improve their situation. We have considered a number of proposals for reform, many of which do not require any great legal or institutional changes. But I have also argued that consistent protection of fishers' rights will ultimately require us to abandon the practice of exclusive flag state jurisdiction, which now represents a serious obstacle to the protection of the basic rights of many of the most vulnerable.

PROTECTING THE VULNERABLE

In October 2020, Rasoul Iran-Nejad, his wife Shiva Mohammad Panahi and their children Anita and Armin drowned when their boat capsized in the English Channel. The body of their fifteen-month-old son Artin was only recovered the following summer. Like many before them, the Kurdish-Iranian family had been attempting to cross the Channel in order to seek asylum in the United Kingdom.[48] This tragedy reminds us that the ocean is a place of danger not only for workers, but for those fleeing persecution or desperate poverty too. The Mediterranean has also been the location of an ongoing humanitarian catastrophe. In 2019 alone, 1,283 people are estimated to have drowned there while attempting to reach safety on the shores of Europe.[49] As a response to this ongoing crisis, our politicians have declared an intention to make our coasts even more inhospitable places for potential migrants or refugees. The UK home secretary Priti Patel, for instance, has recently declared that her ambition is to make the Channel crossing 'unviable',[50] and has ordered officials to explore military methods for preventing people from attempting it. Meanwhile NGOs which have engaged in rescue operations in Europe have been threatened with prosecution for 'aiding illegal immigration',[51] a process of 'criminalising solidarity', the result of which has been a surge in migrant deaths at sea.[52]

The very real danger is that such responses simply push desperate people to make even more dangerous crossings, under cover of night or on smaller and smaller boats. If the sea is a space of rights, we cannot accept a situation where people are criminalised or brutalised for exercising their human right to seek asylum, or indeed for coming to the assistance of those who are fleeing persecution or poverty. Instead we must search for ways of reducing people's vulnerability. Fortunately, this is not a case where we need to argue for new principles, or invent new institutions. But we do need to try and persuade our politicians to drop the populist rhetoric and observe duties that are already clearly inscribed within international laws to which our countries have signed up. Far from allowing them to penalise or demonise those who engage in humanitarian rescue operations, Article 98 of the United Nations Convention on the Law of the Sea actually makes clear that every state should *require* vessels sailing under its flag to rescue anyone 'in danger of being lost' at sea. It also makes clear that coastal states must promote effective search and rescue operations for those in peril.[53] If people are indeed rescued, they become the responsibility of the flag state unless some other safe port can be found. Far from undermining the law by rescuing migrants in danger, then, NGOs are helping states to discharge their duties. They are taking up the slack for governments which are refusing to take their legal and moral responsibilities seriously.

This is not to say that there is not more work to do in rounding out countries' responsibilities. Ideally, the kind of international body that I have argued would be necessary to fully protect the rights of workers at sea could also do important work in safeguarding those seeking a safe haven overseas. In Chapter 8, we will consider the rights that one particular class of migrants – so-called 'climate exiles' – might have. Though climate exiles are distinctive in some ways, the conclusions I will reach about their rights, and about what a fair allocation of the costs of accommodating them might be, have wider relevance. But although it is important that the costs of protecting them are fairly shared, this should never get in the way of individual refugees' ability to seek and achieve refuge. As an ongoing human tragedy, the plight of migrants at sea ought to concern all of us. It demands an effective, and timely, institutional response.

7

THE RIGHTS OF MARINE ANIMALS

Humanity has brought over three-quarters of the world's land area into its own use during the past century, converting it into farms, factories and homes for a burgeoning population.[1] In so doing we have radically shrunk the space available to other species. Activities such as hunting and pollution have also had a huge impact on those we share our world with. The consequences have been devastating. The large animals, or 'megafauna', of many regions have already long since disappeared, and those that remain are often in a highly perilous state. If anything, these trends are accelerating: in the last four decades alone, wild animal populations have declined by an average of 60 per cent.[2] In their place, the population of farmed animals has swelled enormously: 80 billion animals are now bred and slaughtered each year for human consumption.[3] More and more of the world's remaining wilderness is being flattened to grow their fodder. Where there was forest, there is now concrete and tarmac. Where there were wild animals, there are caged animals, bred to be eaten.

As the land comes under ever greater pressure, we are turning our rapacious attention to the ocean instead. In fact, the fish taken from the sea already outnumber the animals we kill for food back on dry land.[4] In some ways sea creatures are especially vulnerable, because they are largely unprotected by the (typically modest) animal welfare standards that apply back on dry land.[5] Marine habitats are under pressure too: mangroves, wetlands and other habitats on the margins between land and sea are now being lost at unprecedented rates. Meanwhile the coral reefs are rapidly bleaching. These trends prompt some unsettling questions: will the sea be 'tamed' in the same way as the land? Will it become an Anthropocene Ocean, dedicated exclusively to meeting our hunger for food and resources? Will we see a wave of extinctions, with the remaining wild sea creatures leading precarious lives on the margins?

Many of us believe that the answers to each of those questions must be a resounding 'no'. The ocean is first and foremost a habitat for a dazzling array of marine life, and it should remain a hospitable and bountiful environment for them long into the future. An account of ocean justice should be able to illuminate why this is such an important goal, rather than seeking merely to divide the spoils of the ocean fairly among humankind. That would be a seriously deficient and short-sighted approach. I will argue in this chapter that an important step towards ocean justice must be to take the rights of marine animals themselves seriously. Respecting and protecting their rights is important for its own sake, over and above anything marine animals might do for us. My goal will be to open up the conversation about what these rights might be, and how they might best be protected.

It is not necessarily the case that all marine animals have identical rights. That would depend on their specific capacities. A whale's rights will plausibly be quite different to those of a starfish, and different again to those of an octopus. Listing the rights that members of every marine species should possess would easily take up an entire book and more, so the aim here will be to illustrate how a case can be made, by concentrating on the rights that members of the cetacean family – whales, dolphins and porpoises – ought to have. Back on dry land, some readers may be familiar with the work of the Great Ape Project, which has seen scholars and activists defending rights to life, to individual liberty and to protection against torture for all chimpanzees, gorillas and orang-utans.[6] My project will be similar in spirit, and I will lend my support to (and argue for extending still further) a Declaration of Cetacean Rights. I want to reiterate that this will be an illustration: nothing I say should be taken to imply that members of *other* species cannot also have important rights, or that cetaceans' rights are somehow more important. But we must start somewhere, and reflecting seriously on the rights of cetaceans should amply persuade us that the conversation about ocean justice cannot stop at the interests of human beings alone.

WHY DO ANIMALS HAVE RIGHTS?

Historically, advocates of animal rights have had a mountain to climb, because it has so often been assumed that justice is a concept that can only intelligibly be applied to humans. This need not mean that principles of justice have no implications for animals whatsoever. A sceptic about animal rights might still agree that it would be an injustice for me to kill your dog. But it would be an injustice *to you*, depriving you of your rightful property, and causing you distress. It would not be an injustice *to the dog*, because from the moral point of view, dogs do not possess rights of their own. According to this view, destroying the rainforests might cause injustice too, if future generations could no longer count on a stable climate, or if indigenous tribespeople were driven from their ancestral homelands. But it would not constitute an injustice towards the other animals that live there — because talk about justice presumes the existence of rights and duties, and non-human animals have neither.

Why, though, should we believe that justice is a concept for humans alone? One answer might be that other animals cannot take part in the conversation about justice. Reflection on the demands of justice or morality is a matter for humans alone, in which other species are incapable of participating. As a result, the upshot of our deliberations – the rights and duties that emerge from discussions about justice and morality – will also apply to humans alone. This is a bad argument, however. For one thing, it is not certain that humans are unique in being able to respond to moral reasons, or even engage in moral debate.[7] It might well be true, of course, that we know of no reliable way to include animals[8] within our deliberations about the nature of justice. But more importantly, the fact that someone cannot take part with us in moral discussion and deliberation surely does not mean they have no rights and duties. Future people cannot discuss justice with us, after all, but they still have a right that we take their interests into account when we make decisions about the fate of the planet. Babies cannot discuss justice with us, but also surely possess rights. Of course, we might say that babies and future people will *one day* be able to discuss justice. But not all of them will: some people will suffer from severe disabilities that make participation in politics very difficult or even impossible. But again, that does not mean they have no rights. Deliberation about justice is important, but even if someone cannot take part in that discussion, they can still have rights worth protecting.[9]

Alternatively, it might be suggested that humans are distinctive because they possess capacities like intelligence, or the ability to use language, which other animals do not. Perhaps *this* explains why we have rights and they don't. Unfortunately for sceptics about animal rights, this does not appear to be true. As we will see in this chapter, whales and dolphins are highly intelligent. They also use complex language. But even if they did not, it is not obvious why they would not have rights. Once again, we must remember that humans vary in their intelligence and their ability to use language (very young babies, for example, cannot speak at all). But we would not – or should not – assume that they cannot possess moral rights.

Suffice to say that the boundaries between the capacities of humans and other animals are much more porous than some of us might like to assume. But in any case, perhaps what really ought to matter is not the ability to use language, or take part in moral debate, so much as the ability of a creature's life to go well or badly. Late in the eighteenth century, the philosopher Jeremy Bentham provided a pioneering argument in favour of better standards of animal welfare. From the point of view of morality, he argued, the crucial issue should not be whether animals are intelligent, or capable of speech, so much as whether they are capable of feeling pain and pleasure. The fact that kicking a dog will cause him pain seems to be sufficient reason not to do it, whether or not he can speak or engage in reasoned debate.[10] Pain is pain, however intelligent its recipient. While Bentham was sceptical about the language of rights, many contemporary scholars and activists believe that enshrining specific animal rights will be an important step forward in securing their protection.

To say that someone has a right to something – a decent life, for example – is to say they have a very weighty claim to it, which cannot be ignored merely for our own convenience. It makes perfect moral sense to say that a dog has a *right* not to be ill-treated, and that he holds this right for his own sake, and not because he is someone's property. Ideally, this right should be protected in law.

Let us put the case for animal rights a little more positively. Members of many other species are *sentient*. By this we mean simply that they can experience various sensations for themselves. If a creature is able to experience pain, if she seems to take whatever steps she can to avoid pain, this seems to justify our saying that she has an *interest* in the avoidance of pain. If she can experience pleasure or other rewarding experiences, she seems by the same token to have an interest in experiencing more of them rather than less.[11] Members of many species also appear to possess self-conscious awareness, or *subjecthood*. They possess, that is, a consciousness of themselves as beings to whom worldly events are happening. They may even possess memories, enabling them to experience feelings such as hope and regret. If a creature can experience emotions like desire and frustration, fulfilment and boredom, then he or she will also plausibly have an interest in a more rather than a less rewarding life. The argument begins with the identification of capacities, which generate interests. These interests, in turn, can ground rights. If an animal can experience intense pain, then he may have a right not to be exposed to such pain. If he can live a full and rewarding life at liberty in the wild, he may have a right to be free from captivity.[12]

For many, the idea that animals can possess rights remains a radical and unsettling one. Sceptics may be perfectly ready to accept the idea that all members of our own species have rights – that is the idea, after all, behind 'human rights'. But they are unwilling to take the extra step of awarding rights to members of other species. I hope to have shown that resistance to the idea of animal rights rests on unstable ground. It is not clear that humans are unique in their capacities. More importantly, it is not obvious that any differences are significant enough to say that we hold rights whereas members of other species do not. I will not claim, however, that all animals have the same rights. After all, I have said that rights are grounded on interests, which in turn are grounded on capacities. And those capacities do differ between species. Sea urchins may not be aware of themselves as distinct individuals, and may not have the rich internal lives that dolphins do. If they are genuinely unaware of where they are and what they are doing, then a right to freedom from captivity might not mean much to them. Life in an aquarium, free from predators, might be perfectly good from the point of view of a sea urchin's well-being, even if for a dolphin it would be unbearable. Sea urchins might, however, have the right to freedom from unnecessary suffering if they are capable of feeling pain. It is plausible that the fuller the mental, physical or emotional capacities a creature has, the fuller the set of rights he or she ought to enjoy. A creature with more capacities will have more interests worthy of protection. A suitable list of rights would have to be carved out for members of each species, on the basis of their specific capacities.

Before I proceed, a couple of quick clarifications. First, my suggestion will be that cetaceans enjoy *moral* rights – that morally speaking, we should recognise clear limits on how we can treat them. They may not, at present, enjoy protection by our laws and our institutions, and so I am certainly not describing *legal* rights that cetaceans already hold. But if we accept that cetaceans do possess moral rights, it is open to us to make the argument that these rights should be protected in law, and thereby *become* legal rights too. The Declaration of Cetacean Rights is an argument that cetaceans possess moral rights, and that these ought to be converted into legal rights; I agree wholeheartedly with that goal.

Second, I am mainly going to concentrate on what we can call *basic* rights. Basic rights are those necessary for someone to lead a minimally decent life.[13] According to major international conventions on human rights, they include the right to life, and rights against cruel treatment and imprisonment, for example. To say that these are basic rights is to say that they are really funda-mental to an acceptable existence, and that without them life might not be worth living. One implication is that basic rights cannot be *outweighed* by other, non-basic rights. My right to own property does not outweigh other people's right to freedom from imprisonment and cruel treatment. This is one reason why slavery is wrong (another, of course, is that people should not *be* property). My right to the free pursuit of a religious belief does not outweigh other people's right to life – which is why the practice of human sacrifice is outlawed, even if I believe it will somehow allow me to ascend to heaven. Though there are sometimes, regrettably, cases in which someone's basic rights can be outweighed, this will only happen when other basic rights are at stake. So basic rights are a serious bit of moral language – and perfectly appropriate, I will argue, to the cetacean case.

JUSTIFYING CETACEAN RIGHTS

In May 2010, scholars and activists gathered at the University of Helsinki, Finland, to proclaim a Declaration of Rights for Cetaceans.[14] As a declaration, it does not yet enjoy the status of international law. Instead it represents an effort to push the protection of whales and dolphins up the political agenda. If enough politicians and opinion-formers give it support, it might one day become a legal reality. Since it is not a formal declaration under international law – which are typically signed by the leaders of states – it can be signed by anybody. I have signed it, and by the end of this chapter you might consider signing it too.

The declaration does resemble the various human rights treaties, however, insofar as it argues that there are important moral rights, and that these ought to be protected under domestic and international law. But it would extend them to the members of the cetacean family – to all whales, dolphins and porpoises – regardless of where in the world they happen to live. The key rights it describes include the right to life; a right to protection from cruel treatment and torture; rights to freedom of movement, including the right of whales and dolphins to remain within their natural environment; a right to the protection of the cetacean environment; and a right to freedom from disruption to their cultures. For the most part, these are best understood as basic rights. The right to life, and to protection from cruelty and imprisonment, are fundamental to any tolerable life. The list also includes non-basic elements, such as the right against disruption to cetacean culture. In this chapter I aim to persuade the reader that these are important moral rights, and that they deserve legal protection. In fact, I will go further than the declaration, and argue that cetaceans possess at least one right which is not included on its list.

Why, then, should we consider whales and dolphins deserving of these rights? Scientists who have worked with cetaceans have long emphasised their remarkable mental capacities. Our knowledge of their capacities is somewhat limited: we know a good deal more about the characteristics typical of some species compared to others, and these knowledge gaps mean that it is difficult to generalise across the whole class of cetaceans. But we do now know that many cetaceans have very considerable capacities for thought and understanding. Bottlenose dolphins have been observed using sponges as tools with which to forage on the ocean floor, and for centuries they have been known to assist human fishers, apparently in return for a share of their catch.[15] As in the case of humans, the historical evolution of cetaceans involved an extraordinary increase in brain size and complexity.[16] Every cetacean possesses a cerebral cortex which is more convoluted, and more packed with neurons, than any human being's.[17] As well as clearly feeling pain and pleasure, they also appear to qualify as self-aware subjects. Dolphins, for example, are capable of recognising themselves as distinct individuals.[18] Experiments have shown that they can understand man-made languages, and grasp pictorial representations of reality, as well as the meaning of gestures such as pointing.[19] They possess their own complex forms of communication and perception too. Besides vision, cetaceans can 'see' the world by using echolocation – a much more useful skill in the murky depths. They are also capable of complex vocal communication. This communication appears to be extremely important to at least some cetaceans: deprived of the ability to communicate with their fellows, scientists have reported dolphins apparently giving up on life.[20]

Because cetaceans are so intelligent, they have achieved considerable social and cultural complexity. Some highly intelligent aquatic creatures – like octopuses – appear for the most part to be rather antisocial. But whales and dolphins have complex and sophisticated social structures. They even seem to

7.1 Spinner dolphins leaping into the air off the coast of Hawaii.

possess their own distinctive 'cultures'. Orcas (or killer whales) have dialects specific to family groups, which are passed down from mother to child. When orcas from different 'pods' meet each other, they perform specific 'greeting ceremonies' before mingling.[21] Humpback whales have been observed developing novel feeding techniques which have then spread rapidly throughout the relevant population.[22] The more we look closely at cetaceans, the more the belief that humans are unique in their dynamic ability to learn new behaviours and practices is shaken.

Indeed, it seems perfectly intelligible to say that cetaceans have intentional practices, to which they are committed. These can have both backward-looking and forward-looking aspects. Schools of whales returning to their original territory after extended trips away 'first sing the old songs of the previous year, and then the new songs'.[23] Orca mothers spend time tutoring their children in shallow-water hunting, meanwhile, offering evidence of a 'forward-looking attitude in the form of a capacity for formulating and carrying out plans'.[24] Even if we restrict subjecthood to creatures with 'the capacity to have a conception of oneself, to formulate long-range plans, to appreciate general facts about one's environment and intelligently employ them in one's plans',[25] there is little doubt that cetaceans qualify. What, though, can we say about the specific rights of cetaceans?

CETACEANS' RIGHT TO LIFE

The first plausible candidate on any list of cetacean rights is a *right to life*. We should understand this as a basic entitlement of whales and dolphins not to be killed, or deprived of the means necessary to their existence. Respecting this right will require us to observe what philosophers call 'negative' duties, which are duties *not* to act towards whales and dolphins in certain ways. It is also plausible that we can have 'positive' duties towards cetaceans, which would involve actually assisting cetaceans who cannot secure their own right to life. But for the most part, I am going to concentrate on negative duties. These will include, most obviously, a duty not to arbitrarily kill whales and dolphins. They will also include a duty to avoid transforming the environment of whales and dolphins in such a way as to make it impossible for them to survive.

If cetaceans do have a basic right to life, this has momentous consequences. Violating the cetacean right to life might not be absolutely forbidden, just as killing humans is not always absolutely forbidden. For instance, in times of war killing some is often necessary in order to avoid far greater numbers of deaths, and in their everyday lives people retain a right of self-defence which means they can have the moral permission to kill others if this is necessary to their survival. But my suggestion is that it is *only* by pointing to some kind of necessity – understood in terms of physical survival – that people could justify killing whales and dolphins. Killing an orca might be justifiable if she has decided to eat you (though rest assured this would be an extremely rare event). Killing her for food might also be permissible if you have no other way to secure your survival. But killing her for sport, or because you would *prefer* for whatever reason to eat orca meat, would not be.

One obvious implication of this position is that the enterprise of commercial whaling was a monumental injustice, which violated cetaceans' right to life

7.2 A hunted whale (probably a fin whale) at the Tyee whaling company, Alaska, c. 1910.

on an enormous scale. Driven by the profit motive, twentieth-century industrial whaling caused the deaths of 99 per cent of the world's blue whales, and
96 per cent of humpback, right and fin whales.[26] Their deaths were brutal, and
involved a gruesome array of weapons and practices, from exploding harpoons
to the trick of capturing infant whales in order to lure their mothers to their
deaths. The carnage generated was not required in order the meet the subsistence needs of humans. It was inspired by the enormous profits to be found by
selling wh   bodies to the fuel, pharmaceutical and cosmetics industries.

          deliberate acts of killing that appear to be ruled out by the
       fe. Killing whales and dolphins as a side effect of fishing
         ts a culpable failure to respect their right of life, assuming
        eeable and avoidable. Every year at least five thousand
        d and killed in the nets used to catch tuna.[27] But the
       reduce dolphin deaths are readily available.[28] To refrain

from using them for reasons of economy is unacceptable in light of the profound consequences for cetaceans. Likewise, many whales are killed every year in 'ship strike' incidents, hit by fast-moving vessels they are unable to avoid. Again, methods for avoiding cetacean deaths are not out of reach by any means. Reductions in speed have been shown to reduce mortalities,[29] and ship hulls can be redesigned to be smoother and less deadly to whales.

Respecting the cetacean right to life can also demand that we avoid interfering with their food supply. Unfortunately, we are seriously impeding the ability of cetaceans to feed themselves. For instance, members of several species of whale depend on tiny crustaceans known as krill for their nutrition. But krill are under serious pressure from industrial fishing,[30] which scoops them up in enormous quantities and grinds them up to produce pet food, dietary supplements or fodder for fish farms. If this means that whales are unable to survive or to rear their young, their right to life is jeopardised.

TORTURE, FREEDOM OF MOVEMENT AND CULTURE

Cetaceans also have a basic right to *freedom from torture* and other forms of cruel treatment. Torture is supremely hard to justify in the human case, not only because it involves intense and unbearable pain, but also because, in inflicting such helplessness on its victims, it represents a horrific (and typically intentional) denial of their agency.[31] Torture replaces a being who can make their own decisions with an unwilling receptable for pain, who can do nothing to change their fate. The possession of sentience and self-awareness ensures that cetaceans, too, will experience torture and other forms of cruelty as both intensely painful and as a radical assault on their agency and autonomy.

Their interest in maintaining their autonomy suggests it cetaceans also have a basic right to *freedom of movement.* crucial in turn to a series of other important rights. Free vital to one's ability to associate with likeminded other plausibly includes a right to stay put if one wishes.[32] protecting the right to freedom of movement means freedom to remain within their chosen natural environment. For that reason, capturing and confining cetaceans will typically represent an injustice. The award-winning film *Blackfish* (2013) vividly captured the terrible consequences of keeping orcas in captivity. We might be able to imagine instances in which confining one or a few cetaceans is necessary in order to prevent a great loss of cetacean life (imagine that it is only by capturing a few dolphins that a cure can be found for some deadly cetacean disease). But even if examples are conceivable, they will be rare in practice. Since freedom of movement is a basic right, we are only justified in restricting it if doing so is necessary to defend the similarly basic rights of many others. Confining cetaceans within theme parks in order to satisfy human curiosity would not meet that test.[33]

The rights to freedom of movement and freedom from torture are basic rights, crucial to even a minimally decent life. But I also want to argue that cetaceans have some *non*-basic rights, over and above those necessary to a minimally decent life. One of the rights suggested by the Declaration of Cetacean Rights is a right against disruption to cetacean culture. We have already seen that there are ample grounds for believing that cetaceans have their own cultures, and that these cultures matter deeply to them. As in the human case, the freedom to associate with like-minded individuals and to pass one's beliefs or practices on to others appears to be highly valuable to them. It may well be that individuals possess no general right that their own culture continues to exist (one reason why is that our descendants must be free to make their own choices about such matters). But individuals may nevertheless have a weighty interest – capable of grounding a right – in being able to maintain cultural and social norms, and transmit them to their fellows.[34] Sometimes we will act wrongly in interfering with this right. Imagine, for instance, a human community that lives scattered across a group of remote islands. It maintains its culture and language by way of regular radio and TV broadcasts. If someone either deliberately or negligently jammed those broadcasts, the community could bly claim that its right to maintain its culture had been thwarted.

This is precisely what we are doing to cetaceans. Sound pollution m seabed drilling, from wind farms and from military testing are seriously interfering with their ability to communicate. (They may also be making life intolerable: there is evidence that sonic pollution is one of the main causes of cetaceans beaching themselves. If so, it violates the basic right against torture too.) Whereas some whales can communicate over distances of 600 miles or more, the noise from ships and wind farms has been found to mask their calls beyond distances of 6 miles. These acoustic disturbances are to all intents and purposes 'shrinking their world'.[35] Sound pollution makes hunting harder, and as such it can also represent an unjust infringement of cetaceans' right to life (it can also make mating problematic, as cetaceans are less able to find each other). Our interference in the lives of cetaceans can often be reduced quite easily, such as through innovations in propeller design.[36] Refusing to make these reasonable accommodations is hard to justify unless our own basic rights are at stake.

I also want to claim that cetaceans possess at least one right that is not included within the Declaration of Cetacean Rights. A good case, it seems to me, can be made for cetaceans' possession of a right to political representation. At present, there is no obvious way in which cetaceans can participate in domestic or global political institutions. Rights to vote or to run for office therefore have no value for them. But this does not mean that we should ignore them when we make political decisions. Just like future people, or those who suffer from medical conditions which make direct participation in political life impossible, non-human animals plausibly possess a right that their interests are adequately taken into account in our political deliberations.[37] We should be designing ocean governance institutions capable of protecting their interests, rather than ignoring them, and this might demand dedicated mechanisms to put their protection at the forefront of political debate. If the interests of marine animals are *not* suitably taken into account within our institutions, those institutions will be less legitimate as a result.

OBJECTIONS AND REPLIES

Some readers will find the conclusions I have reached quite radical and challenging. For example, some might ask whether killing whales should *really* be considered as serious a moral offence as killing a human being. In fact, some philosophers have argued that killing non-human animals may be *less* morally serious than killing humans.[38] One reason for that might be that other animals do not possess a conscious awareness of time. To rob someone of future life is bad – but it is especially bad, we might say, if he or she has hopes and plans for the future. It may be *less* bad if his or her life is a moment-to-moment one, with no hopes or plans for future life. And some marine creatures definitely do seem to lead that kind of moment-to-moment life. Starfish, for instance, probably lack any hopes or ambitions beyond getting to the next food source. In response, I would say that while this might well matter in some cases, it does not appear to be an especially troubling objection in the case of cetaceans. Individual whales and dolphins *do* appear likely to have a sense of time, and even hopes and desires for the future. In that sense it is perfectly intelligible to say that their right to life is a very strong one. It is perfectly conceivable that, if we had some way of understanding their mental processes, we would find that they would deeply regret the prospect of being robbed of future life, and of the ability to continue to live with their loved ones. Much more research would be needed for us to be confident about whether their sense of time is as strong as our own, and so I won't try to rule out the possibility that a human has a somewhat stronger claim not to be robbed of a future. But we do have good grounds to believe that cetaceans have a strong right to life, which should only be overruled in cases of absolute necessity.

I also want to consider an objection that revolves around human culture. In 1986, the International Whaling Commission introduced a moratorium on whaling, which has succeeded in reducing the slaughter of marine mammals. But the practice persists, since several countries – including Norway, Iceland and Japan – continue to hunt whales. In some cases they do so under the auspices of a 'cultural' defence. The objection I want to address suggests that, however regrettable industrial whaling is, we should think differently about the 'cultural' whaling that is still carried out by some communities across the world. Traditional whaling practices may be very important to some people's ways of life, to the extent that the continued existence of their cultures would be threatened if they were outlawed. It has to be said, to begin with, that it can be rather difficult to distinguish between cultural and industrial whaling in practice. Claims about science are also sometimes wrapped into the debate. Japan, for instance, has offered defences of whaling based partly on culture and partly on science, and has recently withdrawn from the International Whaling Commission.[39] Its claims about science are not persuasive. Fundamentally, if whales and dolphins have a basic right to life, then the advancement of marine biology would not provide a sound justification for killing them (we do not kill humans, after all, in order to find out more about their biology). In practice, the killing of tens of thousands of cetaceans does not appear to have advanced science anyway: most expert observers believe that 'scientific' whaling is a cover for a trade in whale meat destined for the dinner plate.

But what about the cultural defence, though? Along with Norway and Iceland, Japan has been a long-standing consumer of whales. Although most Norwegians, Japanese and Icelanders do not eat whale meat, some do, and that tradition may be important to them. It may be especially important to indige-nous communities who have hunted and killed cetaceans for many generations, timing their movements around whales' seasonal migrations, and fashioning arte-facts out of their skin or teeth. Shouldn't we be sympathetic towards the desire to continue those embattled traditions? Sympathetic we might be, but being morally serious about basic rights means we must hold firm to the conclusion that the desire to continue a cultural tradition cannot outweigh a basic right to life. We would not entertain the possibility of killing humans in order to perpetuate a cultural tradition. So why whales? In short, it appears that the cultural defence simply fails to take cetaceans' right to life sufficiently seriously. Things might be different if people's lives *depended* on killing cetaceans for their very existence. Indigenous communities have often combined appeals to both cultural practices and material subsistence when defending whaling. But it is not typically true that indigenous whalers have no alternative means of meeting their subsistence needs without recourse to whaling.[40] If they genuinely do lack alternatives, then they ought to be provided with other means of survival as a matter of urgency. If they possess alternative options, then killing whales cannot be justified.[41]

CETACEANS AND CLIMATE CHANGE

Taking cetaceans' rights seriously will have important implications for how we think about, and respond to, many important oceanic challenges. We can illustrate that point by considering perhaps the greatest challenge of all – climate change. When the world comes together to adopt specific climate goals (Should warming be limited to 1.5 degrees? Two degrees? Or something else?), the rights of whales and dolphins ought to be taken into account. Climate change is already seriously impeding the ability of cetaceans to meet their subsistence needs. In addition to overfishing, krill populations are in decline in part because of the retreat of ice cover in the Antarctic region.[42] Elsewhere ocean warming is leading to serious declines in food availability for dolphins and whales. The dramatic consequences this could have for cetaceans' right to life give us additional reason, should it be required, to pursue highly ambitious emissions reduction strategies.

Taking cetacean rights seriously should also inform our choice of strategies to combat climate change. Take one example. Advocates of 'geoengineering' suggest we can change the natural environment to help the earth or the ocean lock away more carbon, removing it from circulation in the atmosphere. But some geoengineering techniques could have dramatic consequences for cetaceans. One of the most prominent ideas is called 'iron fertilisation'. This involves adding iron to the surface of the ocean, where it should spur an increase in levels of phytoplankton. In theory that could be good news for the many whales that eat phytoplankton. But the consequences are very hard to predict. One result might be a general loss of oxygen in lower levels of the sea, which could have dramatic effects on marine food webs.[43] That could be very bad for members of many other cetacean species. The precautionary principle would suggest we ought to avoid using such techniques unless we have a good understanding of their likely effects, and can safely manage any problems that arise. A concern for the rights of cetaceans should also influence our choice of adaptation strategies. For many coastal communities, the building of sea walls might seem like a reasonable response to rising sea levels. But what if the replacement of natural coastlines with concrete walls makes it more difficult for dolphins to feed, or robs them of safe habitat in which to rear their young? Taking on board the interests of non-human animals such as cetaceans is vital to any just response to climate change.

On the other hand, whales could be important allies in the fight against climate change. This is because whales play a crucial and often underappreciated role in locking away carbon. They physically absorb large quantities of carbon as part of their diet of krill and other small marine animals. Their poop then falls to the ocean floor, where the carbon remains for many years. Remarkably, it would take 1,375 trees a year's growth to absorb the 33 tons of carbon contained in an average great whale's body.[44] When whales eventually die, they fall to the deep ocean floor and this carbon is locked away for centuries. Even more importantly, perhaps, whales act as key conduits for the nutrient cycle, taking iron and nitrogen from the depths and releasing them in surface waters, spurring the (natural) growth of phytoplankton wherever they travel.[45] Phytoplankton in turn sequester far more carbon annually than do the world's rainforests, and it has been estimated that an increase in phytoplankton activity of a mere 1 per cent would capture as much carbon annually as 2 billion new trees.[46] This is not why we should protect whales from hunting or other harmful effects of our actions in the ocean: we should protect them because they have rights. But it is well worth recognising that efforts to help whale populations recover from the catastrophe of commercial whaling could also help enormously to stabilise the climate. Whales are 'ecosystem engineers' and we would do well to make them our allies, not our enemies.[47]

BEYOND CETACEANS?

So far I have suggested that we should defend a list of core rights for cetaceans at least as extensive as that contained in the Declaration of Cetacean Rights. Cetaceans have many moral rights, I have argued, and we should pursue all opportunities to convert them into legal rights that would be protected throughout the ocean. Thinking through cetaceans' interests is a useful way of illustrating the considerable work we have to do in moving beyond the 'anthro-pocentric' (or human-focused) approach taken by many accounts of justice, and indeed by our governing institutions. I have, I hope, vindicated the idea that marine animals can *have* rights, that these can include weighty, 'basic' rights, as well as illustrating some of the likely practical implications if we begin to take these rights seriously.

But I have also been clear that this is just an illustration of the kind of case that can be made. There are many other ocean creatures, with their own capac-ities and interests, which will also have moral rights worthy of protection. For example, we might want to argue that legal rights against killing, torture and imprisonment should also be held by seals, sea cows and octopuses. Building a full account of animal rights will require us to reflect on the different capacities of a great variety of species. Making the case will depend on input from philos-ophers as well as biologists, and defending these rights will demand support from ordinary citizens, from lawyers, pressure groups, and ultimately political leaders.

In some ways the cetacean case is an easy one to make, because the capaci-ties of whales and dolphins overlap to a certain extent with our own. I have sailed alongside whales and dolphins several times, and witnessed them engaging in playful behaviour, from making acrobatic leaps out of the water to riding the boat's bow wave, apparently for fun. Anyone lucky enough to encounter them in the wild may find it easy to recognise that there is a 'person' there, however distinctive their physical form. In other cases, our judgements may be less clear, and there is more space for controversy about how far a species' capacities extend. But these controversies cannot be avoided. Take the case of fish. If, as I believe, fish have a right against cruel treatment, that will likely require us to transform many of our fishing practices. We might have to abandon catching methods that consign individual fish to an unnecessarily painful death, for instance. If fish have a weighty right to life, the consequences will be even more profound. It will not necessarily mean that killing fish for food is always wrong, because there are circumstances where people have no other choice. Millions of people in the global South are at present heavily nutritionally dependent on eating fish. We might regret that fact, and try to change it, but in the meantime, asking them to stop eating fish is not reasonable. But for most of us, my suspicion is that eating fish is to unjustifiably infringe their right to life, and to treat them as mere means to our own ends[48] – including our preference for a varied, interesting diet. That is one major reason why I don't eat fish (though there are many other reasons that have less to do with the rights of fish: among other things, industrial fishing has disturbed the ecological balance of the ocean; devastated much of the seabed and coral reefs; released more carbon than the global aviation industry, through bottom trawling;[49] and killed countless whales and dolphins[50]).

I recognise that this view is controversial, and that many will be unpersuaded that fish have a weighty right to life in the first place. I have already noted that some creatures appear to have moment-to-moment existences, with no conception of the future. Depriving someone of future existence might be worse if they *have* a conception of the future, and less worrisome if they do not. Actually, I am not certain that fish do lead this kind of momentary existence: it may, instead, be one of our prejudices, like the belief that fish do not feel pain (a belief that has stubbornly lingered, in the face of much evidence to the contrary[51]). Once I had the amazing privilege of visiting the Great Barrier Reef with my family – a privilege that might, tragically, be unavailable to our descendants. As we began snorkelling, a large batfish appeared, and remained by the boat throughout our visit. 'Oh, that's Bruce,' our guide observed. 'He always remembers what time we get here.' He fed Bruce before we left, and the fish then swam away, apparently satisfied. So much for the stereotype of the forgetful fish.

Alternatively, we might point to the precarious existence of fish in the wild. Fish are what evolutionary biologists call 'r-strategists'. Whereas humans (just like whales and dolphins) give birth to very limited numbers of young, whom they nurture over an extended period, fish typically lay enormous numbers of eggs and their children are then left to fend for themselves. Most of them are immediately gobbled up by a range of predators. As a result, we might argue that the practice of aquaculture – which involves breeding fish in captivity, fattening them up in huge nets and then eating them – does not really harm them. After all, any individual wild fish is massively unlikely to survive to adulthood. A fish in captivity will eventually be killed for food, but it has a far better chance of making it to adulthood inside a fish farm rather than outside of it. On that view, aquaculture might be morally acceptable – or even preferable – assuming that reasonable welfare standards are in place.[52]

It is not clear what this response establishes, though. Even if aquaculture improves the odds that a given fish will survive to adulthood, it may still infringe its rights. Just as there is a good life for dolphins (and we can be reasonably sure it is not a life in captivity), there is presumably a good life for a fish. And spending its entire life swimming in a net crowded with its fellows, encrusted with lice and excrement, is almost certainly not it. Our failure to recognise the stresses involved for the fish concerned is probably just that: a failure of imagination and understanding. Since this is probably a controversial opinion, though, I will point out that the wider arguments of this book do not stand or fall on the back of it. In the last chapter, I considered the human rights of people involved in the fishing industry. If you believe that there is a future for the fishing industry, this question is a very important one. Even if you believe we should not eat fish – or if you adopt what I think is a more reasonable position, that you should avoid eating fish if you *can* – the fishing industry is not going anywhere soon. As such, questions about human rights in the fishing trade will continue to demand our attention.

8

SEA-LEVEL RISE AND SMALL ISLAND STATES

The border between land and sea is constantly shifting. It contains many liminal zones (from estuaries to wetlands and salt marshes), as well as places that are sometimes land and sometimes not. At times of change, the boundary can lurch dramatically. Until eight thousand years ago, people could walk from (what we now call) England straight to continental Europe, across the region known to archaeologists as Doggerland. When enormous glaciers melted in North America the land bridge was inundated, separating Britain from the rest of Europe and creating what we might – quite wrongly – see as the unalterable map of the modern world.

In the Anthropocene, humans themselves have intervened to redraw marine boundaries. Over the years ingenious Dutch engineers have extended their country's area by around a fifth, and a similar process is now under way in Singapore. For some the result represents a gain, while for others it means a kind of loss. My wife grew up in a house 50 yards from the sea in the small island state of Bahrain. As a child, the ocean was central to her everyday life. Like many locals, her ancestors were merchants, their wooden dhows sailing out into the Persian Gulf, searching for pearls to be sold across the Middle East and as far away as India. Going back there now is always tinged with sadness, because where there was once a shoreline fringed with coral reefs, there are now high-rises and shopping malls. The sea is more than a mile away, its sounds and smells all but forgotten.

In countries like Bahrain, Singapore and the Netherlands, coastal geographies have been *deliberately* altered, to provide more land for housing, farming and industry. But it would be a grave mistake to assume that in the Anthropocene nature is entirely under our control. That would be an example of what the Greeks called *hubris*, the dangerous overconfidence that often precedes a fall. Capitalism is busily transforming the natural world, but our actions are having consequences that we do not clearly foresee, and that many of us will find very difficult to live with. Anthropogenic climate change, in particular, will bring entirely unwanted changes to our shared geography. Rising sea levels are likely to leave many millions of people homeless, and may render entire countries uninhabitable. Without concerted international assistance, the lives and livelihoods of countless vulnerable people will be threatened.

In this chapter we will consider the plight of 'climate exiles' – people rendered homeless, and perhaps even stateless, by sea-level rise. A first priority will be to determine who, if anyone, has a moral duty to admit individual climate exiles, and what kind of protection they are entitled to from the international system. But we also urgently need to consider the implications of sea-level rise for the survival of political communities, especially in the case of small island states. Uniquely, these island states might be rendered completely uninhabitable by rising tides. If so, this could strike a terrible blow to their future as self-governing political communities, with their members potentially dispersed across a number of new host states, and unable, perhaps, to maintain a collective political life or shared institutions. Some commentators have even summoned up the terrible prospect of 'state death', with island communities expunged from the political map entirely. Although the future for small islanders is deeply uncertain, I will argue that this dread scenario can be at least partly dispelled – if we act in the right way. If entire islands are indeed inundated by sea-level rise, their inhabitants will experience very significant losses – losses caused not by them, but by the high-emitters of the world. But the inundation of island states need not mean an end to self-determination or even statehood. Taking the plight of small island states seriously will, however, require us to rethink some long-standing assumptions about the connections between people, territory and states.

THE THREAT OF SEA-LEVEL RISE

A warming planet contributes to sea-level rise in two ways. First, it causes the ocean to expand, because warmer water occupies more space than colder water. Second, it causes glaciers to melt, pouring huge quantities of additional water into the sea. In recent decades melting has become more and more significant, and the collapse of ice sheets in Antarctica and Greenland represents our biggest threat by some distance.[1]

How high could the sea rise? That will depend on our success in cutting back greenhouse gas emissions, and in slowing or even reversing the loss of carbon sinks like rainforests. Even if serious climate policies are put in place immediately, it is virtually certain that sea levels will continue to rise to *some* extent, because our emissions have already 'locked in' a significant degree of warming. But exactly how far they rise is down to us. If our leaders are serious about decarbonising the world economy – and if enough ordinary citizens change their habits – we might limit sea-level rise to around half a metre by the end of this century. Without serious efforts at decarbonisation, we could easily see rises beyond one metre,[2] especially if warming causes the Antarctic ice sheets to collapse on a grand scale.

While one metre might not sound like much, the consequences of even modest sea-level rise could be dramatic. Major world cities could well be submerged by the century's end. The risks posed to places like Miami and New York have received a good deal of attention, but most of the cities that stand to be affected are in Asia, with places like Shanghai, Hong Kong and Osaka facing enormous challenges.[3] Outside of our major cities, large tracts of land would be reclaimed by the sea, if not permanently then at least for hundreds and possibly thousands of years. It is hard to overestimate the challenge this would pose to local communities. Coastal areas no more than 10 metres above sea level are home to roughly 680 million people – one in every eleven people now alive. Nearly a quarter of them live within just one metre of sea level.[4] The warming sea will shrink the space in which millions live, work and grow crops, forcing them to fall back into the interior, pursued by the encroaching coast.

Inundation by the sea is not the only problem posed by rising tides. As the water approaches, salt leaches into nearby farmland, damaging its fertility. Combined with problems like climate-induced desertification, this will severely strain our ability to feed a growing world population. Coastal zones will also face more extreme wave and weather patterns. The Intergovernmental Panel on Climate Change (IPCC) predicts with a high degree of confidence that events such as cyclones or tsunamis will, by the year 2050, go from being once-a-century events in many locations to once-a-year events. Flood damage could increase ten- or even a hundredfold by the year 2100,[5] making living by the coast expensive and precarious.

But sea-level rise will not affect all of us equally. Wave heights in the North Atlantic and the Mediterranean could actually diminish in the coming decades, and in any case people living by those coasts will often have the financial capacity to engage in protective measures – investing in sea walls, flood barriers or the more natural protections to be discussed in the next chapter. By contrast, wave heights will very likely increase across the Southern Ocean and the tropical eastern Pacific, where the capacity to adapt will often be severely strained.[6] Countries in the global South – including China, India, Bangladesh, Vietnam and the Philippines – will be hardest hit by the loss of land for farming and habitation. If the IPCC's most pessimistic scenario comes to pass, the land now inhabited by one-third of the population of countries like Bangladesh and Vietnam will be completely lost to the sea.[7]

This would be a desperate outcome, because most of the world's tropical regions are also relatively poor, meaning their resilience in the face of rapid change will be sorely stretched. Millions of people in the global South are already engaged in a daily battle with poverty, and their governments will struggle to help them through the chaos and disruption caused by rising tides. Migration experts expect a surge in 'internal' displacement, with huge numbers of people forced to find refuge elsewhere in their home states, away from the encroaching ocean. They will often lose property and employment in the process, leaving them vulnerable to marginalisation and exploitation. A major challenge of climate justice will be to channel resources and technical help in the direction of countries in the global South, which for the most part have played a relatively modest role in causing the problem of climate change in the first place. To date, we have not taken the task of financing adaptation in the South sufficiently seriously. But it is undoubtedly one of the greatest challenges that climate change poses to our world.

DISAPPEARING ISLANDS AND THE RIGHT OF REFUGE

Though most of the people who stand to be affected by sea-level rise live in large countries in Southern and Eastern Asia, it poses a quite distinctive challenge to several small island states dotted throughout the ocean. Countries like Kiribati, Tuvalu and the Marshall Islands in the Pacific, and the Maldives in the Indian Ocean, lie so close to sea level that they could be wholly inundated even by relatively modest rises. If that happens, their citizens will face a unique plight. They will not be 'internally' displaced, because there will be no domestic hinterland for them to fall back into. Instead they will be forced to find refuge in someone else's state. They would become what we will call *climate exiles*, dependent on admission to another country for their very survival.[8] At present it is not certain that small island states will be completely submerged, or, if so, which. But in many places the prospects look bleak, especially if a degree of sea-level rise has already been locked in by emissions to date. Anote Tong, the president of Kiribati, has acknowledged that 'our islands, our homes, may no longer be habitable – or even exist – within this century'.[9] Before any such outcome comes to pass, we must think seriously about what small islanders are owed by way of assistance or compensation. If adaptation policies are going to be fair and effective, this will involve listening to islanders themselves – listening to their fears, as well as to their preferences about a possible future post-inundation.

The first priority should undoubtedly be to recognise that climate exiles – or even *potential* exiles – have a right to move to a state that can safeguard their lives and livelihoods. Regardless of whether exiles are ultimately able to maintain their political communities in something like their current form (see

8.1 A teenage girl sits in floodwater caused by sea-level rise, Funafuti Atoll, Tuvalu.

below), this right to move somewhere safe is an important backstop that will protect them from immediate threats to their most basic rights. Unfortunately – despite decades of discussions about climate change and its likely effects – the contemporary refugee system has not yet got to grips with the predicament that climate exiles face. That system was born in the years following the Second World War, when millions were displaced from their homelands and urgently needed asylum elsewhere. It seeks to guarantee a safe haven to people whose own state has turned against them, for reasons including their race, religion or sexuality. The relevant international law defines a refugee as someone who has a well-founded fear of persecution in their home state, and is seeking asylum elsewhere as a result. The problem, however, is that climate exiles do not fit into this picture. Someone made homeless by rising tides is not being persecuted by his or her home state; that state has simply become uninhabitable, for reasons outside of its control. Morally, however, they seem to have just as strong a claim to assistance from the international community as people fleeing persecution. Like refugees conventionally understood, they stand to lose even

163

the most basic protections available to them in their home state.[10] While returning people facing persecution to their home state would expose them to grave risk, in the case of climate exiles it would mean death.

A key goal of the international system should be to extend to climate exiles the same legal protections enjoyed (however imperfectly in practice) by conventional refugees. Whether we *call* them refugees is probably not the most important issue. What matters is that we accept that climate exiles have a moral right to admission in another state, and that this ought to be recognised and protected under international law as a matter of urgency. In fact climate exiles need more than asylum. By contrast to 'regular' refugees – for whom asylum is seen as a temporary measure, on the (often dubious) assumption that they will one day be able to return safely to their homeland – climate exiles would need permanent resettlement. Islands, once submerged, will not become habitable again in the near future. Exiles would have a strong claim, therefore, not only to enter another state, but in due course to become *citizens* of that state. Without a clear path to citizenship, they would be forced to live as a permanent minority, deprived of the same political or social rights as the people they shared their new country with. For people with nowhere else to go, this would be intolerable.

In some quarters the claim that exiles have a right to asylum and even citizenship in a new state will be controversial. But it should not be. Politicians on the right have often decried 'abuses' of the asylum system, and claimed that it should be up to each country to decide whether it will admit refugees, and if so how many. But this tilts the moral calculus much too far in the direction of receiving states. Even if we believed that states generally have the right to make their own decisions about their future, the desire to do so does not outweigh people's basic human right to survival[11] – and this is what is at stake in the case of climate exiles. Unless we are content to live alongside a class of permanent aliens with no pathway to citizenship, asylum must also include the prospect of full and equal membership in the host community.

Still, even if no state should refuse to allow climate exiles to enter at all, we face important questions about which climate exiles should be allowed to migrate where, and in what numbers. Broadly speaking, there are two approaches we could take here. The first would declare that exiles have a right to move to a state *somewhere*. This would presumably have to mean a stable, reasonably well-governed state that would look out for their interests – but it would not necessarily mean a state of their choice. The second approach would declare that exiles have the right to *choose* which state they move to.

The first approach is compatible with an essentially top-down attitude to the problem. In principle, host states could come together and decide how many exiles each of them should admit. They might decide, for instance, that states which have emitted higher than average levels of greenhouse gases should admit higher than average numbers of climate exiles, on the principle of 'you broke it, you fix it'. Or they might decide that wealthier states, or states that are less densely populated, should admit more people rather than fewer, because they have greater capacity to accommodate them. Alternatively, they might try and find some way of balancing responsibility for climate change *and* the capacity to absorb exiles.[12] Either way, we could in theory work out in advance the precise number of exiles any one state should take in. Exiles could then be 'assigned' to each state in accordance with that formula. If the end result was that each exile had a safe place to go, the international community would have delivered on its duties – even if individual climate exiles had no choice in the matter.

In my view, there are several reasons for concern about this top-down response, and they speak in favour of a more bottom-up approach, in which individual exiles have greater control over where they end up living. Clearly, the top-down response would shrink the choices available to individual climate exiles. But that is likely to mean worse outcomes for them. Left to their own devices, exiles might prefer to relocate to states with a similar way of life to their own. They might, for instance, prefer to relocate to other island states that were less vulnerable to rising tides. That would give them a better prospect of continuing their existing ways of life, and perhaps of living with people who share a culture, language or religion with them. Our decisions here could make a significant difference to their well-being, assuming that a good life requires the ability to associate with people who are important to us, and to exert some degree of control over our own lives. The loss of traditional homelands is likely to be wrenching enough without obliging exiles to enter states with cultures, climates or geographies they find alien, even if the fact that those states are wealthy, or high-emitters, would make that in one sense more fitting.

Any just system for rehoming exiles will, I suspect, recognise that they often have significant reasons for preferring admission to one state rather than another.[13] In practice, the views of islanders are often neglected in decisions about how to respond to climate change.[14] This adds insult to injury – and it is unnecessary. Even if exiles have largely been victims of climate change, rather than perpetrators, they could and should be empowered in the adaptation process. We should favour policies that promote their autonomy and active participation, rather than imposing technocratic fixes from above. In practice, I would suggest that exiles' own preferences about where to go ought to be decisive unless the consequences for the admitting state would be highly disruptive.

But we should also acknowledge a worry about the bottom-up approach too. If climate exiles are empowered to enter a state of their choice, it is quite possible they would choose to move en masse to a relatively small number of countries. They might choose to do that because those states were geographically or culturally similar to their former homes, for example, or because they believe they will find better opportunities in some places compared to others. They might move together simply because they prefer not to live apart from friends and family. If this happened, we might worry that some receiving states faced a much greater burden than others. In at least some cases, they might not be the ones we believe *should* bear greater burdens. For islanders to move to other relatively poor and low-emitting island states, for example, would place the burdens of accommodating them on the wrong shoulders.

One response to this is to say that we should not think of climate exiles as being a burden at all. They are human beings, they have the right to live somewhere safe, and in any case – despite what right-wing politicians often say – immigration is typically beneficial for the receiving state. Migrants can be a great asset, they are citizens of the future and, especially in countries with an ageing population, their hard work is likely to be something many countries will continue to depend on. That is an important response, but it doesn't completely dispel the worry about costs. Even if exiles would come to be much-valued citizens at some point in the future, the short- and medium-term costs involved in providing them with education, housing, welfare and health-care services could be considerable, and some states may just lack the capacity to absorb those costs, however regrettable that is. Fiji, for instance, has repeatedly expressed an interest in welcoming exiles from Tuvalu and Kiribati – but it is not obvious that it possesses the resources necessary to accommodate them properly.[15] There are also worries that increasing population pressures in small island states will drive land prices still higher, squeezing the poor out of the housing market. The appeal of the top-down approach, by contrast, is that it promises to share the burdens of accommodating exiles fairly.

The best response at this point is to try to cut the Gordian knot. We should attempt *both* to allow exiles the choice of where to live, *and* to ensure that any costs involved are shared fairly. We should be able to do that, to a significant extent at least, because even if exiles choose to start new lives in some countries rather than others, it is not inevitable that those countries will end up bearing the entirety of any costs that arise.[16] Bodies like the United Nations Adaptation Fund could channel resources in the direction of receiving countries, especially where they lacked the capacity to admit large numbers of exiles without excessive disruption (though to do this, the Adaptation Fund would require much greater resources than it has at present). A better option would be to give a substantial part of the money directly to individual exiles – who would, after all, be the ones who had lost so much – to allow them to stand on their own two feet financially wherever they chose to go. Undoubtedly, this would not fully 'compensate' them for what they had lost. As well as losing homes and businesses, islanders' ability to maintain their identities, practices and allegiances could be severely undermined.[17] The loss of homeland, and the severing of the relationship with land and the ocean, may represent setbacks to their well-being that safe refuge cannot fully make up for. If so, the international community – and especially the high-emitters among us – might well owe exiles some form of meaningful apology, as well as a commitment to share with them in commemorating their enormous loss. At the same time, giving transitional funds to islanders would help put their futures in their own hands, and it would also make their accommodation by new host states a more attractive prospect. Splitting adaptation funds between exiles and their host states offers the best chance of a fair transition. Giving the bulk of the funds to exiles will put them in charge of their own destinies. But sending some funds to host countries will allow them to plan fair transitional policies, reducing the impact on the domestic poor by protecting welfare and educational spending, or investing in good housing.

What I am claiming, then, is that our degree of responsibility for causing climate change, as well as our capacity to pick up transitional costs, are relevant when any costs associated with offering a new home to climate exiles come to be shared. But this should not drive us to a top-down model in which exiles are simply 'assigned' to one country or another. Instead these factors should be taken into account when we try to smooth the process of accommodation for individual climate exiles, by which they and a new host state learn to live with one another. A transitional fund could be set up for climate exiles (and, to a lesser extent, for receiving countries), which states made contributions to in line with both their ability to make sacrifices and their contributions to climate change. I don't want to suggest that this would offer a complete solution to the situation that could arise if many exiles chose to enter one state rather than another. It might be that local services would still be severely strained if too many chose to enter one state at a particular time, and in principle that might justify such a state imposing some limits on immigration, if only temporarily. But sharing any costs of admitting climate exiles fairly could do a great deal to smooth the process of integration, and make it more likely that they will come to exercise control over their own destinies. This kind of proposal also allows us to reframe the political issues in a much more helpful way. If exiles possessed transitional funds of their own, they would be much less likely to be seen by receiving states as a burden (this is a perception that, I have suggested, is often unjustified – but it still exerts a powerful influence on migration politics). Rather than states being 'punished' by the requirement to admit exiles (as right-wing politicians would no doubt claim), admitting them might be an attractive proposition. Most importantly, a policy along these lines would put the future of climate exiles in their own hands. In light of our contributions to climate change, that may be the least we owe them.

SELF-DETERMINATION, STATEHOOD AND TERRITORY

We should also reflect on the *political* losses that exiles could experience. For better or worse, we live in a world of states, in which many people strongly value their ability to govern themselves collectively. In this world of states, the ideal of self-government is strongly linked to control over particular slices of territory. Sea-level rise, however, might be thought to threaten both self-determination and control over territory. The government of the Maldives has suggested, for instance, that sea-level rise may 'cause the denial of the right to self-determination of the Maldives people', and that this would represent a significant part of the harm done to them by climate change.[18] In light of such a prospect, Pacific island leaders insisted in the Suva Declaration of 2015 that their right to exist *as a people* must be protected in any response to sea-level rise.[19]

More starkly, islanders have even been said to face the prospect of what international-relations scholars call 'state death'.[20] Within international law, statehood is taken to be something of a package: it is thought to involve the presence of a permanent population, on a permanent territory, represented by an effective government, and with the ability to engage in foreign relations with other states.[21] But in the case of low-lying island states the presence of a permanent population on a particular piece of territory is under imminent threat. Does this mean that inundation would mean an end to statehood? In times of war, states that have fallen prey to foreign invasion have managed to maintain governments-in-exile for limited periods. They did not cease to be states as a result, and in that sense it seems that statehood can survive in practice even without control over a fixed territory. But wartime invasion is (hopefully) a temporary event. Inundation might be sufficiently long-lasting that the government-in-exile model is no longer appropriate – or so it has been suggested.[22]

The loss of statehood would compound the losses experienced by climate exiles, over and above the loss of land and property, or the loss of cultural connections. As a result, the prospect of inundation takes us into relatively uncharted territory. Would exiles have the right to recreate their states somewhere else? How could they do that, in a world where more or less all land is already occupied by one state or another? If exiles were not able to establish a new land territory, does that mean they could no longer exercise their right to collective self-determination? Would it mean their states, and their island citizenship, would disappear from the historical register?

Although the challenge posed by rising seas is in many ways a desperate one, I am going to offer a counterpoint to any counsel of despair here. Inundation, I will argue, need not mean an end to self-determination, to statehood, or even to the possession of territory. This is not by any means to minimise the losses faced by exiles. These losses are enormous – indeed the very threat of future inundation is in itself a major harm. In neglecting to cut our emissions faster we are doing islanders a great injustice. But many islanders have expressed a deep commitment to self-determination and to independent statehood, come what may. My goal is to take that commitment seriously, and investigate ways in which it might be protected even in the face of rising tides.

Let us begin with the idea of self-determination. At present, island communities are able to make key decisions about their own political futures. They can decide what kind of institutions to run, how to pay for them, and how to include people in the political process. The right of the world's distinct 'peoples' to exercise self-determination is clearly protected within international law. The 1966 Covenant on Civil and Political Rights, for example, declares that all peoples should enjoy the ability 'to freely determine their political status and freely pursue their economic, social, and cultural development'.[23] For many philosophers, what is important about the right to self-determination is not that it allows people to secure justice, or democracy, or economic growth. It is that people have an interest in running institutions that they recognise as *their own*. Those institutions are valuable to a community partly 'because they *created* those institutions together with others, and see those institutions as reflecting their shared projects and contributions'.[24]

The project of collective self-determination is, however, often said to be threatened by inundation. Specifically, the worry is that if climate exiles end up being dispersed between many host states, their ability to govern themselves collectively will suffer. This is not to say that they would no longer be a distinct 'people' (indigenous peoples are still considered peoples even if their territory was long ago annexed by colonisers). Nor is it to say they would no longer have a *right* to self-determination (again, international law is clear that this right is held by peoples *as* peoples, whether they rule over a specific territory or not). But the loss of territory could be a significant blow to the ability to *exercise* the right to self-determination. If islanders no longer have their own collective institutions, what concrete means of determining their own destiny would be open to them?

Consider next the question of statehood. In the contemporary world, the state is the primary vehicle for collective self-determination. Despite the emergence of many global and regional bodies (from the United Nations to the European Union and beyond), states are the pre-eminent actors within both global politics and international law. Peoples who have not yet achieved statehood aspire to it, and those that have achieved it are strongly disinclined to give it up. Statehood is a form of status, and it also brings in tow important legal privileges, including sovereignty over natural resources, the power to conclude treaties, to join the United Nations, and the right to bring cases before the International Criminal Court.[25] But statehood too has been thought to be threatened by inundation. Statehood, remember, is conventionally understood to involve a permanent population, on a permanent territory, represented by an effective government, and with the ability to engage in foreign relations with other states. Once islands are submerged, it has been argued, 'the criteria of territory will no longer be met and the claim to statehood will fail'.[26]

This brings us to the third concept: territory. States typically exercise control over a permanent territory, whereas the loss of territory could mean an end to the possibility of self-determination.[27] Cara Nine, for example, has argued that 'in order to be self- determining, a group may have to have territorial rights – to be granted the authority to establish justice within a certain region'.[28] Without territory, the ability to engage in collective political self-determination may be a non-starter.[29]

The possibility of inundation has been thought, then, to have dramatic – and possibly terminal – implications for both self-determination and statehood. One response, understandably, has been to explore solutions in which exiled island communities could establish *new* states elsewhere, each with its own distinct territory.[30] Even if exiles can no longer live in their former homelands, recreating their states somewhere else on the planet could be a second-best option.

This is a challenging suggestion, because significant tracts of land that are not already the territory of one state or another are notable by their absence (the only major exception is Antarctica, but that is a deeply inhospitable place). Supplying territory for exiled communities would therefore mean existing states giving it up. It has been argued, for instance, that high-emitting states would have violated inundated islanders' right to self-determination – by making their homelands uninhabitable – and should therefore give them territory by way of compensation.[31] It has also been argued that if islanders are deprived of territory for reasons outside of their control, states that possess relatively large portions of territory might have a duty to 'downsize', freeing up territory for new states to be created.[32]

Neither of these arguments tells us *which* parts of a state's territory ought to be given up, though, and there is no easy answer to that question. Within international law, it is widely accepted that states cannot give away, or sell, any part of their territory without the explicit consent of the majority of locals in that region.[33] It seems distinctly possible that consent would not be forthcoming, even if the state promised to compensate anyone affected. For a state to force the issue – by giving away territory regardless of the opinions of locals – would violate the principle of consent. There is also a danger that the choice of which slices of territory to give up would compound existing structural injustices. If a state selected a region on the 'periphery', perhaps because it was less important to the national economy, or even because locals there had least power to object, the costs of creating a new state would fall in the wrong place. Even if islanders have a good claim to new territory, we should not want the costs to fall on the shoulders of those *within* a country who are least able to make sacrifices, or who bear the least responsibility for causing climate change in the first place.[34]

We might still suggest, as Cara Nine has, that exiles could be given 'uninhabited, neglected' tracts of land as a way of avoiding these problems.[35] This might help to a degree, but states may not have significant stretches of uninhabited land to give up, and even if they did they might not be especially attractive to exiles. The prospect of climate exiles gaining new territories of their own begins to look bleak at this point.[36] We might hold firm to the conclusion that some states have a duty to give up land, and hope that a fair method of determining which bits of territory to give up can still be found. I certainly don't want to rule that out. But these difficulties are significant enough that it is worth revisiting some underlying assumptions about the connection between self-determination, statehood and territory.

SELF-DETERMINATION WITHOUT STATEHOOD, STATEHOOD WITHOUT SOVEREIGN TERRITORY?

Is it true that a community cannot be self-determining if it does not exercise independent statehood? For climate exiles, the answer to that question may matter a good deal. But the relationship between self-determination and statehood may be looser than many have assumed. Self-determination implies the ability of a community to decide on its own affairs, in the absence of interference by other communities. Independent statehood is *one* way of delivering that ability. But within the United Kingdom, the self-determination of Scottish or Welsh people has been advanced to some degree through processes of devolution, giving them control over many aspects of public policy. The same is true in Quebec, as well as regions within Brazil, Malaysia, Australia and many other federal states besides. This is not to say that existing federal states are perfect, or that members of their various groups are genuinely equal participants in determining the future of those states. Nevertheless, there are many examples of collective self-determination without independent statehood,[37] and recognising this opens up options we might otherwise ignore. In a world where all useful territory is already inhabited, it might be that the most plausible or even fairest way of advancing the goal of collective self-determination would be to grant exiles internal autonomy or 'nested' self-determination within an existing state. That could still allow them to organise their collective life in a way that reflects their traditions, histories and aspirations.[38] Islanders might either gain their own land within an existing state, or be given rights to participate as a group in political decisions wherever in the state they happen to live.

It is also worth paying attention to examples of indigenous representation in the real world, which may open up further possibilities. In New Zealand, for example, all voters cast a vote for a 'regular' constituency Member of Parliament. But under the 'Maori electorate' system, voters registered as Maori are *also* entitled to cast a vote for an additional representative, usually of Maori descent, who will represent their distinctive interests and experiences, ensuring that their views are suitably visible within national institutions.[39] An alternative way of achieving much the same goal is to establish separate political institutions for indigenous peoples, with which the institutions of the state would then be expected to liaise whenever they came to decide on issues likely to have a significant bearing on their interests. An example of that strategy would be the Sami Parliament in Norway.[40] While the position of small island communities would be in many ways distinctive, these examples do show that the representation of specific peoples within our political institutions is not beyond the bounds of political possibility by any means, even if they happen to be scattered throughout a state's territory.

More radically, it is worth reconsidering the assumption that the loss of land territory would necessarily mean the demise of exiles' original states. For some scholars of international law, it is far from obvious that this is true. Earlier, I mentioned several features thought to be typical of statehood: the presence of a permanent population, on a permanent territory, represented by an effective government, and with the ability to engage in foreign relations with other states. But it might be that these are best thought of as conditions on the *creation* of states. This does not mean that statehood cannot *continue* if one or more of them ceases to apply.[41] To the contrary, in practice international law reveals a strong presumption of the continuation of statehood.[42] One leading scholar of international law has concluded that 'A State is not necessarily extinguished by substantial changes in territory, population or government, or even, in some cases, by a combination of all three.' Provided that the original 'organs of the State' – meaning its government and major institutions – remain in place, a state can continue to exist in the face of considerable change.[43]

This raises the possibility that post-inundation, exiles could continue to be citizens of their original island state whether they achieved self-government within a federal state *or* were dispersed as individual migrants into a variety of receiving states. If they also took on citizenship in their new state, they would be dual citizens – a familiar enough category in our messy world. The point, as the philosopher Jörgen Ödalen has argued, is that the idea of statehood may be more flexible, and more durable, than we would assume from pessimistic predictions of imminent state death.[44] In any case, looking to international law for a clear answer to our question is perhaps a mistake. In practice, we might say, a people will qualify as a state when they are recognised as a state by the international community. Governments-in-exile provide a historical example of 'functioning, yet non-territorial, sovereignty' recognised within international law, and by other states.[45] What this hammers home is that, if inundation comes to pass, recognition of continued statehood for islanders would be a political choice. In principle, the erstwhile inhabitants of an inundated island could continue to be recognised as members of the same state even if they possessed no territory of their own,[46] and regardless of whether they had assumed citizenship within another state. The refusal to recognise their state would be a political choice which required a compelling justification. It would not be an automatic consequence of the loss of original territory.

Similarly, exile communities will be able to represent themselves in international relations to the extent that other states are willing to engage with them, to accommodate embassies and the general apparatus of international relations, and to recognise their diplomats and their passports. During the Second World War, the Polish Government in Exile was based first in Paris, and later in London, from where it maintained diplomatic relations with other states.[47] That fact that France and the United Kingdom hosted the Polish government did not undermine their own claims to sovereignty or territory. Neither does it appear to have been especially burdensome. The recognition of statehood without territory seems to be perfectly possible, then. If members of other communities wrongly violate exiles' right to stay on their own territory, it may be the least we owe them.

I have not claimed, to be clear, that inundation will not generate political losses for climate exiles. Exiles might be deeply wedded to the idea of independent territorial governance on the state model, even if their original territory is lost, and may view self-determination or even statehood without independent territory as a poor second best.[48] But it is important to be clear about the relationship between the ideas of self-determination, statehood and territory, especially if a new territory within which to exercise self-government is not forthcoming. In those circumstances, the continued recognition of island statehood might be an important way of minimising islanders' political losses.

SEA-LEVEL RISE AND MARINE TERRITORY

I have suggested that, even if their land territory was wholly inundated, island communities could continue their existence as distinct states, recognised by fellow countries. But the scope of their self-determination might well be reduced. After all, what would an exile community, its members perhaps scattered between a variety of new host states, exercise self-determination *over*?

There are many possible answers to this question. A state without territory could still, in principle, adopt and enforce laws, even if it is harder to see how those laws would be enforced. It could raise revenues, by selling internet domain name registration, or citizenship, or by operating as a low-tax jurisdiction for multinational businesses. Practices like the sale of citizenship, or the operation of tax havens, are hard to square with a commitment to equality and justice. But if islanders had suffered a grievous wrong, and now found it hard to make ends meet, it is not obvious that we could condemn them for pursuing such options. Fortunately, there are other possibilities – *if* we are prepared to detach the possession of marine territory from the occupation of land.

As Figure 8.2 makes clear, small island states in the South Pacific – including Kiribati, Tuvalu and the Marshall Islands – possess very large Exclusive Economic Zones in relation to their modest land area. What would happen to these EEZs, though, if the islands in question were submerged by sea-level rise? As it stands, the Law of the Sea recognises marine territorial claims made in relation to 'normal' coastal baselines, calculated from the average low-water mark. This means sea-level rise could have dramatic implications for many states' marine territories. In the United States, for instance, sea-level rise could lead to the inundation of much of Florida. If so, the United States EEZ would presumably retreat so that it corresponded with the new shoreline. In most cases, this would produce a smaller national EEZ (though in some cases it could actually lead to a larger one, depending on the quirks of a country's coastline).

But this assumes the country as a whole remains habitable. In international law, uninhabitable islands cannot claim EEZs.[49] At the time when the United Nations Convention on the Law of the Sea was drafted, it was simply not anticipated that inundation could be a major problem. We now know better, and the consequences of this legal detail may prove to be hugely significant. States could, of course, reinforce their shorelines, by building sea walls or other defences against inundation. But in the case of small island states, this is not an attractive option. It would be hugely expensive – quite possibly out of the reach of the communities concerned – and even if successful, it would utterly transform coastal life (for islanders, and for marine animals too).

The alternative is to amend, or at least reinterpret, the Law of the Sea such that EEZs are fixed in place for the foreseeable future, regardless of rising tides. The International Law Association has recommended such a policy as a necessary

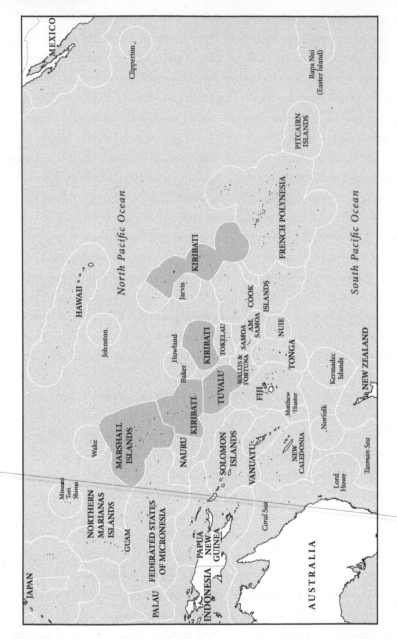

8.2 Exclusive Economic Zones in the Pacific.

protection for island states, which have typically made very modest contributions to sea-level rise, but which are disproportionately vulnerable to it.[50] This poses an interesting quandary for those concerned with equality and justice. Earlier in this book I suggested that the introduction of EEZs was in many ways a retrograde step. It potentially gives great benefits to states with coastlines, but does very little for those without. It has brought only patchy success in conserving marine life within coastal zones, and many states seem to lack the capacity or the inclination to bring about greater sustainability and protect biodiversity. We might argue, therefore, that the EEZs of vanished island states could be turned over to some kind of global authority, capable of advancing goals like democracy, sustainability and justice.

But what if that outcome is unlikely? What if the most likely result of EEZs vanishing from the map is actually that they would simply become part of the High Seas once more, where the ruling principle for harvesting resources is 'first come, first served'? In those circumstances, our quandary looks rather different. *While* EEZs are a feature of our world, there does seem to be something objectionable about the idea that the vast majority of coastal states could maintain their marine territories even if a significant degree of sea-level rise came to pass, while small island states lose theirs as a result of climatic changes for which they bear very little responsibility. If climate exiles are destined for a future as a dispersed minority within a variety of host states, that outcome could be said to add insult to injury.

The alternative is to allow marine territorial entitlements to be preserved. There are a number of ways in which this could be done, depending on what the future holds for climate exiles. If islanders are able to recreate their states elsewhere, their existing EEZs could simply be maintained, even if these stretches of the ocean were quite distant from their new land territory. If islanders are able to exercise self-determination through membership of an existing federal state, then exiles could either maintain the EEZ in their own right, or choose to share it with their new host state (even if they pursued that option, they might retain special privileges over its governance). Alternatively, islanders might disperse individually into a range of existing states, but retain their original island statehood, and their EEZ, alongside their new citizenship.

Some kind of registry of former islanders could be created, alongside mechanisms allowing them to make decisions about the EEZ, and to benefit from any income flowing from it.[51] This stands in stark contrast to a proposal by the former Australian prime minister Kevin Rudd, that Australia might absorb the EEZs of Pacific islands as the price of giving their current inhabitants citizenship. That proposal, roundly criticised by Tuvaluan prime minister Enele Sopoaga as a resurgence of 'imperial thinking' in the region, ignores the fact that islanders have a *right* to refuge. To require them to surrender marine territory as the price of admission would doubly wrong them.[52]

The retention of EEZs by communities that had lost their land territory might strike some as an odd idea. But it has come to be a key demand of many islanders themselves. Leaders from island states in the Pacific, for instance, have argued that their marine territories ought to be preserved regardless of rising tides. The 2015 Taputapuatea Declaration emphasised the ocean-facing nature of Polynesian identity, an identity to which the various peoples of Polynesia remain committed in the face of climate change. As well as resettlement for populations displaced by climate change, it calls on the international community to 'permanently establish the baselines [of its marine territories] in accordance with the UNCLOS, without taking into account sea level rise'.[53] The 2018 Delap Commitment, signed by representatives from Kiribati, the Marshall Islands and Tuvalu, among others, likewise declares their aim: 'To pursue legal recognition of the defined baselines established under the United Nations Convention on the Law of the Sea to remain in perpetuity irrespective of the impacts of sea level rise.'[54] The Pacific Islands Forum has affirmed the same goal.[55]

Ordinary citizens, and social movements, have for their part recommended responses to the challenge of rising tides which empower island communities, rather than leaving them dependent on others for assistance. Most famously, Pacific Climate Warriors, a grassroots network of young Pacific islanders, has become associated with the slogan 'We are not drowning, we are fighting!'[56] They have argued against seeing the inundation of their states, and the relocation of islanders, as a foregone conclusion, and have enjoined world leaders to

take serious actions to limit climate change immediately.[57] As one representative put it, 'We don't deserve to lose our Islands and we will do what we must
to ensure we won't.'[58] Many islanders recognise, nonetheless, that some level of
inundation, and perhaps the total loss of some islands, has already been locked
in. In light of that prospect, they have focused on adaptation measures which
preserve a connection to the homeland and to indigenous culture. The retention of EEZs could prove to be key to the retention of a shared legal and
political identity even if inundation comes to pass.

The problems posed by sea-level rise were not foreseen during the tortuous
emergence of the Convention on the Law of the Sea. We now know, however,
that it represents an enormous threat to livelihoods, identities and community
life on a global scale. Even if we engage in ambitious efforts to reduce the scale
of climate change, a degree of sea-level rise appears inevitable. We will therefore be forced, long before the century is out, to confront questions about the
rights of climate exiles. Three of our principles of ocean justice are relevant
here. Most obviously, we face the challenge of ensuring a *fair transition* for
climate exiles, in which they are able to live secure lives, with dignity and
autonomy. Responding properly to their needs also requires us to identify
principles for *fair burden-sharing*. Finally, I have suggested that our response to
exiles' plight should not treat them as passive recipients of assistance, but as
people who have a right to make decisions about their own future, and an
interest in their continued self-determination as a community. As such the
principle of *democratic inclusion* and active participation is also significant. The
situation climate exiles will find themselves in poses wider questions too, about
the relationship between self-determination, statehood and territory. These
relationships – which were largely taken for granted in the Law of the Sea
Convention – now appear much less settled. Which kinds of entities are entitled to statehood? What might statehood look like for exiled communities? In
tackling those questions, I have suggested that our most cherished ideas about
states, territory and political community might need to be revisited.

9

A BLUE NEW DEAL

In February 2019, Representative Alexandria Ocasio-Cortez and Senator Ed Markey proposed a Resolution to the United States Congress calling for a 'Green New Deal'. That autumn, back in the UK, the idea would play a key role in the Green Party's election manifesto, while the Labour Party's 'It's Time For Real Change' declared the need for a 'Green Industrial Revolution'. Across the Channel, the Democracy in Europe movement launched a major campaign for a Green New Deal for Europe.[1] Despite the inevitable differences of emphasis, these proposals share a common thread, in aiming to tackle both climate change and runaway inequality simultaneously. A 'green revolution' could generate millions of new, well-paid jobs, especially within communities left behind by recent economic shifts.[2]

These interventions have pushed to the centre-stage an idea that has been gaining popularity within academic and activist circles for a decade and more. If major investment is going to be required in order for us to both mitigate and adapt to climate change, then why not also use it to advance important aims of social justice? Our communities are home to many people who have been 'left behind' by globalisation, and by the flight of jobs and economic opportunities from now-marginalised areas. Our collective political response to the challenge of climate change should not further disadvantage – and indeed should seek to empower – people in those communities. To connect back to one of our key principles of ocean justice, we need not simply a transition away from carbon, but a *just* transition, which ensures that those who bear the burdens of reorienting our economies are those who are best able to, and that those who have been left behind are enabled, by a bold climate strategy, to seize new opportunities in creating an economy which transcends its current reliance on carbon.[3]

The idea of a Green New Deal has rapidly attracted support both domestically and internationally. Although it is largely identified with the left, its major aims appear to command widespread public support.[4] But as popular as the idea of a Green New Deal has been, it suffers from its own blind spots. One significant weakness has been that in their focus on reorienting our industries and investing in our communities, advocates of a Green New Deal have had very little to say about the ocean.[5] For the most part their focus has fallen on reforms to land-based sectors of the economy, including farming, housing and industry. This relative neglect of the ocean is indefensible, however. The ocean is crucial both to the global climate system and to our post-carbon future. On the other hand, people living on the coast are on the very frontline of climate-related challenges. As we saw in the last chapter, rising tides threaten to submerge countless homes along the shore. While the encroaching sea will have devastating consequences for many people in the global South, millions of people in the North will be affected too. Coastal communities are often among the most deprived, and their inhabitants are heavily overrepresented in the ranks of those who feel left behind by processes of deindustrialisation. Climate change threatens to leave them still worse off.

Politicians are, fortunately, beginning to recognise that any adequate Green New Deal must contain a significant ocean-oriented component. In September 2019, while still campaigning for the Democratic nomination, Elizabeth Warren agreed that a 'Blue New Deal' would be an indispensable element of a successful green revolution.[6] Any project for renewing, and greening, our economies will have to focus clearly upon the specific deprivations faced by the inhabitants of coastal communities. And, she observed, it will also have to recognise the potential of the ocean industries of the future to tackle climate change. As one group of ocean scholars has put it, 'No blue new deal, no green new deal.'[7] As yet, however, the precise role coastal communities can play is not well understood. This chapter will explore precisely what a 'Blue New Deal' – conceived of as an important, indeed indispensable, element of a broader Green New Deal – might look like. It will first clarify the goals of a Green New Deal more generally, before examining what the priorities of a Blue New Deal focused on coastal communities ought to be.

The focus in these early sections will fall on countries in Europe and North America – not because they are more important, but because this is where the Green New Deal has been most extensively discussed to date. But to be truly successful in putting the ocean economy onto a more sustainable and equitable footing, a Blue New Deal must reach far beyond the shores of the rich North. Our impacts on the sea often have repercussions far beyond each state's marine territory. And for us to fully tackle the climate emergency will require concerted global action. It will also demand a fair sharing of the burdens of the green transition. Many communities in the global South have other problems to contend with, and should not be required to meet the costs of making green transitions on their own. The final section of this chapter, therefore, will examine ways in which Blue New Deals in the South could be better supported through appropriate global institutions and policies.

UNDERSTANDING THE GREEN NEW DEAL

The House Resolution on the Green New Deal envisaged a ten-year national mobilisation aimed at securing a major reduction in carbon emissions by 2030, and at the same time promoting the resilience of both the environment and local communities. One of its key claims is that we face not one but several overlapping crises. Alongside the climate crisis, we also face ongoing challenges associated with the hollowing-out of formerly industrial-focused communities. Those communities have lost both jobs and people as the gravitational centres of economic production have shifted within and between countries. The plight of people who remain living in these communities was deepened by the 2008 financial crisis. In the years since, the shifting tides of our economies have also brought new opportunities to many, especially within the top 10 per cent. But the fact that new jobs are available elsewhere is little consolation to people rooted in communities that have been left behind. Even those with jobs have faced decades of wage stagnation. The financial crisis, meanwhile, exacerbated existing inequalities in income, wealth and economic opportunity between majority populations and people of colour. At the same time, the burden of austerity has fallen disproportionately on women, and especially women of colour.[8]

The transition to a low- or zero-carbon economy will create many winners.[9] Who they are will be determined, in part, by the nature of state policy. Advocates of a Green New Deal often draw an explicit parallel with the massive fiscal stimulus engendered by Franklin D. Roosevelt's New Deal, which rebuilt the American economy in the wake of the Great Depression of 1929 to 1933. But their proposals differ from that earlier New Deal in two important respects. First, the large infrastructure projects of Roosevelt's New Deal eventually came to be associated with considerable environmental damage,[10] whereas the Green New Deal aims to defend the environment and protect biodiversity. Second, Roosevelt's New Deal was chiefly focused on promoting economic growth, whereas advocates of the Green New Deal focus much more explicitly on questions of social justice. Specifically, they insist that the Green version must make a greater effort to ensure a broad sharing of the benefits arising from this new mobilisation of resources. Advocates intend it to counteract systemic injustices, by creating millions of new jobs skewed towards deprived areas.[11] The alternative – that states leave the benefits and burdens of the green transition to fall where they fall – will likely mean further pain for those communities which can least bear it.

The Green New Deal is not the same thing, therefore, as a compensation package for those who will lose out in the transition to a low-carbon economy. Some of those who lose out from the transition will be very well off, and will already possess the capacity to find alternative sources of income and wealth. The Green New Deal is best seen as aimed at those who are relatively disadvantaged, and who have limited opportunities for economic diversification. But just as importantly, the Green New Deal does not aim to extend opportunities *solely* to those who might otherwise lose out from the decarbonisation of our economies.[12] Rather, it aims to extend opportunities to members of all disadvantaged communities, whether they have a historical association with carbon-intensive industries or not. This might involve investment in areas of a country which have suffered from the impact of deindustrialisation more generally, or which were not industry-heavy in the first place. A fair New Deal will be guided by attention to overall levels of well-being, rather than attempting to ensure that there are no losers from the transition away from carbon. Insofar as it will involve massive state investment in the economy, the Green New Deal represents an opportunity to more evenly spread wealth and power in general. In this respect, efforts to include members of marginalised communities – including women, ethnic minorities and informal workers – are especially important.[13]

The policies adopted to advance the goals of a Green New Deal should be sensitive to the nature of the disadvantage experienced by marginalised communities. When a community experiences deindustrialisation, for instance, it will typically be faced with major economic losses, including shortages of jobs and local investment. But our well-being depends on much more than income and wealth. People who lose their jobs can experience losses to their self-esteem, to their social networks and to their physical health.[14] In these cases, it is not clear that financial compensation would be the most appropriate remedy. Instead, it makes sense to explore policies that would place the destinies of members of marginalised communities in their own hands once more, allowing them to make decisions about their future economic life. This suggests a focus on empowerment and agency, and on mitigation and adaption policies which are dynamic and forward-looking.

FROM GREEN TO BLUE

There are three reasons why the ocean will be at the centre of any successful Green New Deal. The first and most obvious is that coastal communities are among the most deprived locales. Although some coastal areas are wealthy, many more have suffered enormously from deindustrialisation, as well as the dwindling of tourist, fishing and boatbuilding businesses. In the United Kingdom, coastal communities have higher proportions of low-wage, low-skill, seasonal and part-time employment than the rest of the country.[15] They include higher-than-average numbers of people with long-term health issues that limit their daily activities, and disproportionate numbers claiming sickness and disability benefits.[16] They have also been among the hardest hit by austerity. Nine of the ten cities most severely affected by public-sector job losses in the UK are coastal, whereas only one of the ten least affected cities is.[17]

Second, coastal communities will be among the hardest hit by climate change. Because they are often relatively disadvantaged to begin with, their capacity to adapt to the coming changes is limited. Most obviously, rising sea levels will hit disadvantaged communities, including many communities of colour, hardest. In the US, this was vividly illustrated in the years following Hurricane Katrina. Sea-level rises will bring about greater coastal erosion, greater vulnerability to storm surges and a much higher risk of rivers and estuaries flooding. In each case, the biggest impact will fall on those communities which can least afford to adapt.[18] In the UK, coastal communities which are reeling from the economic shifts of recent decades will be hit hard by rising tides. Over 2.6 million properties are now at risk from river and coastal flooding in the UK.[19] But austerity measures have reduced the ability of coastal communities to respond effectively to the risk of flooding.[20] A priority of any effective climate strategy must therefore be to enhance their resilience.

Sea-level rise and vulnerability to storms and flooding is not the only impact that climate change will have on coastal communities, however. Because fish are highly sensitive to water temperature as well as to oxygen concentrations, ocean warming is currently causing a major shift of fish stocks towards both North and South. The short-term consequence of such shifts may be positive for some coastal communities, as rarely seen fish arrive in local waters. But the long-term outlook is much less certain. If acidification leads to a collapse in the plankton populations on which many marine food webs depend, fish populations could be hit hard. These challenges will combine with other pressing problems faced by coastal communities, including the growth of offshore 'dead zones', where the spread of harmful algal blooms is encouraged by the runoff of fertiliser from farmland.[21] When considered alongside a legacy of historic over-fishing, the future for many fishing communities appears bleak.

Third, however, it is important to recognise that coastal communities possess massive potential when it comes to powering the shift towards a carbon-neutral economy. Renewable energy will come to be drawn increasingly from the sea. Though they are costlier to install and maintain than their onshore equivalents, offshore wind turbines benefit from faster, and more consistent, winds over the sea. Wind power is already capable of meeting 3 per cent of global electricity demand, and most of that is sourced offshore.[22] Wave power too possesses enormous potential. In the UK, the total supply of wind and wave power that is practically accessible exceeds the country's current overall electricity demand sixfold.[23] The most enormous potential energy sources in the ocean, however, are as yet untapped. The great ocean currents that continually traverse our planet play a crucial part in cycling the nutrients on which marine food webs depend. But they also convey massive quantities of heat energy. If we could find a cost-effective way of tapping into temperature gradients in the oceans, these currents could provide vastly more energy than wind and waves.

Restoring coastal habitats also possesses massive promise as both a mitigation and an adaptation strategy. Whereas the House Resolution emphasises the carbon-storage benefits of land preservation and tree-planting, it does not address the carbon-storage potential of coastal habitats. Huge amounts of wetland have been lost in recent decades as a result of reclamation, urbanisation and the construction of ports and coastal defences. In Europe, fully half of all salt marshes have been destroyed.[24] When wetlands are lost, enormous amounts of carbon can leak back into the atmosphere. Their loss can also substantially increase vulnerability to storms. In the US, coastal habitats are key to protecting communities on the Eastern Seaboard and Gulf of Mexico, while their loss could double the proportion of coastline highly exposed to storms and sea-level rise.[25] But wetland regeneration is an enormous climate opportunity. Wetlands can lock away five times as much carbon as an equivalent area of forest.[26] Saltmarshes in particular are superb at sequestering greenhouse gases. They take in carbon dioxide directly from the atmosphere, and unlike many other forms of vegetation, the sulphates present in salt marshes actively suppress the production of methane.[27]

For all of these reasons, ocean-facing projects should be at the centre of any plan for a Green New Deal. In practice, advocates of such a Deal can face difficult choices. What if some of the most deprived areas in fact bear little promise when it comes to developing green infrastructure? What if the most cost-effective green technologies turn out to support relatively few jobs, or are best located close to existing industrial hubs? These questions suggest that New Deal advocates will sometimes face a trade-off between rapid decarbonisation and widely spreading the benefits of infrastructural investment. But in coastal regions the case for significant investment appears much easier to make. These communities are, on average, more disadvantaged than other areas; they are also going to be among the hardest hit by the effects of climate change; and at the same time they possess significant potential to assist the transition away from carbon. Investing in coastal areas promises to serve both environmental and social justice objectives admirably well.

PRIORITIES FOR A BLUE NEW DEAL

At the national level, a successful Blue New Deal will create new opportunities capable of supporting local communities well into the future. It should focus on industries that are genuinely sustainable, in the sense that they do not place insupportable demands on local or global ecosystems. Better still, it should focus on industries that actively help to reduce the demands our economies make on the environment. Emerging ocean industries can provide replacements for goods and services that are currently highly resource-intensive. We have already discussed the example of energy production, where renewable ocean energy can substitute for fossil fuels. Below, we will discuss the prospects of green aquaculture projects, which can reduce the toll of meat-based agriculture.

At the same time as helping in the green transition, investment should aim to increase the resilience and flexibility of coastal communities, leaving them more capable of withstanding the changes that ocean warming, acidification and sea-level rise are likely to bring in tow. One promising idea is that of Coastal Community Funds, which would see local communities managing their own start-up funds and reinvesting any profits in new local enterprises. In its emphasis on leveraging funding for local, community-defined projects, the House Resolution on a Green New Deal recalls the idea of Community Wealth Building, which focuses on the potential of worker cooperatives, community land trusts and community-controlled financial institutions in restoring the social and economic health of deprived areas.[28] The approach aims to develop under-utilised local resources, and to promote local, broad-based ownership as a means of spurring wider socioeconomic regeneration.[29] Advocates of Community Wealth Building have not yet identified its potential in helping to regenerate coastal areas. But there is evidence that new, sustainable coastal industries can act as seedbeds for broader community regeneration.

This focus provides an important corrective to some short-sighted claims about the benefits of the new Blue Economy. A considerable public relations effort has gone into suggesting that industries like industrial-scale fish farming represent a bright future for coastal regions, because of the profits they can generate. But profits are not everything – especially if they are spirited away by large multinational corporations. We must insist that sustainable coastal industries benefit the wider community, and we should hold fast to the emphasis on broader social objectives (including employment, community empowerment, nutritional security and access to healthy wild spaces), rather than adopting a myopic focus on the bottom line.[30] We should also place a premium on activities that sustain, and even help regenerate, coastal ecosystems rather than further degrading them. The examples I provide in this suggestion are all cases where greater investment could help communities as a whole to both participate in the climate mitigation effort and reduce their own vulnerability to climate-related challenges.

One major priority should be the protection and restoration of coastal habitats. Wetlands possess massive potential as a defence against storm surges.

They can provide far more effective storm protection than sea walls, which are considerably more expensive. In the US, it has been estimated that every dollar spent on wetland restoration can save ten dollars in storm damage, far outperforming other methods of coastal defence.[31] Improved coastal protection will be vital in protecting people from sea-level rise. In many places – such as Texas – coastal habitats currently protect disproportionately high numbers of poor families.[32] Protected coastal habitats can also support sustainable ocean industries. In Louisiana, an oyster reef restoration project is expected to significantly reduce the force of waves at the shore, to generate many new jobs and to bring $8.4 million to the local economy.[33] In New York City, the restoration of oyster and wetland habitats has been identified as a fruitful strategy in protecting against sea and storm damage.[34] In some places, wetland restoration may also reap dividends in stimulating local tourism. Wetlands can be tremendously biodiverse habitats, and play a particularly important role in supporting bird-life. Exposure to vibrant wild spaces also sustains human well-being.

A second priority area should be seaweed farming. Seaweed aquaculture is widely practised in Asia, but has not yet made a major impact in Europe or North America. Although it is best suited to calm waters, one advantage of seaweed aquaculture is that it does not involve large start-up costs. It also possesses major environmental benefits. Growing seaweed can safely lock away large quantities of carbon. On one estimate, a network of seaweed farms covering just 5 per cent of American coastal waters could safely absorb as much carbon as that emitted by 30 million cars.[35] Seaweed can also be an effective replacement for fossil fuels, in its capacity as a biofuel. In stark contrast to some land-based biofuel sources, seaweed aquaculture does not increase competition for arable land, does not require herbicide or pesticide use, and supports a high level of biodiversity.[36] Seaweed can also help reduce greenhouse gas emissions in its role as a foodstuff. One reason why cattle-farming is such a big contributor to climate change is that cows belch out large amounts of methane, which is a potent contributor to global warming. But cattle fed seaweed supplements emit drastically lower quantities of methane, reducing the climate impact of beef farming considerably.[37] Finally, coastal vegetation has an important role in securing coastal communities against the effects of rising sea levels. Seaweed aquaculture in Norway, for instance, has been shown to reduce wave heights by up to 60 per cent, and hence to offer valuable protection against coastal erosion.[38]

Third, shellfish aquaculture possesses promise as a potentially low-carbon industry. 'Bivalves' such as oysters, mussels and clams remove carbon from the ocean when forming their shells, and lock it away for many years.[39] Although bivalve production does have a carbon footprint, it is tiny compared to that of any farmed meat. Shellfish aquaculture scores well on other important measures too. Unlike both land-based farming and fish farming, shellfish aquaculture does not involve confining animals. At its most basic, mussel farming, for instance, can involve simply lowering a rope into the ocean. Mussel larvae will attach themselves to it, and grow wild over the course of a year before the rope is drawn in to harvest them. Although the mussels are of course killed and eaten, during their lives there are none of the animal welfare concerns that plague industrial farming. Moreover, shellfish aquaculture does not involve killing other creatures for fodder – because the bivalves in question feed themselves, filtering nutrients from the water. This is a stark contrast to fish-farming operations, where salmon and shrimp are fed enormous quantities of wild fish. Shifting consumption to shellfish can therefore ease the problem of unsustainable overfishing, rather than making it worse. Finally, shellfish can also play an important role in regenerating coastal ecosystems through their role in filtering seawater, stabilising sediments and controlling algal blooms.

A fourth priority area should be the greening of ports. As international trade has intensified, new ports have proliferated around the world, and existing ports have grown – which is one factor behind the loss of wetlands worldwide. Ports are often associated with significant deteriorations in air quality, and hence with elevated rates of cardiovascular disease, respiratory problems and other health issues.[40] Can we find ways of reducing ports' environmental impact, while still driving the redevelopment of local communities? That is what the 'Green Port' approach aims to do.[41] Several Japanese ports have already reinvented themselves as recycling hubs. Major ports in the Netherlands have moved into recycling and green energy production, using waste products to generate biofuels and tapping offshore wind energy.[42] These projects could create many new jobs. They can also bring significant health benefits to locals – who are often disadvantaged, and, at least in the US, disproportionately likely to be people of colour. The implementation of a Clean Air Action Plan in the Los Angeles/Long Beach area, for instance, has already brought about dramatic reductions in childhood asthma and adult cancer rates.[43] If the Green Ports scheme was rolled out more widely – which will require substantial initial investment – ports could transform themselves from hotspots of pollution and high emissions into key sites for the green transition, bringing significant economic, health and environmental benefits to local economies.

FROM LOCAL TO GLOBAL

To date, discussions about the idea of a Green New Deal have been especially prominent in the US, the UK and the European Union. But governments there possess the financial might to fund new green industries at the local level, should they choose to do so. In the global South, it is much less obvious that this is the case. If the world is to shift from its carbon-intensive trajectory, however, and ease the demands it places on ecosystems more widely, the Green New Deal – and its Blue dimension – must be global in ambition. To see why, consider the challenge of climate change. Some rich countries have already made progress in decarbonising their economies, by switching to renewable forms of energy. But if we focus on the full range of goods their citizens consume, it is less clear that their carbon footprints are declining substantially. Citizens in wealthy countries now consume large quantities of goods manufactured in the global South, where emissions and other environmental impacts are less tightly regulated.[44] If corporations from rich countries shift production to the global South, this does not mean their customers in the global North are 'consuming' less carbon. It just means any emissions linked to their consumption are released somewhere else on the planet. From the point of view of climate change, shifting emissions from one place to another makes little difference. A healthy climate requires reductions in total *global* emissions, wherever they are caused. This means it is not enough to roll out green technologies in rich countries. Efforts to help countries in the global South to reduce the carbon intensity of their own domestic industries will be required too. A successful green transition will not mean 'environmentalism in one country'. It will be a truly global effort.

This represents a significant challenge, because countries in the South often lack the financial capacity to invest heavily in new green industries. Having emerged from colonialism into a global economy whose rules continue to favour the rich and powerful, they often have distinctly limited access to investment capital, are heavily indebted and have other pressing problems to deal with – such as endemic poverty. Morally, it would be unjust for the global community to place the burdens of green transitions on the shoulders of those who can least afford to bear them.[45] Pragmatically, requiring poor countries to finance their own green transitions likely means that those transitions will be seriously delayed. If the world is to shift to a zero-net carbon economy by 2050 – as it must if we are to avoid very damaging levels of climate change – we have around a decade in which to fundamentally reorient investment in our economies. If we are to meet this goal, national and international institutions must rapidly find ways of enabling people in the South to take crucial steps towards their own individual green transitions. And the ocean economy must be a major part of that process. The African Union has recently noted that coastal communities in Africa are disproportionately affected by poverty, a lack of education and a lack of capacity to invest in their own futures. But at the same time, it has argued that the development of sustainable coastal industries offers promise when it comes to improving their situation.[46]

How, though, can countries in the South be supported in their own individual Blue New Deals? One possibility is to open up existing climate-funding mechanisms more fully to ocean ecosystems. The United Nations' 'REDD+' scheme is the most obvious candidate. It provides payments to countries that agree to preserve 'carbon sink' ecosystems such as forests from destruction, or which plant new forests capable of sucking more carbon out of the air. Those payments reflect the amount of carbon safely locked away in those ecosystems, so that the more is protected or planted, the higher the payments flowing to the countries where those ecosystems exist. REDD+ has already begun to send money to heavily forested countries such as Brazil and Indonesia. Its extension to coastal areas has been patchy, however, and this represents a lost opportunity. Mangroves in particular are hugely effective at locking away carbon – they 'sequester' carbon fifty times faster than land-based forests, and store two to four times as much carbon per acre[47] (they are also hugely important breeding grounds for fish, and can provide very effective shore stabilisation and coastal protection, though REDD+ focuses on carbon alone).

We might suppose, then, that mangroves would be prime candidates for global conservation funding. But the integration of mangroves into the REDD+ scheme is incomplete. In some places mangroves have been included, but so far REDD+ has steered funding to places where trees are at least 4 metres in height, and this excludes many scrub mangroves which are exceptional at locking away carbon. The scheme also 'rewards' carbon stored within the first 30 centimetres of soil alone. Since mangroves typically lock carbon away far more deeply than that, this means the incredible contribution they can make to climate stabilisation is not recognised.[48] These rules could be amended so that mangroves are more fully integrated into the scheme. If so, rather than losing mangroves at an alarming rate, we might see their protection and even restoration across many coastlines in the South. In Vietnam, Vien Ngoc Nam and his colleagues have shown how rapidly mangroves managed to recover from the Vietnam War, during which the US dropped huge quantities of the defoliant Agent Orange. They have captured large amounts of carbon in the process.[49] In much of Asia, tropical Africa and Latin America, the potential for restoring or extending mangroves is substantial.

REDD+, though, has long been a controversial programme. One objection has been that it commodifies nature. Countries are paid to protect ecosystems not because they are intrinsically valuable, but because a price has been put on locking away carbon. Forests deliver 'carbon credits' to those who own them. Those credits can then be traded like any other commodity. In practice, a wealthy country could choose to 'buy' some of those credits from a country with forests, rather than having to reduce its own emissions. The fact that money would then flow towards the global South is a good result, other things being equal. But somewhere in the process, it seems that nature has been turned into one more currency. To respond to this worry adequately would, I believe, require us to systematically rethink the goals of schemes such as REDD+. The point should not be that countries like Brazil, say, are providing an 'ecosystem service' that is being consumed elsewhere, which they should then be paid for. The point is that climate stability on our planet requires carbon sinks like forests and mangroves to be preserved or even extended – but this comes at a cost. However valuable it is to the world as a whole, conservation can prevent locals from escaping from disadvantage. If forests are cleared, locals can raise cattle and sell meat. If mangroves are destroyed, shrimp farms can be set up in their place. Conservation is beneficial for all of us, but for locals it means the prospects of escaping from poverty and inequality may recede still further. Since wealthy countries have greater capacity to make these sacrifices, and since conservation is in their interests too, they ought to be the ones picking up the tab (plus, of course, it is the emissions of the industrialised North that have made conservation necessary, and for some this will add further weight to the claim that they should carry the costs). Payments to countries with forests or mangroves are best seen, in my view, not as payments for services rendered, but as a vital measure to ensure that the costs of conservation are fairly shared.

Schemes like REDD+ are valuable, then, because they can help to dissolve the dilemma between conservation and economic 'development' in the global South. Even if locals would prefer to follow the path of conservation, it is unfair to ask – and unrealistic to expect – locals to stay in poverty on our behalf. If rich countries want people in the global South to conserve and even extend vital ecosystems, they need to take on the lion's share of the costs of conservation. Sending money to countries which maintain or extend carbon sinks will help them to open up other, less environmentally damaging, routes out of poverty.[50]

REDD+ is framed in an unhelpful way, then, to say the least. Still, if we have a crucial decade in which to make the transition to net zero, arguments for

9.1 A mangrove restoration project in Jakarta, Indonesia.

the abolition of REDD+ look like fiddling while Rome burns. If we did not have REDD+, we would need to establish something not entirely dissimilar to it, capable of channelling funds urgently in the direction of countries that are being asked to preserve key ecosystems notwithstanding their desire to escape from disadvantage. And we would need to do that very rapidly. The best path is therefore to seek to ensure that REDD+ is funded properly, so that it can make a proper difference in defusing the conservation/development dilemma in the global South. At the same time, we should reform the scheme to address some persistent criticisms about its practical effects. Back on dry land, REDD+ and its predecessor schemes have sometimes been associated with the exclusion and even dispossession of indigenous communities. Under the logic of 'payments for ecosystem services', the more carbon a forest absorbs, the more money it attracts. Local elites have an incentive to maximise the growth of that forest, and if that means pushing indigenous people out – on the (often misinformed) belief that their traditional practices damage the forest – so much the worse for them. For this reason, some have worried that the extension of REDD+ to coastal habitats will lead to a wave of 'ocean grabbing', in which traditional and sustainable fishing practices are squeezed out as mangroves or seagrass meadows are planted.[51]

If the point of the REDD+ scheme should be to ensure that the less well off do not lose out through conservation, this would be the opposite of progress. Success should mean greater security and economic independence for locals, rather than less. In many cases, the problem has been the top-down nature of decision-making. Traditional, small-scale fishers are not typically the enemies of coastal ecosystems. But conservation schemes have often been elite-driven, with local communities, their practices and perspectives seen as an inconvenience at best.[52] The challenge is to ensure that local communities are fully involved in efforts to protect vital ecosystems, and that they genuinely benefit from any funds that arise from them. Fortunately, some countries in the global South are leading the way in showing how this can be done. India's Joint Mangrove Management programme, for instance, has involved local communities and non-governmental organisations in efforts to preserve and restore mangrove forests, and participatory and women-centred mangrove conservation programmes are now under way in Bangladesh, Thailand, Cambodia and the Philippines.[53] As well as protecting local ecosystems, these projects can support employment, social networks and nutritional security.

If such projects are successful in reconciling conservation with progress in tackling poverty and other social problems, the framework could be extended to other kinds of coastal ecosystem. Seagrass beds and tidal flats can sequester enormous quantities of carbon, as well as providing an important habitat for marine animals like sea turtles and manatees. Though it is less obviously focused on restoring a natural ecosystem, seaweed aquaculture could also make a contribution to arresting climate change, with the potential to capture two and a half million tons of carbon dioxide per year.[54] While some forms of seaweed have a short life – and hence release carbon back into the ocean relatively quickly – others have a much longer 'turnaround time' and therefore can effectively lock carbon away for many years.[55]

Still, it may turn out that existing funding pathways (such as REDD+) are inadequate to the task of bankrolling the greening of the ocean economy, and that we will need to explore other sources of funds besides. 'Green bonds' are a key possibility. A bond is a financial instrument that allows an institution like a state, corporation or bank to borrow large sums of money. Bonds are bought by investors, whose outlay will be repaid at a specified time in the future, with interest. Green bonds could potentially see large amounts of finance flowing from individuals, pension funds or sovereign wealth funds, which could be used to enhance ocean ecosystems.[56] They may also help reorient our economies more generally in a more climate-conscious direction. Reflecting on a successful Nigerian pilot scheme, the country's former minister of the environment, Amina Mohammed, has suggested they are 'not just a way to raise money but a means of unlocking the very conversation that was needed— about the role of environmental stewardship and of climate in national economic development'.[57] At present, global interest rates are low, and investors are desperate for secure investments guaranteeing even a modest return. This represents an ideal opportunity for ramping up green bond schemes. Although bonds need to be repaid – perhaps fifty or a hundred years in the future – what we need now is an urgent injection of investment into ocean conservation schemes or sustainable ocean industries. Green bonds are already a reality – but the finance they offer is not yet sufficient. One ambitious proposal that could help meet the shortfall is for a World Climate Bank, which would issue enormous quantities of bonds, and thereby provide governments or suitable international bodies with sufficient money to bankroll a green transition.[58] Regeneration projects aimed at capturing carbon and enhancing biodiversity in coastal zones would be an excellent candidate for such spending. Alternatively, a dedicated Ocean Sustainability Bank could unlock a further stream of funding for monitoring and protecting ocean ecosystems.[59]

In the wake of the Covid crisis, there will be a temptation for governments to rein in spending and impose a new brand of austerity. That would be a mistake, and not only because it would once more impose years of straitened living on the world's poor. Borrowing can pay for itself, if the money is spent on building infrastructure and future-proofing our economies.[60] It's hard to image a better way of spending the proceeds of borrowing than revitalising coastal economies and coastal ecosystems throughout the world. Doing so will bring new opportunities to ocean-facing communities, as well as protecting them from the emerging threat of sea-level rise. The goal of the Blue New Deal should be to regenerate coastal ecosystems at the same time as providing a boost to poor and marginalised communities. We cannot take it for granted that the emerging 'blue economy' will promote climate stability and ecological regeneration. That will require concerted global action, providing much-needed investment to countries of the global South which can offer so much when it comes to revitalising the ocean.

Ocean recovery should be central to any viable plan for a just transition beyond carbon and towards ecological repair. For that reason a significant Blue element will be a crucial part of any successful Green New Deal. A Blue New Deal, however, is not the same thing as 'Blue Growth'. The Blue Growth narrative has often served as code for more intensive exploitation of the ocean, even if that means the consolidation of the fishing industry in fewer and fewer hands, environmentally damaging practices in fish farming, or destructive seabed mining. At its worst, the industrialisation of the ocean economy would bring rewards to the haves rather than the have-nots, and drive marine wildlife to the margins of an Anthropocene Ocean. A Blue New Deal cannot mean that. Instead it must involve a simultaneous commitment to both environmental protection and restoration, and the pursuit of social justice. It should recognise that the benefits that the ocean delivers to us are complex and multifaceted, and in many cases cannot easily be captured by a focus on the bottom line. The Blue New Deal must recognise the tremendous social, cultural and health benefits of healthy coastal ecosystems. It must also empower the disempowered, give greater opportunities and voice to marginalised coastal communities, and spur the regeneration of the ocean, restoring biodiversity *and* helping us achieve climate stability.

10

BEYOND THE BLUE NEW DEAL

The chapters in the second half of this book have argued for a raft of important reforms to ocean governance, including better legal protections for cetaceans and other marine animals; a suite of policies aimed at turning the rights of workers at sea from idea to reality; and robust protections for climate exiles. The last chapter identified ways in which states can take the lead in enhancing the sustainability of coastal areas – reforms which, I suggested, could have major payoffs both for human coastal communities and for marine ecosystems. In many cases countries already have the resources to sustain their own Blue New Deals, while elsewhere international action – and major global investment – will be required to help build local capacity.

Taken together, these reforms would move us much closer to ocean justice. The ocean would become a more secure space of rights, for both humans and other animals. The threats climate change poses to lives and livelihoods would be reduced. Coastal communities would be empowered to take on control of their own sustainable ocean industries. The environmental impact of a Blue New Deal should not be underestimated: given that the ocean is an interconnected ecosystem, restoring greater health to one area could have positive results everywhere.

Nevertheless, the reforms discussed so far do not quite match the scale of the challenges we face at sea. They would not, by themselves, fully avert the looming crises of environmental destruction and growing inequality. To do that we will have to countenance more radical institutional changes. Transforming the ocean economy, and making the ocean a bastion of biodiversity rather than the next site for destructive industrialisation, will mean transforming the law and politics of the ocean too. In this final chapter I will outline some 'blue sky thinking' – or, perhaps we should say, blue water thinking – for the future of the ocean. These will include some very radical proposals, and I won't claim that it is probable that the world will act on them. Vested interests often stand in the way of progress, and those who benefit from the status quo frequently manage to convince us that change is not even possible, never mind desirable. There is no underestimating the power of the industrial fishing and fossil fuel lobbies, or the potential for politicians' ears to be bent by advocates of deep-sea mining or other new technologies. But the point of thinking seriously about justice is not to describe what is *likely* to happen. If it was, we would end up offering endless justifications for the status quo, or something very like it. As should be abundantly clear by now, the status quo in ocean governance is failing us. To restrict ourselves to describing only the modest shifts from our current pathway that seem readily accessible would mean reconciling ourselves to a world in which the Blue Acceleration continues, in which the lion's share of the rewards from 'blue growth' are reaped by a privileged few, in which our global ocean is progressively emptied of wildlife and colonised by the monocultures of industrial fish farming, and in which the resources of the seabed are mined regardless of the environmental consequences.

We have to aim higher than that. We do not have to accept that an Anthropocene Ocean is inevitable – that the ocean will be progressively 'tamed', or despoiled, in the same way that much of the land has been.[1] The human conquest of the land has had terrible consequences for the other species we share it with – and it has hardly been an unalloyed success for us either. Our domestication of nature has brought about a hugely unequal economy, and has unleashed a series of global challenges – from pollution to pandemics to climate change – that we are struggling to cope with. This book is written in the hope of a different future for the ocean. But turning that hope into a reality demands a decisive break with business as usual – because business as usual in the ocean will mean a massive loss of biodiversity and the proliferation of environmental problems that we cannot fully control. If you agree with me that something has to change, the next step is to imagine what a better future would look like. Once we have a positive vision of a just ocean in mind, we can then argue about how it could be brought closer to reality. My aim in this chapter is to set our sights high, to imagine another future and to ask: why not?

ALL CHANGE ON THE HIGH SEAS

We have seen that individual countries – with appropriate international assistance, when required – can transform their coasts, making their EEZs more sustainable and diverse, at the same time as supporting local communities navigating recent economic turmoil. There are grounds for believing these Blue New Deal policies could be highly successful, making a rapid, positive difference to coastal communities while replacing environmentally destructive practices with more sustainable ones. Nevertheless, most of the ocean does not fall into the domain of one EEZ or another. Two-thirds of its surface area (and the vast majority of its volume) is classified as the High Seas, where no state holds sway. Underneath it lies the deep seabed, which is governed by the International Seabed Authority and is hence beyond national jurisdiction too. Together, these two zones represent what international law calls the Area Beyond National Jurisdiction (ABNJ) – an area so vast that it contains fully 95 per cent of the habitable space on earth, as well as millions of as-yet-undiscovered species.[2]

The current governance regime for ABNJ is not, however, fit for purpose. It was drafted at a time when many of the most sweeping challenges we face – from climate change and acidification to plastic pollution – were not yet recognised. At the same time, the Law of the Sea Convention is excessively deferential to the freedoms of individual states, leaving them solely responsible, for the most part, for the actions of vessels sailing under their flags and giving them the choice of whether they want to join Regional Fisheries Management Organisations or not. Meanwhile, the prospect of the commercial mining of the deep seabed creeps ever closer. The International Seabed Authority has already granted thirty licences for the exploration of seabed minerals in the Area, to a series of private and state actors. But recent scientific advances have made it abundantly clear that seabed mining could have terrible and long-lasting effects on life on the deep seabed, and that the ISA's rules are not sufficiently developed to prevent serious damage. As a result the International Union for the Conservation of Nature has called for a complete moratorium on mining and commercial exploration on the deep seabed.[3] There is an urgent need to pause and reconsider.

As I write, commercial interest in the genetic codes of the remarkable organisms to be found in the deep ocean continues to grow. While the technology needed to harness deep-sea resources has been developing, it has become more and more apparent that a new set of rules is required both in order to mitigate any environmental impacts and to share any resulting benefits and burdens fairly. In recent years the world's governments have been locked in negotiations over a new legal agreement covering 'Biodiversity Beyond National Jurisdiction' (BBNJ). A draft BBNJ Treaty was published in the summer of 2019,[4] and a revised draft later that year. If it enters into law, this treaty would provide a new governing framework for the exploitation of marine life in the High Seas and on the deep seabed. It would help fill a critical 'governance gap' left unaddressed by the Law of the Sea Convention, which in the light of recent challenges is beginning to look less like a patchwork of ocean governance and more like a cobweb full of gaping holes.

The text of the draft BBNJ Treaty, as it stands, contains some ambitious language. While the principle of 'common heritage' was controversially omitted from the first draft, it re-emerges in the second, at the insistence of countries in the global South. Algeria's representative Mohammed Bessedik spoke on behalf of the African Group of countries when he emphasised 'the importance of this principle, not only for humankind but also for the high seas and marine life as a whole', and declared that a treaty without the principle would be one without a soul.[5] The draft treaty aims to take an 'integrated' approach to ocean governance, and to build the resilience of ocean ecosystems. It suggests states must cooperate to conserve ocean ecosystems, and build new regional or global institutions wherever necessary to fill governance gaps. It emphasises the importance of Marine Protected Areas, and the necessity of carrying out Environmental Impact Assessments before High Seas biological resources are exploited. These are all positive signals, though many difficult decisions remain to be made (anyone can read the draft treaty,[6] and if you do so, you will imme-diately notice that it represents a menu of options still to be argued over).

Although it is a work in progress, it is already apparent, sadly, that the draft treaty will not measure up to the scale of problems we face in the Area Beyond National Jurisdiction. Article 4 of the draft treaty makes clear that it would 'not undermine' or 'prejudice' any of the rights or jurisdictions already given to states under the existing Law of the Sea Convention. The phrase 'not under-mine' is somewhat ambiguous,[7] but it may very well mean, among other things, that an eventual treaty would not limit the practice of exclusive flag state jurisdiction – even though that practice has long provided legal cover for environmental destruction and labour abuses. It may well mean that it would not constrain the rights of coastal states over their Exclusive Economic Zones either – even though what happens in EEZs can have a major impact on what happens on the High Seas. Likewise, it may mean the treaty will not compete with the existing competences of regional fisheries organisations – even though they have signally failed to arrest the collapse of many fish populations. In fact, Article 8 makes clear that the treaty will not apply to fish at all, which leaves a gaping void in any treaty aimed at protecting biodiversity on the High Seas. While the draft treaty envisages a process for setting up Marine Protected Areas on the High Seas, meanwhile, it is unclear whether it will reserve the legal authority necessary to make their rules binding on everyone, or whether the recognition of MPAs will be left to individual flag states. If flag states remain free to pick and choose which MPAs they recognise, they will continue to represent 'paper parks', protecting ecosystems in theory but not in practice.[8]

We also lack grounds for confidence that the draft treaty would arrest the accelerating inequalities in the ocean economy. The draft treaty does declare, in language redolent of the original 1970s debates preceding UNCLOS, its aim to 'Contribute to the realization of a just and equitable international economic order'. Likewise, it insists that the use of marine genetic resources 'shall be for the benefit of mankind as a whole'. But it is not yet clear how this will be guaranteed in practice. Rich states have argued that if High Seas genetic resources are exploited, any benefits to be shared with the global South could be 'non-monetary' in form. In theory, this could mean as little as the mere sharing of knowledge about marine biodiversity. Countries in the global South have insisted that benefit-sharing must actually involve money flowing in the direction of poor and landlocked countries, but both monetary and non-monetary options are left on the table in the draft treaty as it stands. More strikingly still, the treaty holds out the possibility that the sharing of benefits could be an optional process rather than a compulsory one.[9] Reversing growing inequalities at sea will require much more ambition than that.

Why exactly has the draft treaty avoided tackling some of the major weaknesses of ocean governance to date? I have discussed this with people centrally involved in working on the new treaty, and I believe the answer lies with a fear that powerful states will walk away otherwise, leaving the document to become one more failed treaty, meeting with insufficient support to become a binding piece of international law. The situation recalls the months leading up to the original Law of the Sea Convention, and the bolting on to it, later, of an Implementing Agreement that did so much to water down its more radical elements. Then too the drafters prioritised the 'continued participation' of all or most states, even if this meant a significant diminution of ambition. Having *some* rules on the exploitation of the genetic diversity of the High Seas, the theory goes, is better than having no rules – or letting them fall under the existing default principle of 'first come, first served'. But the sense that current negotiations are replaying the failures of the past – and in particular the gradual dismantling of the global South's radical vision for the original Law of the Sea Convention – is hard to shake. Karl Marx once wondered whether history was destined to produce a sense of déjà vu, causing events 'to be re-enacted twice over, once as grand tragedy and the second time as rotten farce'.[10] The negotiations for a new BBNJ Treaty are not quite farcical. But the sense that we have not learned from history hangs over them like a fog. In that context, we must be forgiven for imagining what a better solution would look like. The status quo, after all, leaves us hurtling towards ecological disaster and rampant inequality. It is hard to see how the draft treaty fundamentally alters that predicament, for all of the good intentions behind it. If arguing that we should press the brakes and take a different path is not 'realistic', then one response is: so be it. But another response is that in politics, what is realistic depends to a significant extent on what we believe we can achieve, and how we think others will act. If we can change enough minds, what is unrealistic today can come to seem distinctly possible tomorrow.

A WORLD OCEAN AUTHORITY

Why not begin with the idea that the Area Beyond National Jurisdiction should be governed by all of us, in the interests of present and future generations, of the humans who depend on the sea and the animals that actually make it their home? Why not reiterate that nobody depends on the resources of the High Seas, and shift the burden of argument so that, rather than constraints on exploitation needing to be justified, it is exploitation itself that would require a very powerful defence?[11] If we were prepared to make that move, we could begin to see a future for the High Seas and the seabed below as an enormous reserve, democratically and sustainably governed in accordance with key principles of ocean justice. That would demand a new governing body, an institution tasked with acting as a guardian for the deep ocean. A World Ocean Authority could be empowered to make all decisions about the use of the High Seas, and mandated to defend principles such as democratic inclusion, sustainability and fair benefit- and burden-sharing.

If the exploitation of its resources was sometimes permissible – if we could be sure that this would not compromise the diversity and health of the ABNJ – it would only take place on the condition that it genuinely helped people in the global South to catch up with the rich North. In that sense, a World Ocean Authority could deliver on the half-century-old vision of global South advocates for a New International Economic Order, who saw the deep sea as the potential birthing place of a radically transformed global economy. But those advocates could not have foreseen what we now know about the likely consequences of activities such as deep-sea mining, and in all likelihood, the precautionary principle would see an end to the vast majority – and quite possibly all – mining activities in the ABNJ, as well as a radical curtailing of fishing (see below). The goals of the authority would be largely protective, rather than focusing on allowing orderly exploitation. Our duty to cooperate to protect biodiversity in the wider ocean is an important plank of the common heritage principle. In the words of the South African representative to the United Nations General Assembly, that 'principle is about solidarity; solidarity in the preservation and conservation of a good we all share and therefore should protect'.[12]

It may be difficult to envisage exactly what an ocean governed in this way would look like. But the idea that we have duties to collaborate to protect crucial parts of our global ecosystem, and that this can require collective forms of governance in which individual state interests are put to one side, is already reflected in the successful Antarctic Treaty system. During the early twentieth century, the so-called 'white continent' was the target for territorial claims from countries such as Norway, Chile and the United Kingdom. But the 1959 Antarctic Treaty put those claims on ice, and created a set of institutions that still govern the continent as a place of peace, science and environmental protection. A 1991 Protocol on Environmental Protection declared Antarctica a 'natural reserve, devoted to peace and science', and prohibited all mining there.[13] So-called 'claimant states' have not quite renounced their territorial claims on the continent, and it is possible that some states may one day walk away from the Antarctic Treaty and begin exploiting its resources. Meanwhile, the treaty system itself is not perfect – it gives too little weight to voices from the global South, for instance. But imperfect as it is, the Antarctic model dispels any suggestion that the ABNJ cannot be peacefully and sustainably governed.

The challenge of designing inclusive and just institutions for the ocean has already attracted some attention. A number of proposals for innovative forms of oceanic governance are worthy of mention. As long ago as 1997, the then United Nations secretary-general Kofi Annan proposed the re-establishment of the long-defunct UN Trusteeship Council, a body which, he claimed, might serve as 'the forum through which member states [could] exercise their collective trusteeship for the integrity of the global environment and common areas such as the oceans, atmosphere and outer space'.[14] The following year, the Independent World Commission on the Oceans recommended that the High Seas should be managed as an enormous public trust 'to be used and managed in the interest of present and future generations',[15] and since then several scholars have proposed that we establish ocean trusts of some form or other.[16]

My argument for a World Ocean Authority is more radical in several respects, however. The proposals mentioned above still see individual states as the chief actors within ocean politics, charged one by one with conserving the ocean's resources and accountable for the most part to their own citizens for any successes and failures. On one version, an International Ocean Trust would set general standards for the protection of the High Seas. But individual states would be accountable to their *own* citizens for ensuring their activities on the High Seas were not unduly harmful.[17] On a rival proposal, civil society bodies might have the legal standing to hold states accountable for their activities on the High Seas – but states would remain the primary agents and decision-makers in its governance.[18] On my proposal, the World Ocean Authority would stand above states, which would not have the power to veto or depart from its rules. Under its auspices the ocean would, for the first time, be collectively and democratically governed as an important domain of global politics in its own right. It is worth pointing out that this proposal is compatible with giving some people a kind of special standing in some decisions. For instance, the peoples of some Pacific islands are quite distinctive in having a long history of regularly navigating the High Seas, and relying on it for their livelihoods (a look at the map in Chapter 8 will show why: their EEZs are clustered around, and actually enclose, some stretches of the High Seas). A World Ocean Authority could grant special representation rights to such communities, guaranteeing them a role in important local decisions, and it would also be well advised to learn from their long-running knowledge of the region (as well as other indigenous storehouses of knowledge throughout the ocean).[19] Above all, the authority would help shift the ocean from being an afterthought or marginal concern within the contemporary world, to a major focus of global – as opposed to merely international – cooperation.

The World Ocean Authority would not *own* the High Seas or the seabed beneath it. Morally, none of us can do that. If anything, we have a duty to preserve those places for the creatures who actually live there. This is one thing that is attractive about the idea of an ocean trust: the trustees who administer a trust do not own the assets in it, but instead have a legal duty to maintain those assets in the interests of the relevant beneficiaries. In principle, that could mean all of life on earth. An authority of the type I am proposing would also give robust institutional form to the idea that the ocean is part of our common heritage – and as I noted in Chapter 4, the idea that we have a common stake in the ocean's future is compatible with recognising it as the common heritage of many other species too. One thing that is less attractive about proposals for ocean trusts, though, is the fact that they tend to be conceived of in a purely legalistic way. Their advocates have typically envisioned sections of the ocean being run by impartial trustees with a clear legal brief, with concerned citizens or other actors retaining the power to hold them to legal account if that brief is not adhered to. My proposal, by contrast, is democratic in character. It would task an authority with including, and representing, a whole variety of actors in ocean governance. Rather than the governance of the ocean being left to legal trustees, individual citizens, local communities and indigenous groups should be given a direct voice in the collective management of the ocean, and not just a remedial right to seek legal redress whenever states fail to act on their duties.[20] Given the centrality of the ocean to our lives, and the ramifications that effective or ineffective ocean governance will have for our future, people the world over have a right to participate in oceanic governance. The authority should serve as a vehicle for a broad popular engagement in the future of the ocean.

The authority would hold the exclusive power to determine who can exploit the wider ocean, when and how. The idea of reserving such powers to a dedicated international body is not a completely new one: the International Seabed Authority, at least as originally envisaged by countries from the global South, was supposed to determine whether the resources of the seabed beyond national jurisdiction could be exploited, by whom and in what circumstances. Shifting global politics eventually led to its powers being systematically degraded, in the 1994 Implementing Agreement, to the extent that it now looks like little more than a registry for claims to exploit the seabed. But the principle that exploitation should be conditional on the consent of a legitimate ocean authority is the right one. My argument, though, would extend the World Ocean Authority's powers to the seabed *and* the ocean above it. The seabed is not a separate ecosystem, after all; it interacts with what goes on in the water above it. Our governance needs to be joined up to reflect that fact.

If the authority took its sustainability brief seriously, it is likely that most forms of exploitation on or under the High Seas would be forbidden, at least for the foreseeable future. Many ecologists believe that fishing on the High Seas is ecologically unsustainable, and that in the absence of large fuel subsidies it simply wouldn't occur anyway.[21] Paying large fishing conglomerates millions to wreak havoc with the marine food web makes no kind of sense. By contrast, closing the High Seas to fishing entirely could spur a wider regeneration of fish populations.[22] Rather than a patchwork of optional Marine Protected Areas, in essence the entire High Seas would be one enormous Marine Reserve. The exploitation of seabed resources, meanwhile, would have to pass serious tests of environmental safety. Given the slow recovery time of many organisms on the deep seabed, it seems unlikely that seabed mining activities would ever pass the test.

Some economic activities in the Area Beyond National Jurisdiction might still be permissible. In earlier chapters I have noted that corporations are rushing to identify and patent the genetic codes of deep-sea creatures, whose ability to live under extreme conditions means they may hold the secret to the medicines or technologies of the future. In principle, doing so will not harm those creatures themselves. But for one person to claim a patent will reduce others' ability to use these codes themselves (that, after all, is what patents are for). This is why the discussion about benefit-sharing mechanisms is so important, and explains why they are one of the issues the draft treaty on BBNJ is still grappling with – although early indications are that the benefit-sharing mechanisms it embraces will turn out to be excessively kind to those who profit from such activities. The World Ocean Authority would have the power to determine the fate of genetic codes from in or under the High Seas. It might decide to refuse to allow any patents to be claimed over genetic codes at all, if that was the best way of ensuring that the benefits from any future medical treatments, for instance, truly accrued to the have-nots as well as to the haves. Or it could grant patents, on the condition that meaningful forms of benefit-sharing and technology transfer were in place that enabled people in the South to overcome the barriers to entry in high-tech scientific industries. It might even sell patents to the highest bidder, and use the money to fund its conservation activities. But that would be a decision to be made democratically, by the entire international community. What is key is that exploitation would not take place unless it was genuinely in the interest of the worst off as well as the most advantaged.

The main goal of the World Ocean Authority would not be to raise money, but to protect the ocean. But there would be no shortage of ways to spend any money it did raise from licensing sustainable ocean activities. It could fund marine conservation projects in the EEZs of countries from the global South, including the effective policing of Marine Protected Areas, the monitoring of illegal fishing and the restoration of key, hyper-fertile habitats such as coral reefs. It could fund 'just transition' projects, easing the social costs of adjusting to a more modest set of demands on the ocean. Consider again the idea of a ban on High Seas fishing. In practice, the countries that would lose most from any such ban would be South Korea, Taiwan and Japan, which can probably afford to offset any losses to their fishing fleets[23] (rather than in effect paying those fleets to fish on the High Seas, those countries could invest in more sustainable ocean industries instead). But some countries that fish on the High Seas are in a less fortunate position, and might require help in engineering a just transition. It is not clear that a World Ocean Authority would raise the kind of money that advocates of a New International Economic Order believed would soon flow from the deep seabed, and it is best seen as a guardian of the wider ocean rather than a body seeking to make gains from its exploitation. But to the extent that it could raise funds, the dream that the wider ocean could act as the midwife to a more egalitarian world order is not a forlorn one by any means.

EXCLUSIVE ECONOMIC ZONES

Anyone persuaded by the argument so far might ask: why not place the entire ocean – or at least the ocean outside of narrow territorial seas – under the jurisdiction of a World Ocean Authority? After all, much of the ocean's biodiversity is contained within the Exclusive Economic Zones that surround the world's coasts. I've suggested that the arguments for giving coastal states EEZs are actually surprisingly weak. If we want to protect local attachments, or subsistence needs, allowing coastal states to retain 12-mile territorial seas would probably be enough. From the point of view of equality and sustainability, by contrast, the introduction of EEZs has left a great deal to be desired. Those who care about equality should regret the way it has brought great benefits to many, but little or no benefits to landlocked countries, whereas countries in the global South have often signed away access to their coastal resources for a small share of their economic value. Those who care about sustainability should regret the fact that, although the Law of the Sea Convention suggests coastal states have a duty to conserve the resources in their EEZs, those words are not backed up with meaningful legal consequences for those which choose not to.

So why not simply abolish EEZs, and turn them over to a World Ocean Authority too? Personally, I find that prospect an attractive one. But I also recognise that it is likely to be highly divisive. States in both the North and the South appear strongly disinclined to give up territory once they have acquired it. Leaders from the global South welcomed the introduction of EEZs, and even if they have rarely brought the advantages that were hoped for, their amalgamation into a global authority would almost certainly be presented as a return of imperialism in another guise. The argument that a World Ocean

Authority would do a better job of both protecting our ocean and promoting a more egalitarian world order would have to be made, step by step. In the meantime, I don't want the argument for a World Ocean Authority to stand or fall on a claim quite that contentious. Even if EEZs are likely to be a feature of our world for some time to come, we do not have to accept that they will continue to work in their current form. Instead, I will explore several ways in which the rules governing EEZs could be adapted in order to better advance the goals of equality and sustainability. These are all compatible with, and in many cases would help support, the Blue New Deal policies I described in the last chapter.

A first priority should be to strengthen each country's duty to conserve biodiversity within its EEZ. The principle that fish 'stocks' should be 'optimally utilized' should be dropped. The priority should be to allow fish populations to find their own equilibrium. Harmful fishing subsidies should be outlawed. To the extent that fishing is still possible, destructive practices such as bottom trawling and the use of cyanide and dynamite should be outlawed. Each state should designate a significant proportion of its EEZ as Marine Protected Areas, in which all destructive practices, and all fishing, should be outlawed (they would, therefore, be much closer to Marine Reserves in nature). All too often MPAs operate as 'paper parks', in which devastating fishing practices are still allowed, or in which staffing and monitoring resources are wholly inadequate. As a result, most MPAs fail to make a significant difference in practice.[24] Successful MPAs share key features such as size, strong enforcement, durability and an insistence on 'no-take' policies rather than modest constraints on fishing.[25] An ambitious target – to protect between 30 and 50 per cent of each EEZ in this way – should become the norm.[26] When considered alongside a World Ocean Authority on the High Seas, which makes up almost two-thirds of the ocean by surface area, this would mean that around 80 per cent of the ocean was made up of strongly protected Marine Reserves or the equivalent.[27] Putting such radical policies in place could lead to a regeneration of marine life in a surprisingly short period of time.

There have been some indications that national governments are waking up to the challenges involved in protecting our ocean. But words need to be

10.1 A green sea turtle swimming in the Hol Chan Marine Reserve, Belize.

matched by action. In December 2020, an international 'High Level Panel' agreed to a new set of targets for a Sustainable Ocean Economy. The leaders of Australia, Canada, Chile, Fiji, Ghana, Indonesia, Jamaica, Japan, Kenya, Mexico, Namibia, Norway, Palau and Portugal signed up to a set of key principles for governing their countries' EEZs. Among other things, they committed to end illegal fishing, prohibit harmful subsidies, scale up seaweed farming as an alternative to unsustainable fuel and feedstocks, and improve the extent and health of vital coastal ecosystems such as mangroves and kelp beds.[28] That is a promising development. But public pressure will be vital to make sure those targets are backed by meaningful action.

It is crucial too that the impact of conservation measures is fairly shared. This will require mechanisms to help countries in the global South – and disadvantaged regions within the countries of the North – absorb the costs of conservation. As I argued in the last chapter, the point is not that 'ecosystem services' have to be paid for by those who 'consume' them. The point is that in

215

many places there is a conflict between conservation and the desire to escape from disadvantage, and people should not be forced to make that choice. A bountiful ocean ecosystem, safely sequestering carbon in mangroves or seagrass meadows, allowing the recovery of fish, whales and other marine animals, is in all of our interests, as well as the interests of marine animals themselves. But the costs of the transitions involved must not be allowed to fall on the shoulders of the worst off. Major conservation financing will be necessary, in the short to medium term. In the long run, these conservation activities will bring enormous benefits, both locally and globally.

A second priority should be an embargo on offshore fossil fuel extraction. It was hugely disappointing that, just weeks after its prime minister, Erna Solberg, had signed up to the principles of the High Level Panel on ocean sustainability, Norway announced sixty-one new licences for offshore oil and gas exploration.[29] That is as clear an example of giving to the ocean with one hand and taking away with the other as we could wish for. The world already has access to more oil and gas than it can safely use. Spending billions on finding still more supplies on the seabed, where extraction may cause long-term environmental damage, makes no sense at all. Countries should follow Denmark's example and announce a clear date by which offshore fossil fuel extraction will come to an end. In fact, they should be more ambitious than the Danish government has been. Theresa Scavenius, the founder of the new Danish climate-oriented political party Momentum, told me: 'The target is a good start but it doesn't match the urgency of the situation. We need to stop extracting fossil fuel much earlier than 2050 if the country is going to meet its climate targets.' Our governments are wary of taking such measures because they will wipe billions from shares in fossil fuel companies, and impact on the world's pension funds (although some have already taken steps to divest from fossil fuels). But the fossil fuel market is a bubble, and one day it is going to burst – unless we are prepared to reconcile ourselves to a scorched planet. Better to plan now for a future beyond carbon, and switch investment to safe and renewable technologies such as offshore wind power. Efforts to tackle demand for fossil fuels through methods such as carbon taxes have a role to play, but ultimately we will have to put an end to the supply of fossil fuels. States should have a legal duty to wind down their fossil fuel industries, and redirect the enormous tax breaks they offer to the industry in the direction of sustainable energy. In some cases, this might demand international assistance, where poor countries are heavily reliant on fossil fuel exports and will struggle to open up new opportunities.[30] If we know that a transition away from carbon is necessary, the right time to start is yesterday. But today is a good second best.

Third, states should place much greater emphasis on 'social' objectives when governing their EEZs. Coastal management has often been essentially neoliberal in form, with overwhelming priority placed on maximising the economic yield from marine industries. That is a wholly short-sighted approach, especially when the profits in question have enriched some but not others. We should move away from the kinds of policies that have enriched a privileged few (foremost among them large fishing corporations, biotech firms and fossil fuel companies), and seek instead policies that genuinely advance the well-being of all, including the poor and marginalised.[31] This suggests there is a premium on the kinds of Blue New Deal policies I discussed in the last chapter, which are capable of supporting many new green jobs, spreading wealth throughout the community and giving those communities a greater degree of control over their own destinies. Despite the many promises, the benefits of neoliberal economic policies do not 'trickle down' to the whole community. In many cases, investment in small-scale businesses will do a far better job of making sustainable coastal industries work for all.

Fourth, we should revisit the idea that states with extensive and bountiful coastlines have a duty to share access with those that do not. With the advent of the Law of the Sea Convention, landlocked countries were shut out of most of the ocean economy, and they have never found their way back (although the convention suggests that countries that cannot fully exploit the fish in their EEZs ought to offer access to landlocked countries instead, for instance, this has never been delivered on in any systematic way. For the most part, access has been sold to Distant Water Fleets from high- or middle-income countries instead.) It is not inevitable that states without coastlines should be shut out of sustainable ocean industries, or indeed from access to the sea more generally. But tackling their disadvantage will require some creative thinking. One proposal is that landlocked countries could be offered guaranteed, free transit through coastal countries, as a kind of 'land bridge' to the sea. Extortionate transit costs – the payments a state demands simply for allowing goods to be shifted across its territory to the sea – should also be outlawed. In addition, landlocked states could be enabled to participate in sustainable industries such as seaweed farming or offshore renewable energy. Either way, their ability to engage with the ocean and with international trade would be enhanced at little cost to others.[32]

AN OCEAN RENEWED

Many readers of this book will balk at the overall message of this final chapter. While they may be persuaded of many of the more modest proposals argued for in previous chapters, as well as the prospects for a Blue New Deal, the proposals here would take us into much less familiar territory. Is it at all likely that a World Ocean Authority, with the powers I have suggested, could emerge? Is it at all likely that states would agree to limit their activities within their own EEZs in the many ways I have suggested? Will 80 per cent of the ocean ever be strongly protected? Radical proposals for change are often criticised for being 'infeasible', and for standing in the way of the more piecemeal changes that are actually within our reach. If we have to choose between a good chance of making moderate progress towards ocean justice, and a slim chance of making more dramatic progress, why not opt for the former? The French philosopher Voltaire is meant to have said (in turn quoting an older Italian proverb) that we should not let 'the best' be the enemy of 'the good'. The search for perfect policies, he was implying, should not interfere with the everyday task of identifying good ones. Shouldn't our proposals for reform be tempered by a large dose of realism?

One response to this worry is to point out that the best and the good are not always incompatible. It is not clear that the more modest proposals I have made in previous chapters and the more radical proposals I have made here need to compete with each another. We can argue that inundated states should retain their EEZs (as long as EEZs last) and also argue that the prerogatives an EEZ brings in tow should be reformed. We can argue that the rights of marine animals, and of workers at sea, should be better protected in a whole host of ways, whether the governance of the deep sea comes to be transformed by a World Ocean Authority or not. Likewise, whether states retained 12-mile territorial seas or 200-mile EEZs, they would still have considerable scope to pursue Blue New Deal policies by restoring coastal ecosystems, greening their ports, engaging in sustainable aquaculture and investing in renewable ocean energy.

But I also want to push back against the claim that more radical reforms are not feasible. One reason we should be suspicious about claims of infeasibility is that they are often disproved in practice. Many people argued that Britain's National Health Service would not work and yet it is one of its great success stories. Many people have argued that minimum wage legislation would produce mass unemployment – it has not. Philosophers and rulers once thought that elected government would be impossible on any scale larger than a city, and that people from different religions could not live together in peace – they were wrong on both counts. Another reason we should be suspicious is that claims that a given policy is infeasible often turn out to mean not that they are strictly impossible, but that they are too *costly*.[33] If so, it is important to ask: costly for whom? In the years leading up to the Law of the Sea Convention, similar claims were made about the feasibility of extending egalitarian and democratic principles to the governance of the seabed. But it was not as though we discovered that doing so would be impossible in any strict practical sense. The institutions and rules proposed by advocates of a New International Economic Order probably would have worked more or less as envisaged. What we learned, if anything, is that rich countries possessed the power to block reforms they did not see as being in their interests (or which they believed would be inimical to a 'healthy' global economy, which meant much the same thing), by threatening to walk away from international agreements that (as they saw it) unduly limited their prerogatives in the ocean economy.

Radical reforms to ocean governance *will* be costly, at least in the short term, for many rich countries. Those countries will find themselves unable to consume oceanic resources as they have done to date, free of charge and for the most part without constraint, and for that reason it would not be surprising if many of their governments objected, inspired by powerful vested interests in the economy. It is important not to pretend that radical reforms will be to everyone's immediate benefit. But sticking to our current path will be even more costly, at least in the long term. It will clearly be costly for the have-nots, who will continue to be excluded from the table when the spoils of the Blue Acceleration come to be shared out. In that sense we should have the courage to spell out just what many claims about feasibility really imply. When addressed to people in the global South, by people in the North, they turn out to mean nothing more or less than: *You cannot really expect us to share our privileges with you?* Spelling that out clearly is an important first step for anyone who wants to show that another way is possible. But the status quo may also be costly for all of us, in the long term. Although some of the privileged may believe they will be able to protect themselves from the impacts of rampant climate change and ecological destruction, they have no guarantee of that, not least because our understanding of the possible consequences of the demands we are placing on the ocean remains rather rudimentary. And it is still less clear that we will be able to protect our children's and grandchildren's interests in a world of runaway climate change and rampant inequality.

The proposals I have made in this chapter – for reformed governance on both the High Seas and within Exclusive Economic Zones – could have dramatic effects, turning around the fortunes of at least four-fifths of the ocean. This is not to say that they will be sufficient to protect the ocean environment. The ocean will continue to be at the mercy of decisions made back on dry land, and especially the decisions we make in the coming years about how far and how fast to decarbonise our economies. But we should not underestimate what is still possible. The goal of radical ocean policies should not only be to preserve the ocean biodiversity that exists today. In practice, when we think about conservation, we often fall victim to what ecologists call 'shifting baseline syndrome'.[34] We try earnestly to preserve as much of what currently exists as possible. Since our efforts are never entirely successful, the next generation will try to preserve as much as possible of what then remains – and so on. Whatever each new generation inherits is taken as the benchmark for what should be, even though this benchmark continually diminishes. Over time, people become used to an ecosystem which is, in historical terms, significantly diminished, and diminishing still. The possibility of *regenerating* the bountiful and resilient ecosystems that once existed – or allowing them to regenerate themselves – quietly drops out of the picture.

But our goal really could be to regenerate or 'rewild' the ocean – or better still, to allow it to rewild itself. Not only is the regeneration of the ocean possible, it could happen much faster than you think. Some ecologists believe that concerted action to protect the ocean (which will mean, for the most part, leaving it to its own devices) could see marine life rebounding significantly within a single human generation (although the chances of recovery are significantly lower if we fail to take radical action to tackle climate change).[35] That is not pure speculation, because we have seen it happen in practice. During both the First and Second World Wars, industrial fishing was significantly downscaled: mines and submarines made fishing too dangerous, and the war effort drew both people and boats away. By the end of both wars, fish populations had recovered dramatically.[36] That was an experiment that was forced on us, but it shows what is possible. More recently, Marine Protected Areas that are adequately policed have acted as fountains of marine life, with fish spilling out into other areas in unexpectedly high numbers. Strongly protected Marine Reserves can even help reduce climate change, as rebounding fish and shellfish populations cycle more carbon into the depths of the ocean.[37] Suitably protected, the High Seas could function in the same way in the restoration of marine life, but on a much larger scale. Closer to our shores, oyster reefs and kelp forest habitats have proven capable of recovering in less than a decade, when allowed to. Mangroves and saltmarshes have regenerated within a mere ten to twenty years.[38] Species that are especially long-living (including the cetaceans that swim the ocean, and the strange organisms that live on the deep seabed) will take much longer to recover, and for that reason they demand much more determined protection. But as the example of the humpback whales shows, a significant rebound in numbers is possible,[39] allowing them to go on cycling nutrients throughout the ocean, singing their strange songs while sustaining a rebirth of ocean life. A recovery of vibrant ocean life is possible, and it could not be more important.

AFTERWORD

The Stockholm Resilience Centre – a research institute that works to promote global sustainability – maintains a website called Radical Ocean Futures.[1] An innovative collaboration between artists and scientists, the site encourages users to reflect on what the ocean might look like in the year 2070. Most of the fictionalised ocean futures it describes are decidedly dystopian. One imagines a scenario where sea-level rise has wiped countries like Bangladesh and the Netherlands from the map entirely, although some brave folk are now living in glass domes on the ocean floor. In another imagined future, overfishing, combined with a geoengineering project gone badly awry, has produced an eerie, empty ocean. In still another, the ocean has been converted into a giant industrial plant designed to process jellyfish into human food.

These visions are in some ways fanciful, because we don't know quite what the ocean will look like half a century from now. But the project is an important one nonetheless. It is vital to pause to reflect on what kind of ocean we want, rather than stumbling blindly towards one future or another. It's also crucial to recognise the kind of ocean we are likely to end up with if we hold fast to our current trajectory. The ocean we are likely to have, if current trends continue, is not an attractive one at all. What we could call the Anthropocene future would see the ocean steadily emptied of wild marine life, and instead filled with farmed fish from just a few species – although even those species would be threatened by acidification, warming, the growth of marine dead zones with low or no oxygen, and plastic pollution. In many ways this would also be a neoliberal future, insofar as it would see an extensive privatisation of ocean resources and even, perhaps, marine territory.[2] Neoliberalism thrives on the removal of decision-making power from sites of public accountability and democracy, and so we could also expect ocean governance to be depoliticised, with major decisions made by corporations, behind closed doors. Any profits to be had would flow to the wealthy, whereas people who had been used to accessing the ocean for traditional, subsistence activities – or simply for recreation – could expect to find themselves shut out of its spaces and its politics.

We can, however, imagine alternative ocean futures – and this book has been an exercise in doing just that. The alternative future it has depicted is an egalitarian and participatory one, in which the ocean economy is oriented less around the pursuit of profit (and especially profit which flows towards those who are already winners), and more around the pursuit of key social goals such as the alleviation of poverty, nutritional security, community regeneration and the health or spiritual benefits of exposure to a vibrant ocean. Within each coastal zone, countries would pursue their own Blue New Deals (with help from the international community where necessary), restoring coastal ecosystems and revitalising coastal communities. At the same time the governance of the High Seas would be completely transformed, and more rigorous rules applied to EEZs in order to turn around their ecological fortunes. If the two strategies were pursued simultaneously – if 80 per cent of the ocean was strongly protected – it would become a haven for resilient and bountiful life once more, while also supporting the livelihoods of the many people who depend on it. In many ways this vision resonates with the image of a just ocean economy which was painted by advocates of a New International Economic Order in the 1960s and '70s. In that period, leaders in the global South argued that the ocean economy could be the fountainhead for a fairer global economy, in which disadvantaged communities would be active participants, and in which the ideal of freedom of the sea would no longer operate as a cover for corporate pillage. But the picture I have painted in this book does differ from that vision in some respects. In the 1960s and '70s, our understanding of the

ecological challenges faced by the ocean – and the likely environmental consequences of activities like seabed mining – was rudimentary at best. Knowing
what we now do about the overlapping challenges faced by the ocean, and
armed with a suitable degree of respect for the interests of the creatures that
inhabit it, our approach to ocean governance should now focus less on fair
exploitation and more on effective protection.

This means breaking out of the mindset of the Blue Acceleration, which
presents the ocean as the next exciting resource frontier, ripe for investment.
That mindset continues to treat the ocean as a cornucopia, much as in the
early 1600s Grotius imagined that we could reap and reap the fruits of the sea
without altering its condition at all. We have already systematically degraded
the land and its ecosystems, and created a host of environmental problems in
the process. If we are to find a just and sustainable future on earth, I have
argued that we cannot go on to treat the ocean in the same way. In this sense,
as in so many others, the land and the sea are inextricably linked. One great
danger of the Blue Acceleration mindset is that it encourages us to defer important questions about how to repair land-based ecosystems (the blithe assumption that we can exploit the ocean with impunity means that important
decisions about sustainability and equity back on dry land never quite need to
be faced). Once we realise that the ocean cannot and should not be industrialised in the same way as the land, by contrast, we are forced to engage with
broader questions about the future of our economies and indeed of our planet
as a whole. My belief is that the new ocean politics I have described in this
book, which would robustly protect at least four-fifths of the ocean, will leave
us in a far better place when we come to face those questions.

What, though, can you, the reader, do to help? To some extent that will
depend on the resources open to you, though there are likely to be some
changes that everyone can make. At the purely individual level, it is important
that we try to reduce the demands we place on the ocean and its ecosystems.
One way to do that would be to consume less fish if you can. Many people, as
we have seen, are nutritionally dependent on fish, in the sense that removing it
from their diet would leave them with few alternative sources of protein and

225

vital micronutrients. But most of us are not in that position, and could shift our diet away from fish quite easily. That might mean cutting fish out of our diets completely, or it might mean cutting down. If the latter, it is worth taking care to avoid fish that are associated with destructive practices such as bottom trawling, with the bycatch of dolphins and other marine animals (tuna is a particular problem here), or with human rights abuses (as we have seen, this may mean avoiding farmed shrimp or prawns, unless you can be reasonably confident about the supply chains involved). Farmed fish, meanwhile, are almost certainly not the solution when it comes to addressing the environmental impacts of the fishing industry.

Another priority should be a reduction in our consumption of single-use plastics, given that so much of it ends up in the sea. More positively, you could engage in beach clean-up operations, removing harmful items from our coastlines. Given the connection between climate change and ocean warming and acidification, we should already be thinking about ways of reducing our carbon footprints. This might involve cutting down on travel, switching to electric vehicles where possible, installing renewable sources of home heating and electricity, and reducing or ending our consumption of meat (given that meat 'production' has such an outsized association with greenhouse gas emissions, as well as intensifying deforestation and the competition for land more generally).

If you are lucky enough to own significant personal wealth, then you could try to invest it in 'green' (or blue) assets. Even those of us who are not wealthy may have some power to make a difference in this respect. If you have a workplace pension, put pressure on your pension fund to end any investments it still makes in fossil fuels, and to make positive efforts to seek out sustainable industries capable of supporting local livelihoods, including in the transition away from carbon. If you have a bank account, challenge your bank about whether they are still investing in offshore fossil fuels, or have made the switch to renewable technologies. In your role as a consumer, pressure corporations, including supermarket chains, to pay more attention to issues including workers' rights, bycatch and marine pollution. Although corporations are powerful and individuals are typically not, shareholders care about reputational damage, and will not want to be singled out for the damage they do to marine ecosystems. As a result, knowledge can be power – and the ability to reach out and spread your knowledge to others especially so. Fossil fuel companies are still engaging in 'greenwashing', claiming they will achieve carbon neutrality in the near future without taking the radical steps that would make that possible. Unless and until our governments take a firmer line with them, consumer pressure and direct action may be the best ways of encouraging them to change their ways and switch their massive investments into renewable technologies before the fossil fuel bubble bursts once and for all.

It is probably in the political sphere that we can have the greatest impact. The governance of the ocean needs to become an everyday political issue in the same way that issues such as education, welfare and policing are, rather than being relegated to the political margins. Given politicians' laser-eyed focus on targeting the floating voter, this will probably only happen when they see a concern for the ocean's future making a difference to our voting intentions, or to their mail boxes. In many countries, Green parties have begun to put the protection of the ocean at the heart of their policy platforms, and this is very much to be welcomed. A series of NGOs have also worked hard to place ocean politics on the agenda. It is crucial that parties which neglect ocean issues, and which refuse to make vital decisions about the future of the ocean, should be persuaded that this will harm their political fortunes. Practical actions might include lobbying local politicians, donating to parties which put ocean protection in their manifestos, supporting ocean-facing NGOs, and persuading your fellow citizens of the significance of these issues.

In many countries in both the North and South of our planet, the ocean is already attracting new advocates who are bursting with ideas about how to restore coastal ecosystems and support local communities in their transitions to a sustainable future. We can make a difference by engaging with those advocates, spreading their message and even becoming advocates for the ocean in our own right. In this way, we can work together to make the case for a Blue New Deal and a new, more egalitarian, politics for our ocean.

NOTES

INTRODUCTION

1. Camilo Mora et al., 'How Many Species are there on Earth and in the Ocean?', *PLoS Biology*, vol. 9, no. 8 (2011), e1001127.
2. Patricio Bernal, 'State Ocean Strategies and Policies', in Hance Smith et al. (eds), *Routledge Handbook of Ocean Resources and Management* (Abingdon: Routledge, 2017), pp. 33–54, at p. 45.
3. Kristina Gjerde, 'Challenges to Protecting the Marine Environment beyond National Jurisdiction', *International Journal of Marine and Coastal Law*, vol. 27 (2012), pp. 839–47, at p. 839.
4. Elizabeth Kolbert, *The Sixth Extinction: An Unnatural History* (London: Bloomsbury, 2014).
5. Jane Lubchenco and Steven Gaines, 'A New Narrative for the Ocean', *Science*, 364:6444 (2019), p. 911.
6. Jean-Baptiste Jouffray et al., 'The Blue Acceleration: The Trajectory of Human Expansion into the Ocean', *One Earth*, vol. 2 (2020), pp. 43–54.
7. On the income and wealth of the top 10 per cent, see Facundo Alvaredo et al., 'The Elephant Curve of Global Inequality and Growth', *AEA Papers and Proceedings*, vol. 108 (2018), pp. 103–8. On their emissions, see Thomas Piketty and Lucas Chancel, *Carbon and Inequality: From Kyoto to Paris*, Paris School of Economics Working Paper (2015).
8. Sudhir Anand and Paul Segal, 'Who Are the Global Top 1%?', *World Development*, vol. 95 (2017), pp. 111–26.
9. Greenpeace International, *Deep Trouble: The Murky World of the Deep Sea Mining Industry* (London: Greenpeace International, 2020), p. 25.
10. Robert Blasiak et al., 'Corporate Control and Global Governance of Marine Genetic Resources', *Science Advances*, vol. 4, no. 6 (2018), eaar5237, p. 2.

1. THE CRUCIBLE OF LIFE

1. Jesús Arrieta et al., 'What Lies Underneath: Conserving the Oceans' Genetic Resources', *Proceedings of the National Academy of Sciences*, vol. 107, no. 43 (2010), pp. 18318–24.
2. Dorrik Stow, *Oceans: A Very Short Introduction* (Oxford: Oxford University Press, 2017), p. 42.
3. Yadigar Sekerci and Sergei Petrovskii, 'Mathematical Modelling of Plankton–Oxygen Dynamics Under the Climate Change', *Bulletin of Mathematical Biology*, vol. 77, no. 12 (2015), pp. 2325–53.

4. Stow, *Oceans: A Very Short Introduction*, p. 80.
5. Meryl Williams et al., 'Making Marine Life Count: A New Baseline for Policy', *PLoS Biology*, vol. 8, no. 10 (2010), pp. 1–5.
6. Michael Orbach, 'Beyond the Freedom of the Sea: Ocean Policy for the Third Millennium', *Oceanography*, vol. 16, no. 1 (2003), pp. 20–29, at p. 21.
7. Philip Steinberg, 'It's So Easy Being Green: Overuse, Underexposure, and the Marine Environmentalist Consensus', *Geography Compass*, vol. 2, no. 6 (2008), pp. 2080–96, at pp. 2086–7.
8. Stow, *Oceans: A Very Short Introduction*, p. 153.
9. *The Mahābhārata Volume 2*, trans. J.A.B. van Buitenen (Chicago: University of Chicago Press, 1975), p. 589.
10. Salit Kark et al., 'Emerging Conservation Challenges and Prospects in an Era of Offshore Hydrocarbon Exploration and Exploitation', *Conservation Biology*, vol. 29, no. 6 (2015), pp. 1573–85, at p. 1574.
11. John Kaldellis et al., 'Environmental and Social Footprint of Offshore Wind Energy. Comparison with Onshore Counterpart', *Renewable Energy*, vol. 92 (2016), pp. 543–56, at p. 544.
12. Stow, *Oceans: A Very Short Introduction*, p. 137.
13. James Hein and Kira Mizell, 'Ocean Minerals', in Hance Smith et al. (eds), *Routledge Handbook of Ocean Resources and Management* (Abingdon: Routledge, 2017), pp. 296–309, at p. 306.
14. Yimin Ye et al., 'Rebuilding Global Fisheries: The World Summit Goal, Costs and Benefits', *Fish and Fisheries*, vol. 14, no. 2 (2013), pp. 174–85, at p. 176.
15. Christopher Golden et al., 'Nutrition: Fall in Fish Catch Threatens Human Health', *Nature News*, vol. 534, no. 7607 (2016), p. 317.
16. World Bank, *The Global Program on Fisheries: Strategic Vision for Fisheries and Aquaculture* (Washington DC: World Bank, 2011).
17. Jerome Verny and Christophe Grigentin, 'Container Shipping on the Northern Sea Route', *International Journal of Production Economics*, vol. 122, no. 1 (2009), pp. 107–17, at p. 110.
18. IBRD/World Bank, *The Potential of the Blue Economy* (Washington DC: World Bank, 2017), p. 21.
19. Laleh Khalili, *Sinews of War and Trade: Shipping and Capitalism in the Arabian Peninsula* (London: Verso, 2020).
20. Patrick Manning, *Migration in World History*, 2nd edn (Abingdon: Routledge, 2013), pp. 109–10.
21. Brian Rouleau, 'Seafaring Communities, 1800–1850', in D'Maris Coffman et al. (eds), *The Atlantic World* (Abingdon: Routledge, 2015), pp. 131–48, at p. 138.
22. Epeli Hau'ofa, 'Our Sea of Islands', in Eric Waddell, Vijay Naidu and Epeli Hau'ofa (eds), *A New Oceania: Rediscovering Our Sea of Islands* (Suva: Beake House, 1993), p. 16.
23. Paul Gilroy, *The Black Atlantic* (London: Verso, 1993).
24. Jay Golden et al., 'Making Sure the Blue Economy is Green', *Nature Ecology & Evolution*, vol. 2 (2017), pp. 1–3, at p. 2.
25. Paula Casal and Nicole Selamé, 'Sea for the Landlocked: A Sustainable Development Goal?', *Journal of Global Ethics*, vol. 11, no. 3 (2015), pp. 270–79.
26. Tommy Koh, 'A Constitution for the Oceans' (1982). Available at http://www.un.org/depts/los/convention_agreements/texts/koh_english.pdf (accessed 26 June 2019).
27. Michael Faye et al., 'The Challenges Facing Landlocked Developing Countries', *Journal of Human Development*, vol. 5, no. 1 (2004), pp. 31–68, at p. 32.
28. Paul Collier, *The Bottom Billion* (Oxford: Oxford University Press, 2007), pp. 53–8.
29. Figures for France, United States, Australia and United Kingdom include overseas dependencies. Note that China claims a much larger EEZ, but its claims are contested by neighbouring states.
30. Peter Nolan, 'Imperial Archipelagos', *New Left Review*, no. 80 (2013), pp. 77–95, at p. 79.
31. Ibid., p. 82.

32. Ibid., pp. 85–90.
33. J. Virdin et al., 'The Ocean 100: Transnational Corporations in the Ocean Economy', *Science Advances*, vol. 7, no. 3 (2021), eabc8041.
34. Robert Blasiak et al., 'Corporate Control and Governance of Marine Genetic Resources', *Science Advances*, vol. 4, no. 6 (2018), eaar5237.
35. Alastair Couper et al., *Fishers and Plunderers* (London: Pluto Press, 2015), p. 79.
36. Alexis Rife et al., 'When Good Intentions Are Not Enough . . . Insights on Networks of "Paper Park" Marine Protected Areas', *Conservation Letters*, vol. 6, no. 3 (2013), pp. 200–212.
37. IPCC, *Climate Change: The Physical Science Basis* (Cambridge: Cambridge University Press, 2013).
38. Jason Hall-Spencer et al., 'Volcanic Carbon Dioxide Vents Show Ecosystem Effects of Ocean Acidification', *Nature*, vol. 454, no. 7200 (2008), pp. 96–9, at p. 99.
39. Terry Hughes et al., 'Global Warming and Recurrent Mass Bleaching of Corals,' *Nature*, vol. 543, no. 7645 (2017), pp. 373–7.
40. Michael Angelidis, 'Waste Disposal and Ocean Pollution', in Smith et al. (eds), *Routledge Handbook of Ocean Resources*, p. 388.
41. Stow, *Oceans: A Very Short Introduction*, p. 145.
42. Robert Diaz and Rutger Rosenberg, 'Spreading Dead Zones and Consequences for Marine Ecosystems', *Science*, vol. 321, no. 5891 (2008), pp. 926–9.
43. Angelidis, 'Waste Disposal and Ocean Pollution', pp. 381–95, at p. 387.
44. Marcus Eriksen et al., 'Plastic Pollution in the World's Oceans: More Than 5 Trillion Plastic Pieces Weighing over 250,000 Tons Afloat at Sea', *PLoS One*, vol. 9, no. 12 (2014), e111913.
45. Chris Wilcox et al., 'Threat of Plastic Pollution to Seabirds is Global, Pervasive, and Increasing', *Proceedings of the National Academy of Sciences*, vol. 112, no. 38 (2015), pp. 11899–904.
46. Marta Coll et al., 'Ecosystem Overfishing in the Ocean', *PLoS One*, vol. 3 (2009), e3881.
47. FAO, *The State of the World's Fisheries and Aquaculture* (Rome: Food and Agriculture Organization, 2009), p. 9.
48. John Wiedenmann, 'Exploring the Effects of Reductions in Krill Biomass in the Southern Ocean on Blue Whales Using a State-Dependent Foraging Model', *Ecological Modelling*, vol. 222, no. 18 (2011), pp. 3366–79, at p. 3366.
49. S. Sandilyan and K. Kathiresan, 'Mangrove Conservation: A Global Perspective', *Biodiversity and Conservation*, vol. 21, no. 14 (2012), pp. 3523–42.

2. FREEDOM AT SEA

1. For a detailed history of the Indian Ocean, see David Abulafia, *The Boundless Sea: A Human History of the Oceans* (London: Penguin, 2019), part two.
2. Hassan Khalilieh, *Islamic Law of the Sea: Freedom of Navigation and Passage Rights in Islamic Thought* (Cambridge: Cambridge University Press, 2019), pp. 215–16.
3. Michael Orbach, 'Beyond the Freedom of the Sea: Ocean Policy for the Third Millennium', *Oceanography*, vol. 16, no. 1 (2003), pp. 20–29, at p. 21.
4. Philip Steinberg, *The Social Construction of the Ocean* (Cambridge: Cambridge University Press, 2001), pp. 64–7.
5. W. Frank Newton, 'Inexhaustibility as a Law of the Sea Determinant', *Texas International Law Journal*, vol. 16 (1981), pp. 369–432, at p. 380.
6. Bo Theutenberg, 'Mare Clausum et Mare Liberum', *Arctic*, vol. 37, no. 4 (1984), pp. 481–92, at p. 484.
7. See for instance Orbach, 'Beyond the Freedom of the Sea', p. 21.
8. Steinberg, *The Social Construction of the Ocean*, p. 78.
9. Khalilieh, *Islamic Law of the Sea*, chapter 1.
10. See for example Hersch Lauterpacht, 'The Grotian Tradition in International Law', *British Yearbook of International Law*, vol. 23 (1946), pp. 1–53, and Arthur Nussbaum, *A Concise History of the Law of Nations* (London: Macmillan, 1954).

11. Martti Koskenniemi, 'International Law and the Emergence of Mercantile Capitalism: Grotius to Smith', in Pierre-Marie Dupuy and Vincent Chetail (eds), *The Roots of International Law* (Leiden: Brill Nijhoff, 2014), pp. 1–37, at p. 1. See also Ileana Porras, 'Constructing International Law in the East Indian Seas: Property, Sovereignty, Commerce and War in Hugo Grotius' *De Jure Praedae*', *Brooklyn Journal of International Law*, vol. 31 (2006), pp. 741–804.

12. Hugo Grotius, 'The Free Sea', in *The Free Sea*, trans. Richard Hakluyt (Indianapolis: Liberty Fund, 2004 [1609]), p. 10.

13. Hugo Grotius, *Commentary on the Law of Prize and Booty*, trans. Gwladys Williams (Indianapolis: Liberty Fund, 2006 [1604]), p. 9.

14. Grotius, *The Free Sea*, p. 34.

15. Ibid., p. 47.

16. Ibid., p. 24.

17. Lauterpacht, 'The Grotian Tradition in International Law'.

18. Khalilieh, *Islamic Law of the Sea*, pp. 215–18.

19. Sarah Pemberton, *Locke's Political Thought and the Oceans* (Lanham, MD: Lexington Books, 2017), p. 4. See also Theutenberg, 'Mare Clausum et Mare Liberum'.

20. Quoted in Newton, 'Inexhaustibility as a Law of the Sea Determinant', p. 383.

21. John Selden, *Of the Dominion, or, Ownership of the Sea*, trans. Marchamont Nedham (London: Marchamont Nedham, 1652), p. 3.

22. Ibid., p. 169.

23. Ibid., p. 141, 143.

24. The Scottish jurist William Welwood had made the same point still earlier (William Welwood, 'Of the Community and Propriety of the Seas', in David Armitage (ed.), *Hugo Grotius: The Free Sea* (Indianapolis: Liberty Fund, 2004 [1613]), pp. 63–74), and the Portuguese friar Serafim de Freitas had also cast doubt on Grotius's claims about inexhaustibility. See Monica Brito-Vieira, '*Mare Liberum* vs. *Mare Clausum*: Grotius, Freitas, and Selden's Debate on Dominion over the Seas', *Journal of the History of Ideas*, vol. 64, no. 3 (2003), pp. 361–77.

25. Pemberton, *Locke's Political Thought and the Oceans*, p. 9.

26. See for example Theutenberg, 'Mare Clausum et Mare Liberum', pp. 490–91; Scott Shackelford, 'Was Selden Right? The Expansion of Closed Seas and Its Consequences', *Stanford Journal of International Law*, vol. 47, no. 1 (2011), pp. 1–50.

27. Christopher Rossi, 'A Particular Kind of Dominium: The Grotian Tendency and the Global Commons in a Time of High Arctic Change', *Journal of International Law and International Relations*, vol. 11, no. 1 (2015), pp. 1–60, at pp. 27–8.

28. Koskenniemi, 'International Law and the Emergence of Mercantile Capitalism', p. 19.

29. David Armitage, 'Introduction', in *The Free Sea*, trans. Richard Hakluyt (Indianapolis: Liberty Fund, 2004), pp. xi–xx, at p. xx.

30. See John Locke, *Second Treatise of Government* (Cambridge: Cambridge University Press, 1988 [1689]).

31. Steinberg, *The Social Construction of the Ocean*, p. 97; Newton, 'Inexhaustibility as a Law of the Sea Determinant', p. 387.

32. Selden, *Of the Dominion*, chapter 20.

33. Grotius, 'The Free Sea', p. 29.

34. Hugo Grotius, *The Rights of War and Peace* (Indianapolis: Liberty Fund, 2005 [1625]). Grotius also declared that countries could possess coastal waters in a 1637 letter to Monsieur de Reigersberg. See Virginie Blanchette-Seguin, 'Preserving Territorial Status Quo: Grotian Law of Nature, Baselines and Rising Sea Level', *New York University Journal of International Law & Politics*, vol. 50 (2017), pp. 227–63.

35. Samuel von Pufendorf, *De Jure Naturae et Gentium* (Washington DC: Carnegie Foundation, 1934 [1762]), pp. 560–61.

36. Ibid., p. 562.

37. Emmerich de Vattel, *Law of Nations* (Washington DC: Carnegie Foundation, 1916 [1758]), p. 106.

NOTES to pp. 40–51

38. Ibid., pp. 107–8.
39. Khalilieh, *Islamic Law of the Sea*, pp. 215–18.
40. Heinz Kent, 'The Historical Origins of the Three-Mile Limit', *American Journal of International Law*, vol. 48, no. 4 (1954), pp. 537–53.
41. Callum Roberts, *The Unnatural History of the Sea* (Washington DC: Island Press, 2007), pp. 122–34.
42. Ibid., pp. 32–40.
43. Lawrence Hamilton and Melissa Butler, 'Outport Adaptations: Social Indicators Through Newfoundland's Cod Crisis', *Human Ecology Review* (2001), pp. 1–11, at p. 2.
44. Trevor Branch and Terrie Williams, 'Legacy of Industrial Whaling', in James Estes et al. (eds), *Whales, Whaling and Ocean Ecosystems* (Berkeley: University of California Press, 2006), pp. 262–78, at p. 263.
45. Roberts, *The Unnatural History of the Sea*, p. 109.
46. Scott Barrett, *Environment and Statecraft: The Strategy of Environmental Treaty-Making* (Oxford: Oxford University Press, 2003), chapter 1.
47. Alex Oude Elferink, 'De Groot – A Founding Father of the Law of the Sea, Not the Law of the Sea Convention', *Grotiana*, vol. 30 (2009), pp. 152–67, at p. 165.
48. Grotius, *Commentary on the Law of Prize and Booty*, p. 332.
49. For a useful discussion of Pufendorf's views, see Cara Nine, 'Rights to the Oceans: Foundational Arguments Reconsidered', *Journal of Applied Philosophy*, vol. 36, no. 4 (2019), pp. 626–42.
50. Grotius, *Commentary on the Law of Prize and Booty*, p. 23.
51. For discussion see John Salter, 'Hugo Grotius: Property and Consent', *Political Theory*, vol. 29, no. 4 (2001), pp. 537–55, at p. 539.
52. Grotius, *Commentary on the Law of Prize and Booty*, p. 23.
53. Anna Stilz, *Territorial Sovereignty: A Philosophical Exploration* (Oxford: Oxford University Press, 2019), p. 62.
54. Rashid Sumaila et al., 'Winners and Losers in a World where the High Seas is Closed to Fishing', *Scientific Reports*, vol. 5, no. 8481 (2015), pp. 1–6, at p. 4.
55. Hugo Grotius, 'Defense of Chapter V of the Mare Liberum', in *The Free Sea*, pp. 75–129, at p. 116.

3. ENCLOSING THE OCEAN

1. Mark Zacher and James McConnell, 'Down to the Sea with Stakes: The Evolving Law of the Sea and the Future of the Deep Seabed Regime', *Ocean Development & International Law*, vol. 21, no. 1 (1990), pp. 71–103, at p. 79.
2. Bernard Oxman, 'The Territorial Temptation: A Siren Song at Sea', *American Journal of International Law*, no. 100 (2006), pp. 830–51, at p. 832.
3. John Noyes, 'The Territorial Sea and Contiguous Zone', in Donald Rothwell et al. (eds), *Oxford Handbook of the Law of the Sea* (Oxford: Oxford University Press, 2015), pp. 91–113. UNCLOS also allows for the declaration of 'contiguous zones', within which the coastal state can prevent or punish 'infringement of its customs, fiscal, immigration or sanitary laws and regulations' (UNCLOS Article 33(1)).
4. A coastal state does have the right to enforce its decisions on resource use, for instance by excluding foreign fishing vessels if it chooses. But otherwise, its domestic laws are not generally presumed to apply outside of its territorial seas. Gemma Andreone, 'The Exclusive Economic Zone', in Rothwell et al., *Oxford Handbook of the Law of the Sea*, pp. 159–80, at p. 177.
5. There is an important qualification to be discussed below: when states do not possess the capacity to harvest the total allowable catch of fish, they are meant, under UNCLOS, to give other states access to their EEZs.
6. Oxman, 'The Territorial Temptation', p. 833.
7. Liam Campling and Alejandro Colas, *Capitalism and the Sea* (London: Verso, 2021), p. 68.

8. Antonius Gagern and Jeroen van den Bergh, 'A Critical Review of Fishing Agreements with Tropical Developing Countries', *Marine Policy*, vol. 38 (2013), pp. 375–86, at p. 377.

9. Christopher Rossi, 'A Particular Kind of Dominium: The Grotian Tendency and the Global Commons in a Time of High Arctic Change', *Journal of International Law and International Relations*, vol. 11, no. 1 (2015), pp. 1–60, at p. 53. Note that between 200 and 350 nautical miles, UNCLOS envisages a benefit-sharing mechanism under which up to 7 per cent of the proceeds from exploitation would be shared with the International Seabed Authority. To date, exploitation has thus far occurred exclusively within the 200-mile zone. Ted McDorman, 'The Continental Shelf', in Rothwell et al., *Oxford Handbook of the Law of the Sea*, pp. 181–202, at p. 198.

10. A. John Simmons has suggested that prominent accounts of territory do not show states to have good claims to ownership over the resources of the seabed, although they might have claims to jurisdiction over people within immediate coastal zones (Simmons, *Boundaries of Authority*, Oxford: Oxford University Press, 2016, pp. 196–9). Margaret Moore has suggested that control over the resources of the seabed is not crucial to communities' self-determination – which, on her account, is key to territorial claims – and that the optimal solution would be for these resources, and fish stocks, to be managed internationally (Moore, *A Political Theory of Territory*, Oxford: Oxford University Press, 2015, pp. 167, 169–70). Cara Nine has suggested that territorial rights over (largely) uninhabited places such as Antarctica and the Arctic region cannot be justified (Cara Nine, 'Territory in a World of Limits: Exploring Claims to Oil and Ice', in Liam Leonard et al. (eds), *Environmental Philosophy* (Bingley: Emerald Group Publishing, 2013), pp. 137–55).

11. John Selden, *Of the Dominion, or, Ownership of the Sea*, trans. Marchamont Nedham (London: Marchamont Nedham, 1652).

12. Hugo Grotius, *The Rights of War and Peace* (Indianapolis: Liberty Fund, 2005 [1625]).

13. Sometimes occupation was defined in transparently self-serving ways. Europe's colonisation of much of the rest of the world often leant on the argument that its adventurers had found bits of territory that no one was occupying at the time: indigenous populations might from time to time be noticed, but would usually turn out not to be 'occupying' the land in quite the right way. The path was clear for these territories to be ruled by communities capable of occupying them properly.

14. Anna Stilz, *Territorial Sovereignty: A Philosophical Exploration* (Oxford: Oxford University Press, 2019).

15. Surabhi Ranganathan, 'Ocean Floor Grab: International Law and the Making of an Extractive Imaginary', *European Journal of International Law*, vol. 30, no. 2 (2019), pp. 573–600.

16. Quoted in McDorman, 'The Continental Shelf', p. 184.

17. Philip Jessup, 'The Palmas Island Arbitration', *American Journal of International Law*, vol. 22, no. 4 (1928), pp. 735–52.

18. C.H.M. Waldock, 'The Legal Basis of Claims to the Continental Shelf', *Transactions of the Grotius Society*, vol. 36 (1950), pp. 115–48, at p. 139.

19. Jessup, 'The Palmas Island Arbitration'.

20. Ranganathan, 'Ocean Floor Grab', p. 17.

21. Hugo Grotius, 'Defense of Chapter V of the Mare Liberum', in *The Free Sea*, trans. Richard Hakluyt (Indianapolis: Liberty Fund, 2004 [1615]), pp. 75–129, at p. 116.

22. Callum Roberts, *The Unnatural History of the Sea* (Washington DC: Island Press, 2007), p. 193.

23. John Locke, *Two Treatises of Government* (Cambridge: Cambridge University Press, 1988 [1688]), p. 289.

24. J.C. Phillips, 'The Exclusive Economic Zone as a Concept in International Law', *International and Comparative Law Quarterly*, vol. 26, no. 3 (1977), pp. 585–618, at p. 601.

25. For instance, fishers from landlocked countries came to be excluded from the vast majority of the world's most productive fishing grounds. Helmut Tuerk, 'Landlocked and Geographically Disadvantaged States', in Rothwell et al., *Oxford Handbook of The Law of the Sea*, pp. 325–45, at p. 326.

26. Moore, *A Political Theory of Territory*, pp. 168–9.
27. It is important not to assume that artisanal or small-scale fishing activities are sustainable by definition. For counter-examples, see Julie Hawkins and Callum Roberts, 'Effects of Artisanal Fishing on Caribbean Coral Reefs', *Conservation Biology*, vol. 18, no. 1 (2004), pp. 215–26.
28. 1945 Presidential Proclamation No. 2668. Policy of the United States with Respect to Coastal Fisheries in Certain Areas of the High Seas.
29. 1945 Presidential Proclamation No. 2667. Policy of the United States with Respect to the Natural Resources of the Subsoil and Sea Bed of the Continental Shelf.
30. Garrett Hardin, 'The Tragedy of the Commons', *Science*, 162.3859 (1968), pp. 1243–8, at p. 1244.
31. Susan Cox, 'No Tragedy of the Commons', *Environmental Ethics*, vol. 7, no. 1 (1985), pp. 49–61.
32. Elinor Ostrom, 'The Challenge of Common-Pool Resources', *Environment: Science and Policy for Sustainable Development*, vol. 50, no. 4 (2008), pp. 8–21.
33. Surabhi Ranganathan, 'Global Commons', *European Journal of International Law*, vol. 27, no. 3 (2016), pp. 693–717.
34. H. Scott Gordon, 'The Economic Theory of a Common-Property Resource – The Fishery', *Journal of Political Economy*, vol. 62, no. 2 (1954), pp. 124–42, at p. 135.
35. Ibid., p. 135.
36. Yimin Ye, 'Global Fisheries: Current Situation and Challenges', in Hance Smith et al. (eds), *Routledge Handbook of Ocean Resources and Management* (Abingdon: Routledge, 2017), pp. 215–31, at p. 223.
37. Food and Agriculture Organization, *World Review of Fisheries and Aquaculture* (Rome: Food and Agriculture Organization, 2010).
38. Daniel Pauly and Dirk Zeller, 'Catch Reconstructions Reveal that Global Marine Fisheries Catches are Higher than Reported and Declining', *Nature Communications*, vol. 7, no. 10244 (2016), pp 1–9, at p. 2.
39. European Parliament Directorate General for Internal Policies, *Global Fishing Subsidies* (Brussels: European Parliament, 2013).
40. Global Ocean Commission, *From Decline to Recovery: A Rescue Package for the Global Oceans* (Oxford: Global Ocean Commission, 2014), p. 41.
41. Gabrielle Carmine et al., 'Who is the High Seas Fishing Industry?', *One Earth*, vol. 3, no. 6 (2020), pp. 730–38.
42. David Agnew et al., 'Estimating the Worldwide Extent of Illegal Fishing', *PLoS One*, vol. 4, no. 2 (2009), pp. 1–8, at p. 3; Alkaly Doumbouya et al., 'Assessing the Effectiveness of Monitoring Control and Surveillance of Illegal Fishing: The Case of West Africa', *Frontiers in Marine Science*, vol. 4 (2017), pp. 1–50.
43. See for instance Henry Butler and Jonathan Macey, 'Externalities and the Matching Principle', *Yale Law and Policy Review*, vol. 14 (1996), pp. 23–66.
44. Andreone, 'The Exclusive Economic Zone', p. 167.
45. Salit Kark et al., 'Emerging Conservation Challenges and Prospects in an Era of Offshore Hydrocarbon Exploration and Exploitation', *Conservation Biology*, vol. 29, no. 6 (2015), pp. 1573–85, at p. 1574.
46. Jillian Ambrose, 'Denmark to End New Oil and Gas Exploration in North Sea', *Guardian* (4 December 2020).
47. John Hannigan, *The Geopolitics of Deep Oceans* (Cambridge: Polity, 2016), p. 65.
48. Lawrence Juda, 'World Marine Fish Catch in the Age of Exclusive Economic Zones and Exclusive Fishery Zones', *Ocean Development & International Law*, vol. 22, no. 1 (1991), pp. 1–32, at p. 7.
49. Gagern and van den Bergh, 'A Critical Review of Fishing Agreements', p. 379.
50. Ibid., p. 379.
51. Ramon Bonfil et al., *Distant Water Fleets: An Ecological, Economic and Social Assessment* (Vancouver: University of British Columbia Fisheries Centre, 1998), p. 24.

52. Gagern and van den Bergh, 'A Critical Review of Fishing Agreements', p. 378.
53. Nathan James Bennett, Hugh Govan and Terre Satterfield, 'Ocean Grabbing', *Marine Policy*, vol. 57 (2015), pp. 61–8.
54. Jacqueline Alder and Ussif Sumaila, 'Western Africa: A Fish Basket of Europe Past and Present', *Journal of Environment and Development*, vol. 13, no. 2 (2004), pp. 156–78, p. 169.
55. Alastair Couper et al., *Fishers and Plunderers* (London: Pluto Press, 2015), p. 54.
56. Gohar Petrossian and Ronald V. Clarke, 'Disaggregating Illegal Fishing Losses for the 22 Countries of the West African Coast', *Maritime Studies* (2020), online early, pp. 1–11.
57. Katherine Seto and Brooke Campbell, 'The Last Commons: (Re)constructing an Ocean Future', in William Cheung, Yoshitaka Ota and Andres Cisneros-Montemayor (eds), *Predicting Future Oceans* (Amsterdam: Elsevier, 2019), pp. 365–76, at p. 370.
58. Christopher Béné, Bjørn Hersoug and Edward Allison, 'Not By Rent Alone: Analysing the Pro-poor Functions of Small-scale Fisheries in Developing Countries', *Development Policy Review*, vol. 28, no. 3 (2010), pp. 325–58.
59. Tuerk, 'Landlocked and Geographically Disadvantaged States', pp. 325–45, at p. 333.
60. Charles Quince, *The Exclusive Economic Zone* (Wilmington, DE: Vernon Press, 2019).
61. Developed countries are the destination for 85 per cent of fish exports. Wilf Swartz et al., 'Sourcing Seafood for the Three Major Markets: The EU, Japan and the USA', *Marine Policy*, vol. 34 (2010), pp. 1366–73, at p. 1367.

4. REMAKING THE WORLD ORDER AT SEA

1. Adom Getachew, *Worldmaking After Empire: The Rise and Fall of Self-Determination* (Princeton: Princeton University Press, 2019), chapter 5.
2. Quoted in Tayo Akintoba, *African States and Contemporary International Law: A Case Study of the 1982 Law of the Sea Convention and the Exclusive Economic Zone* (The Hague: Martinus Nijhoff, 1996), p. 137.
3. Quoted in Peter Payoyo, *Cries of the Sea: World Inequality, Sustainable Development and the Common Heritage of Humanity* (The Hague: Martinus Nijhoff, 1997), p. 69.
4. Boleslaw Boczek, 'Ideology and the Law of the Sea: The Challenge of the New International Economic Order', *Boston College International and Comparative Law Review*, vol. 7, no. 1 (1984), pp. 1–30, at p. 13.
5. William Wertenbaker, 'A Reporter at Large: The Law of the Sea', *New Yorker* (1 August 1983), pp. 41–5, at p. 45.
6. Emmanuel Bello, 'International Equity and the Law of the Sea: New Perspectives for Developing Countries', *Verfassung und Recht in Ubersee*, vol. 13, no. 3 (1980), pp. 201–12, at p. 212.
7. Jan Jansen and Jürgen Osterhammel, *Decolonization: A Short History* (Princeton: Princeton University Press, 2017), p. 10.
8. Nils Gilman, 'The New International Economic Order: A Reintroduction', *Humanity* (Spring 2015), pp. 1–16, at p. 5.
9. James Hein and Kira Mizell, 'Ocean Minerals', in Hance Smith et al. (eds), *Routledge Handbook of Ocean Resources and Management* (Abingdon: Routledge, 2017), pp. 296–309, at p. 296.
10. W. Frank Newton, 'Inexhaustibility as a Law of the Sea Determinant', *Texas International Law Journal*, vol. 16 (1981), pp. 369–432, at pp. 371–2.
11. Dennis Arrow, 'Seabeds, Sovereignty and Objective Regimes', *Fordham International Law Journal*, vol. 7, no. 2 (1983), pp. 169–243, at p. 172.
12. John Mero, *The Mineral Resources of the Sea* (Amsterdam: Elsevier, 1965). In the end, Mero's prediction of an imminent seabed bonanza did not come to pass. There is evidence, in fact, that the economic opportunities were at times deliberately exaggerated. In the early 1970s, the CIA hatched a plan to raise from the seabed a Soviet nuclear submarine called the *Red Star*, which had sunk near Hawaii. To explain away its activities on the seabed, John Hannigan reports, 'The CIA planted dozens of enthusiastic articles about the prospects for

mining the vast mineral wealth on the ocean floor in scientific journals and major periodicals.' John Hannigan, *The Geopolitics of Deep Oceans* (Cambridge: Polity, 2016), p. 84.

13. Proclamation 2667 of 28 September 1945, entitled 'Policy of the United States with Respect to the Natural Resources of the Subsoil and Sea Bed of the Continental Shelf', and Proclamation 2668, entitled 'Policy of the United States with respect to Coastal Fisheries in Certain Areas of the High Seas'.

14. United Nations Convention on the Continental Shelf (29 April 1958), Article 1.

15. Ted McDorman, 'The Continental Shelf', in Donald Rothwell et al. (eds), *Oxford Handbook of the Law of the Sea* (Oxford: Oxford University Press, 2015), pp. 181–202, at p. 190.

16. Arrow, 'Seabeds, Sovereignty and Objective Regimes', p. 174.

17. 1967 Outer Space Treaty, Preamble. The 1979 Moon Agreement (though signed by relatively few countries) went further in declaring the moon to be part of our common heritage.

18. Surabhi Ranganathan, 'Global Commons,' *European Journal of International Law*, vol. 27, no. 3 (2016), pp. 693–717, at p. 708.

19. Arvid Pardo, Speech to the United Nations General Assembly, November 1967. UN Doc A/C.1/PV.1516.

20. Annica Carlsson, 'The US and UNCLOS III – The Death of the Common Heritage of Humankind Concept?', *Maritime Studies* (July–August 1997), pp. 27–35, at p. 28.

21. Antonio Cassese, *International Law in a Divided World* (Oxford: Clarendon Press, 1986), p. 377. As Alex Oude Elferink has put it, the idea that ocean resources 'could be brought under a coordinated management regime of the interested States or the international community as a whole is foreign to De Groot's thinking'. Oude Elferink, 'De Groot – A Founding Father of the Law of the Sea, Not the Law of the Sea Convention', *Grotiana*, vol. 30 (2009), pp. 152–67, at p. 166.

22. Euripides Evriviades, 'The Third World's Approach to the Deep Seabed', *Ocean Development and International Law Journal*, vol. 11, no. 3/4 (1982), pp. 201–64, at p. 211.

23. Arvid Pardo, Speech to the United Nations General Assembly, November 1967.

24. Elisabeth Mann Borgese, 'The New International Economic Order and the Law of the Sea', *San Diego Law Review*, vol. 14 (1977), pp. 584–96, at p. 590.

25. Payoyo, *Cries of the Sea*, p. 163.

26. Mann Borgese, 'The New International Economic Order and the Law of the Sea', p. 584.

27. Elisabeth Mann Borgese, *Ocean Governance and the United Nations* (Centre for Foreign Policy Studies, Dalhousie University, 1995), p. 236.

28. Mann Borgese, 'The New International Economic Order and the Law of the Sea', p. 586.

29. Robert Friedheim and William Durch, 'The International Seabed Resources Agency Negotiations and the New International Economic Order', *International Organization*, vol. 31, no. 2 (1977), pp. 343–84, at p. 344.

30. Mann Borgese, 'The New International Economic Order and the Law of the Sea', p. 590.

31. Friedheim and Durch, 'The International Seabed Resources Agency Negotiations', p. 352.

32. Tommy Koh, 'A Constitution for the Oceans' (1982), p. xxxiv. Available at http://www.un.org/depts/los/convention_agreements/texts/koh_english.pdf.

33. Ibid., p. xxxiv.

34. Payoyo, *Cries of the Sea*, p. 307.

35. Lawrence Juda, 'UNCLOS III and the New International Economic Order', *Ocean Development and International Law*, vol. 7, nos. 3–4 (1979), pp. 221–55, at p. 241.

36. See e.g. Arrow, 'Seabeds, Sovereignty and Objective Regimes', p. 174; Friedheim and Durch, 'The International Seabed Resources Agency Negotiations', p. 352.

37. Mero, *Mineral Resources of the Sea*, p. 5.

38. Friedheim and Durch, 'The International Seabed Resources Agency Negotiations', p. 361.

39. Quoted in Payoyo, *Cries of the Sea*, p. 312.

40. Carlsson, 'The US and UNCLOS III', p. 29.

41. Friedheim and Durch, 'The International Seabed Resources Agency Negotiations', p. 356.

42. Carlsson, 'The US and UNCLOS III', p. 29.

43. Mann Borgese, 'The New International Economic Order and the Law of the Sea', p. 589.

44. Arrow, 'Seabeds, Sovereignty and Objective Regimes', p. 183.
45. Ibid., p. 178.
46. Scott Shackelford, 'Was Selden Right? The Expansion of Closed Seas and Its Consequences', *Stanford Journal of International Law*, vol. 47, no. 1 (2011), pp. 1–50, at p. 26.
47. Carlsson, 'The US and UNCLOS III', p. 28.
48. Payoyo, *Cries of the Sea*, p. 395.
49. Ibid., p. 466.
50. Quoted in Helmut Tuerk, *Reflections on the Contemporary Law of the Sea* (The Hague: Martinus Nijhoff, 2012), p. 41.
51. Payoyo, *Cries of the Sea*, p. 420.
52. Ranganathan, 'Global Commons', p. 712.
53. Linwood Pendleton, 'Greening the Ocean Economy', in Smith et al. (eds), *Routledge Handbook of Ocean Resources*, pp. 199–211, at p. 204.
54. David Freestone, 'Marine Biodiversity in Areas beyond National Jurisdiction', in International Ocean Institute (ed.), *The Future of Ocean Governance and Training: Essays in Honour of Elisabeth Mann Borgese* (Leiden: Brill Nijhoff, 2018), pp. 151–5, at p. 154.
55. As Dire Tladi argues, 'The common management idea is perhaps the most central element of the common heritage of mankind principle.' Tladi, 'The Common Heritage of Mankind and the Proposed Treaty on Biodiversity in Areas beyond National Jurisdiction: The Choice Between Pragmatism and Sustainability', *Yearbook of International Environmental Law*, vol. 25, no. 1 (2015), pp. 113–32, at p. 126.
56. Alexandre Kiss, 'The Common Heritage of Mankind: Utopia or Reality?', *International Journal*, vol. 40, no. 3 (1985), pp. 423–41, at p. 435.
57. See the helpful discussion in Prue Taylor, 'The Concept of the Common Heritage of Mankind', in Douglas Fisher (ed.), *Research Handbook on Fundamental Concepts of Environmental Law* (Cheltenham: Edward Elgar Publishing, 2016), pp. 306–35.
58. Prue Taylor, 'The Common Heritage of Mankind: Expanding the Oceanic Circle', in Dick Werle (ed.), *The Future of Ocean Governance and Capacity Development: Essays In Honor of Elisabeth Mann Borgese* (Leiden: Brill Nijhoff, 2018), pp. 142–50, at p. 149.
59. Joe Guinan and Martin O'Neill, *The Case for Community Wealth Building* (Cambridge: Polity, 2020).
60. Kiss, 'The Common Heritage of Mankind', p. 433.
61. See for instance Arianna Broggiato, 'Fair and Equitable Sharing of Benefits from the Utilization of Marine Genetic Resources', *Marine Policy*, vol. 49 (2014), pp. 178–85, at p. 179; Taylor, 'The Common Heritage of Mankind: Expanding the Oceanic Circle'.

5. SEVEN PRINCIPLES OF OCEAN JUSTICE

1. Chris Armstrong, 'Ocean Justice: SDG 14 and Beyond', *Journal of Global Ethics*, vol. 16, no. 2 (2020), pp. 239–55.
2. Kirsty Nash et al., 'To Achieve A Sustainable Blue Future, Progress Assessments Must Include Interdependencies Between the Sustainable Development Goals', *One Earth*, vol. 2, no. 2 (2020), pp. 161–73.
3. Kristina Gjerde et al., 'Ocean in Peril: Reforming the Management of Global Ocean Living Resources in Areas Beyond National Jurisdiction', *Marine Pollution Bulletin*, vol. 74, no. 2 (2013), pp. 540–51, at p. 545.
4. Jennifer Telesca, *Red Gold: The Managed Extinction of The Giant Bluefin Tuna* (Minneapolis: Minnesota University Press, 2020).
5. Cassandra Brooks et al., 'Challenging the Right to Fish in a Fast-Changing Ocean', *Stanford Environmental Law Journal*, vol. 33 (2013), pp. 289–324, at p. 298.
6. Callum Roberts, *The Unnatural History of the Sea* (Washington DC: Island Press, 2007), p. 365.
7. Karen McVeigh, 'Revealed: 97% of UK Marine Protected Areas Subject to Bottom-Trawling', *Guardian*, www.theguardian.com (9 October 2020).

8. Dire Tladi, 'The Common Heritage of Mankind and the Proposed Treaty on Biodiversity in Areas Beyond National Jurisdiction: The Choice Between Pragmatism and Sustainability', *Yearbook of International Environmental Law*, vol. 25, no. 1 (2015), pp. 113–32, at p. 116.

9. See Deborah Rowan Wright, *Future Sea* (Chicago: Chicago University Press, 2020), pp. 119–20.

10. Anne-Marie Brady, 'A Pyrrhic Victory in Antarctica?', www.thediplomat.com (4 November 2016).

11. Chelsea Harvey, 'Once Again, New Antarctic Reserves Fail to Win Backing', www.sciencemag.org (2 November 2020).

12. See https://ocean.economist.com/governance/articles/the-need-to-protect-at-least-30-of-the-ocean-by-2030 (accessed 22 February 2021).

13. See https://sdgs.un.org/goals/goal14 (accessed 18 January 2020).

14. Bethan O'Leary et al., 'Effective Coverage Targets for Ocean Protection', *Conservation Letters*, vol. 9, no. 6 (2016), pp. 398–404. Enrich Sala and Kristin Rechberger, 'Protecting Half the Ocean?', in Raj Desai et al. (eds), *From Summits to Solutions: Innovations in Implementing the Sustainable Development Goals* (Washington DC: Brookings Institution Press, 2018), pp. 239–64.

15. Reniel Cabral et al., 'A Global Network of Marine Protected Areas for Food', *Proceedings of the National Academy of Sciences*, vol. 117, no. 45 (2020), pp. 28134–9.

16. David Freestone, 'Marine Biodiversity in Areas Beyond National Jurisdiction', in International Ocean Institute (ed.), *The Future of Ocean Governance and Training: Essays in Honour of Elisabeth Mann Borgese* (Leiden: Brill Nijhoff, 2018), pp. 151–5, at p. 151.

17. Michael Orbach, 'Beyond the Freedom of the Sea: Ocean Policy for the Third Millennium', *Oceanography*, vol. 16, no. 1 (2003), pp. 20–29, at p. 27.

18. Kristina Gjerde, 'Challenges to Protecting the Marine Environment beyond National Jurisdiction', *International Journal of Marine and Coastal Law*, vol. 27 (2012), pp. 839–47, at p. 844.

19. Quoted in ibid., p. 840.

20. Rashid Sumaila et al., 'Fisheries Subsidies and Potential Catch Loss in SIDS Exclusive Economic Zones: Food Security Implications', *Environment and Development Economics*, vol. 18, no. 4 (2013), pp. 427–39.

21. Robert Blasiak et al., 'Corporate Control and Global Governance of Marine Genetic Resources', *Science Advances*, vol. 4, no. 6 (2018), eaar5237, p. 2.

22. Robert Goodin, 'Enfranchising All Affected Interests, and its Alternatives', *Philosophy & Public Affairs*, vol. 35, no. 1 (2007), pp. 40–68.

23. Ana Spalding and Ricardo de Ycaza, 'Navigating Shifting Regimes of Ocean Governance', *Environment and Society*, vol. 11 (2019), pp. 5–26, at p. 7.

24. On the idea of representing animals, see Alfonso Donoso, 'Representing Non-Human Interests', *Environmental Values*, vol. 26, no. 5 (2017), pp. 607–28.

25. Saying this requires us to take what philosophers call a 'wide person affecting view'. For an explanation and defence of that view, see Nils Holtug, *Persons, Interests, and Justice* (Oxford: Oxford University Press, 2010), pp. 106–62.

26. Nadia Urbinati and Mark Warren, 'The Concept of Representation in Contemporary Democratic Theory', *Annual Review of Political Science*, vol. 11, no. 1 (2008), pp. 387–412.

27. Anja Karnein, 'Can We Represent Future Generations?', in Inigo Gonzalez-Ricoy and Axel Gosseries (eds), *Institutions for Future Generations* (Oxford: Oxford University Press, 2016), pp. 83–97, at p. 86.

28. See https://www.humanrightsatsea.org/who-are-we (accessed 22 February 2021).

29. Scholars of environmental studies might be tempted to add a further principle here, called the 'ecosystem principle'. Such a principle would suggest that environments such as the ocean are complex, interdependent ecosystems, and should be governed as such. I do not treat that as a separate principle here, but it is compatible with what I say in this chapter.

30. Simon Dietz and Eric Neumayer, 'Weak and Strong Sustainability in the SEEA: Concepts and Measurement', *Ecological Economics*, vol. 61 (2006), pp. 617–26, at p. 619.

31. For a recent argument in favour of the objective list approach to well-being, see Christopher Rice, 'Defending the Objective List Theory of Well-Being', *Ratio*, vol. 26, no. 2 (2013), pp. 196–211.
32. I am setting out some complex philosophical issues quite quickly here, and readers might want some pointers to the broader literature on well-being and flourishing. For a defence of an 'objective' account of well-being, which defines flourishing in terms of whether a person can or cannot perform or enjoy certain states (such as health, good personal relationships and so on), see Guy Fletcher, *The Philosophy of Well-Being* (Abingdon: Routledge, 2016). On my view, well-being is not wholly objective, but can also depend on 'subjective' processes such as endorsement or identification. That suggests our account of well-being should really be a 'hybrid' one. For a defence of such an account, see Steven Wall and David Sobel, 'A Robust Hybrid Theory of Well-being', *Philosophical Studies*, vol. 178, no. 9 (2020), pp. 2829–51. Finally, it is worth noting that accounts of well-being which are at least partly objective appear to be close cousins of the 'capability approach' to equality. For a very influential defence of that approach, see Amartya Sen, *Choice, Welfare and Measurement* (Oxford: Blackwell, 1982), pp. 353–69.
33. Branko Milanovic, *Global Inequality* (Cambridge, MA: Harvard University Press, 2016).
34. I have made an argument along these lines, though at much greater length, in Chris Armstrong, *Justice and Natural Resources: An Egalitarian Theory* (Oxford: Oxford University Press, 2017), chapter 2.
35. Elisabeth Mann Borgese, 'The New International Economic Order and the Law of the Sea', *San Diego Law Review*, vol. 14 (1977), pp. 584–96, at p. 587.
36. Easkey Britton et al., 'Blue Care: A Systematic Review of Blue Space Interventions for Health and Wellbeing', *Health Promotion International*, vol. 35, no. 1 (2020), pp. 50–69.
37. Ruby Grantham, Jacqueline Lau and Danika Kleiber, 'Gleaning: Beyond the Subsistence Narrative', *Maritime Studies*, vol. 19, no. 4 (2020), pp. 509–24.
38. Ronan Foley et al. (eds), *Blue Space, Health and Wellbeing: Hydrophilia Unbounded* (London: Routledge, 2019).
39. For a fuller account of the various costs created by conservation projects, and how they should be shared, see Armstrong, *Justice and Natural Resources*, chapter 10.
40. Chris Armstrong, 'Sharing Conservation Burdens Fairly', *Conservation Biology*, vol. 33, no. 3 (2019), pp. 554–60.
41. I discuss the argument about benefits in more detail, using rainforest protection as an example, in Chris Armstrong, 'Fairness, Free-riding and Rainforest Protection', *Political Theory*, vol. 44, no. 1 (2016), pp. 106–30.
42. Yimin Ye, 'Rebuilding Global Fisheries: The World Summit Goals, Costs and Benefits', *Fish and Fisheries*, vol. 14, no. 2 (2013), pp. 174–85, at p. 179.
43. Roberts, *The Unnatural History of the Sea*.
44. Ibid., p. 365.
45. United Nations Framework Convention on Climate Change, *Paris Agreement*, Preamble.
46. Ibid., Article 6, Article 4.

6. PROTECTING WORKERS AT SEA

1. This is part of a larger pattern: fewer than 1 per cent of crimes at sea are believed to result in criminal convictions. Ian Urbina, 'Murder at Sea: Video Captures 4 Murders, But the Killers Go Unpunished', *New York Times*, 20 July 2015.
2. Kate Hodal and Chris Kelly, 'Trafficked into Slavery on Thai Trawlers to Catch Food for Prawns', *Guardian*, 10 June 2014.
3. Irini Papanicolopulu, *International Law and the Protection of People at Sea* (Oxford: Oxford University Press, 2018), pp. 29–30; Alastair Couper et al., *Fishers and Plunderers* (London: Pluto Press, 2015), pp. 121–37.
4. Naomi Bang, 'Casting a Wide Net to Catch the Big Fish: A Comprehensive Initiative to Reduce Human Trafficking in the Global Seafood Chain', *University of Pennsylvania Journal of Law & Social Change*, vol. 17 (2014), pp. 221–55, at p. 223.

5. I will use the term 'fishers' to describe these workers, rather than the more familiar 'fishermen' because, although most of those who catch fish out at sea are men, women and children are also present in the industry.

6. See https://www.marineinsight.com/maritime-law/a-guide-to-applying-for-us-visa-for-seafarers (accessed 14 May 2020).

7. The International Labour Organization's *Maritime Labour Convention* of 2006 is an example.

8. Papanicolopulu, *International Law and the Protection of People at Sea*, p. 39.

9. See https://www.ilo.org/dyn/normlex/en/f?p=1000:11300:0::NO:11300:P11300_INSTRUMENT_ID:312333 (accessed 14 May 2020).

10. Enrique Cajigas, 'Panama', in Deirdre Fitzpatrick and Michael Anderson (eds), *Seafarers' Rights* (Oxford: Oxford University Press, 2005), pp. 381–406, at pp. 388, 391.

11. Jonathan Hyslop, '"Ghostlike" Seafarers and Sailing Ship Nostalgia: The Figure of the Steamship Lascar in the British Imagination, *c.* 1880–1960', *Journal for Maritime Research*, vol. 16, no. 2 (2014), pp. 212–28, at p. 216.

12. Joseph Conrad, 'Well Done', in Joseph Conrad, *Notes on Life and Letters*, ed. J.H. Snape with Andrew Burza (Cambridge: Cambridge University Press, 2004), pp. 142–52, at pp. 143–4.

13. David Chappell, 'Ahab's Boat: Non-European Seamen in Western Ships of Exploration and Commerce', in Bernhard Klein and Gesa Mackenthun (eds), *Sea Changes: Historicizing the Ocean* (New York: Routledge, 2004), pp. 75–89, at pp. 75–6.

14. Hyslop, '"Ghostlike" Seafarers and Sailing Ship Nostalgia', p. 213.

15. Couper et al., *Fishers and Plunderers*, p. 33.

16. Liam Campling and Alejandra Colas, *Capitalism and the Sea* (London: Verso, 2021), p. 147.

17. Alastair Couper, 'Historical Perspectives on Seafarers and the Law', in Fitzpatrick and Anderson, *Seafarers' Rights*, pp. 3–35, at p. 26.

18. Supang Chantavanich et al., 'Under the Shadow: Forced Labour Among Sea Fishers in Thailand', *Marine Policy*, vol. 68 (2016), pp. 1–7.

19. See https://www.ilo.org/global/standards/information-resources-and-publications/lang--en/index.htm (accessed 11 January 2018).

20. Melissa Marschke and Peter Vandergeest, 'Slavery Scandals: Unpacking Labour Challenges and Policy Responses within the Off-shore Fisheries Sector', *Marine Policy*, vol. 68 (2016), pp. 39–46, at p. 40.

21. International Labour Organization, *Employment Practices and Working Conditions in Thailand's Fishing Sector* (Bangkok: ILO, 2013), p. 46.

22. Jason Szep and Stuart Grudgings, 'Special Report: Thai Authorities Implicated in Rohingya Muslim Smuggling Network', *Reuters* (17 July 2013).

23. Annuska Derks, 'Migrant Labour and the Politics of Immobilisation: Cambodian Fishermen in Thailand', *Asian Journal of Social Science*, vol. 38 (2010), pp. 915–32, at p. 922.

24. See https://www.hrw.org/report/2018/01/23/hidden-chains/rights-abuses-and-forced-labor-thailands-fishing-industry (accessed 17 November 2020).

25. Marschke and Vandergeest, 'Slavery Scandals', p. 40.

26. Philip Robertson, *Trafficking of Fishermen in Thailand* (Bangkok: International Organization for Migration Thailand, 2011).

27. See https://www.hrw.org/report/2018/01/23/hidden-chains/rights-abuses-and-forced-labor-thailands-fishing-industry (accessed 17 November 2020).

28. Erol Kahveci, 'Neither At Sea Nor Ashore: The Abandoned Crew of the Obo Basak', *Annuaire de Droit Maritime* (2006), pp. 281–322.

29. Benjamin Skinner, 'The Fishing Industry's Cruellest Catch', *Bloomberg Business Week* (23 February 2012).

30. Penny Howard, 'Sharing or Appropriation? Share Systems, Class and Commodity Relations in Scottish Fisheries', *Journal of Agrarian Change*, vol. 12, nos. 2–3 (2012), pp. 316–43, at p. 337.

31. Couper et al., *Fishers and Plunderers*, p. 37.

32. Severin Carrell, 'Slavery Risk Warning over UK's Scallop Fisheries', *Guardian* (1 February 2018).

33. For a good analysis of exploitation, see Nicholas Vrousalis, 'Exploitation, Vulnerability, and Social Domination', *Philosophy & Public Affairs*, vol. 41, no. 2 (2013), pp. 131–57.
34. Robert Goodin, 'Structures of Complicity', unpublished manuscript (2019).
35. Henrik Österblom et al., 'Transnational Corporations as "Keystone Actors" in Marine Ecosystems', *PLoS ONE*, vol. 10, no. 5 (2015), e0127533.
36. Alastair Couper, 'Implications of Maritime Globalisation for the Crews of Merchant Ships', *Journal for Maritime Research* (February 2000), pp. 1–8, at p. 3.
37. Douglas Guilfoyle, *Shipping Interdiction and the Law of the Sea* (Cambridge: Cambridge University Press, 2009).
38. Couper et al., *Fishers and Plunderers*, p. 167.
39. For a valuable account of the nature of structural injustice, see Iris Marion Young, *Responsibility for Justice* (Oxford: Oxford University Press, 2011), chapter 2.
40. Thomas Mensah et al., 'Proposals for Legal Reform', in Fitzpatrick and Anderson, *Seafarers' Rights*, pp. 539–59, at p. 548.
41. See https://www.msc.org/en-us/standards-and-certification/fisheries-standard (accessed 3 March 2021).
42. Katrina Nakamura et al., 'Seeing Slavery in Seafood Supply Chains', *Science Advance*, e1701833 (2018), pp. 1–10, at pp. 3, 7.
43. Bang, 'Casting a Wide Net to Catch the Big Fish', pp. 238–43.
44. See http://www.fao.org/port-state-measures/en (accessed 4 March 2021).
45. Robin Churchill, 'Seafarers' Rights at the National Level', in Fitzpatrick and Anderson, *Seafarers' Rights*, pp. 131–67, at p. 134–5.
46. 1926 Slavery Convention, Article 5. As Adom Getachew has pointed out, there is a dubious history to this distinction between slavery and forced labour. Colonial powers in the 1920s were prepared to outlaw 'slavery proper' (presumably practised by others), but were not willing to subject practices of forced labour within their own colonies to international scrutiny. Getachew, *Worldmaking After Empire: The Rise and Fall of Self-Determination* (Princeton: Princeton University Press, 2019), p. 59.
47. Guilfoyle, *Shipping Interdiction and the Law of the Sea*, p. 76.
48. Zoe Tidman and Conrad Duncan, 'Four Drowned Migrants in English Channel Were Part of Same Iranian Family, *Independent*, www.independent.co.uk (28 October 2020).
49. See https://reliefweb.int/sites/reliefweb.int/files/resources/IOM_Mediterranean_3Jan2020.pdf (accessed 23 January 2021).
50. Lizzie Dearden, 'Channel Crossings: Priti Patel was Warned Government Policies were Pushing Migrants into Dangerous Voyages Nine Months Ago', *Independent*, www.independent.co.uk (11 August 2020).
51. Marina Petrillo, Lorenzo Bagnoli and Claudi Torrisi, 'The Prosecutor's Case Against the Rescue Ship *Open Arms*', https://openmigration.org/en (29 March 2018).
52. Cetta Mainwaring and Daniela DeBono, 'Criminalising Solidarity: Search and Rescue in a Neo-Colonial Sea', *Politics and Space* (2021), online early.
53. United Nations Convention on the Law of the Sea, Article 98.

7. THE RIGHTS OF MARINE ANIMALS

1. James Watson et al., 'Catastrophic Declines in Wilderness Areas Undermine Global Environment Targets', *Current Biology*, vol. 26, no. 21 (2016), pp. 2929–34.
2. WWF, *Living Planet Report 2018* (Gland, Switzerland: WWF International, 2018).
3. See https://ourworldindata.org/meat-production#number-of-animals-slaughtered (accessed 24 February 2021).
4. Dinesh Wadiwel, 'Do Fish Resist?', *Cultural Studies Review*, vol. 22, no. 1 (2016), pp. 196–242, at pp. 196–7.
5. Ibid., p. 198.

6. Paola Cavalieri, 'The Meaning of the Great Ape Project', *Politics and Animals*, vol. 1 (2015), pp. 16–34.

7. For a discussion, see Steve Sapontzis, 'Are Animals Moral Beings?', *American Philosophical Quarterly*, vol. 17, no. 1 (1980), pp. 45–52.

8. In what follows, I will often talk of 'animals' rather than using the more cumbersome phrases 'other animals' or 'non-human animals'. But this is of course a shorthand: humans are animals too and we should not pretend otherwise.

9. It might be thought that animals cannot have duties, if they cannot understand and act on moral principles. But whether this is true or not, animals could still possess rights. See for example Joel Feinberg, 'The Rights of Animals and Future Generations', in William Blackstone (ed.), *Philosophy and Environmental Crisis* (Athens, GA: University of Georgia Press, 1974), pp. 43–68.

10. Jeremy Bentham, *An Introduction to the Principles of Morals and Legislation* (London: Macmillan, 1789). If animals are subjects of their own lives, then 'he' or 'she' are more appropriate terms than 'it', even if the word 'it' is often used to describe individual animals.

11. Peter Singer, *Practical Ethics*, 2nd edn (Cambridge: Cambridge University Press, 1993).

12. To keep things relatively simple, I will concentrate on the capacities of sentience and subjecthood in what remains of this chapter. But in principle, rights could be grounded on a much wider cluster of capacities, including sentience, subjecthood, autonomy, rationality and others besides. For an illustration of how we can move from a cluster of capacities to defending specific rights, see Kirstin Andrews et al., *Chimpanzee Rights: The Philosophers' Brief* (Abingdon: Routledge, 2018), chapter 6.

13. For more on the idea of basic rights, see Henry Shue, *Basic Rights: Famine, Affluence, and US Foreign Policy* (Princeton: Princeton University Press, 1980).

14. See www.cetaceanrights.org (accessed 29 November 2019).

15. Bianca Romeu, 'Bottlenose Dolphins that Forage with Artisanal Fishermen Whistle Differently', *Ethology*, vol. 123, no. 2 (2017), pp. 906–15.

16. Lori Marino, 'Brain Structure and Intelligence in Cetaceans', in Philippa Brakes and Mark Simmonds (eds), *Whales and Dolphins: Cognition, Culture, Conservation and Human Perceptions* (London: Routledge, 2013), pp. 115–27.

17. David Levin, 'Towards Effective Cetacean Protection', *Natural Resources Lawyer*, vol. 12, no. 4 (1979), pp. 549–97, at p. 557.

18. Diana Reiss and Lori Marino, 'Mirror Self-Recognition in the Bottlenose Dolphin: A Case of Cognitive Convergence', *Proceedings of the National Academy of Science*, vol. 98, no. 10 (2001), pp. 5937–42.

19. Louis Herman et al., 'Representational and Conceptual Skills of Dolphins', in Herbert Roitblat, Louis Herman and Paul Nachtigall (eds), *Language and Communication: Comparative Perspectives* (Hillsdale, NJ: Erlbaum Associates, 1993), pp. 403–42.

20. Levin, 'Towards Effective Cetacean Protection', p. 556.

21. Luke Rendell and Hal Whitehead, 'Culture in Whales and Dolphins', *Behavioral and Brain Sciences*, vol. 24 (2001), pp. 309–82, at p. 315.

22. Ibid., p. 312.

23. Paola Cavalieri, 'Whales as Persons', in Susan Armstrong and Richard Bozler (eds), *The Animal Ethics Reader*, 2nd edn (London: Routledge, 2008), pp. 204–10, at p. 207.

24. Ibid., p. 207.

25. Jan Narveson, 'Animal Rights', *Canadian Journal of Philosophy*, vol. 7, no. 1 (1977), pp. 161–78, at p. 166.

26. William Burns, 'The Berlin Initiative on Strengthening the Conservation Agenda of the International Whaling Commission: Towards a New Era for Cetaceans?', *Journal of International Wildlife Law and Policy*, vol. 6, no. 3 (2003), pp. 255–76, at p. 73.

27. Callum Roberts, *The Ocean of Life: The Fate of Man and the Sea* (London: Penguin, 2012), p. 324.

28. Ibid., p. 324.

29. David Laist et al., 'Collisions Between Ships and Whales', *Marine Mammal Science*, vol. 17, no. 1 (2001), pp. 35–75.

30. Roberts, *The Ocean of Life*, p. 253.

31. For a philosophical discussion of torture and its wrongfulness, see David Sussman, 'What's Wrong with Torture?', *Philosophy & Public Affairs*, vol. 33, no. 1 (2005), pp. 1–33.

32. Kieran Oberman, 'Immigration, Global Poverty and the Right to Stay', *Political Studies*, vol. 59, no. 2 (2011), pp. 253–68.

33. For an investigation of the poor physical and mental health outcomes of orcas in captivity, see Lori Marino et al., 'The Harmful Effects of Captivity and Chronic Stress on the Well-Being of Orcas (Orcinus Orca)', *Journal of Veterinary Behavior*, vol. 35 (2020), pp. 69–82.

34. The philosopher will add: so long as those norms are compatible with justice. There can be no right to transmit traditions that by definition harm others.

35. Roberts, *The Ocean of Life*, p. 172.

36. Ibid., p. 179.

37. Alasdair Cochrane, *Should Animals Have Political Rights?* (Cambridge: Polity, 2020).

38. On the link between psychology unity and the interest in continued existence, see Jeff McMahan, 'The Comparative Badness for Animals of Suffering and Death', in Tatjana Visak and Robert Garner (eds), *The Ethics of Killing Animals* (Oxford: Oxford University Press, 2016), pp. 65–85, at p. 78.

39. See https://iwc.int/statement-on-government-of-japan-withdrawal-from-t (accessed 2 April 2021).

40. Rachel Wichert and Martha Nussbaum, 'The Legal Status of Whales: Capabilities, Entitlements and Culture', *Sequencia*, vol. 72 (2016), pp. 19–40, at p. 26. See also Paula Casal, 'Is Multiculturalism Bad for Animals?', *Journal of Political Philosophy*, vol. 11, no. 1 (2003), pp. 1–22, at p. 5. As Casal has pointed out to me, the countries which practise the most extensive killing of whales – including Iceland, Norway, Denmark, Canada and Japan – are among the richest in the world.

41. Defenders of indigenous whaling sometimes suggest that even if *individuals'* continued existence is not at stake in the debate about whaling, the continued existence of their *communities* is. People may not be able to recognise themselves as members of the same tribe or community if they can no longer kill whales and use or consume their bodies. Those communities have already suffered hugely from their absorption into majority, 'modern' societies, an often-forced absorption that might even qualify as a kind of cultural genocide. Should they be subject to still more pressure, even while majority communities themselves kill and eat animals on a massive scale? This is an important challenge. It would certainly be hypocritical to criticise the killing of cetaceans but leave modern factory farming unmentioned. Though this book focuses on the ocean, I would certainly criticise both, and in terms of its scale factory farming is undoubtedly one of the biggest threats to animal welfare and the health of our planet more generally. It is also possible that the condemnation of cultural whaling has been used cynically as a stick for Western communities to beat 'traditional' communities with, while presenting themselves, rather improbably, as saviours. This reminds us that the way we frame the case for animal rights is very important. We should be even handed in our attention, and we should listen seriously to people's own descriptions of the importance of cultural practices in their own lives. But it does not shake my view that the preservation of culture is not as fundamental as the right to life. Taking cetaceans' right to life seriously means we should reject cultural defences of whaling, just as we should reject cultural defences of human sacrifice.

42. Angus Atkinson et al., 'Long-term Decline in Krill Stock and Increase in Salps within the Southern Ocean', *Nature*, vol. 432, no. 7013 (2004), pp. 100–103.

43. *Scientific Synthesis of the Impacts of Ocean Fertilization on Marine Biodiversity* (Montreal: Secretariat of the Convention on Biological Diversity, 2009), pp. 23–9.

44. Ralph Chami et al., *Nature's Solution to Climate Change*, International Monetary Fund Finance and Development, December 2019, p. 35.

45. Joe Roman et al., 'Whales as Marine Ecosystem Engineers', *Frontiers in Ecology and the Environment*, vol. 12, no. 7 (2014), pp. 377–85, at pp. 379–81.

46. Chami et al., *Nature's Solution*, p. 36.

47. Andrew Pershing et al., 'The Impact of Whaling on the Ocean Carbon Cycle: Why Bigger was Better', *PLoS One*, vol. 5, no. 8 (2010), e12444.

48. Christine Korsgaard, *Fellow Creatures: Our Obligations to the Other Animals* (Oxford: Oxford University Press, 2018), pp. 220–26.
49. Lili Pike, 'The Surprise Catch of Seafood Trawling: Massive Greenhouse Gas Emissions', www.vox.com (18 March 2020).
50. See for instance Laura Mannocci et al., 'Assessing the Impact of Bycatch on Dolphin Populations: The Case of the Common Dolphin in the Eastern North Atlantic', *PLoS One*, vol. 7, no. 2 (2012), e32615.
51. Troy Vettese, Becca Franks and Jennifer Jacquet, 'The Great Fish Pain Debate', *Issues in Science and Technology*, vol. 36, no. 4 (2020), pp. 49–53.
52. This picture of aquaculture is in many ways highly simplified. One reason is that people prefer to eat farmed or 'ranched' fish, such as tuna, salmon, trout and shrimp/prawns, which are themselves predators. Enormous quantities of fish are killed to provide food for them. The name often given for these fish – 'trash fish' – stands by itself as a terrible indictment of our attitude towards them.

8. SEA-LEVEL RISE AND SMALL ISLAND STATES

1. Intergovernmental Panel on Climate Change, *Climate Change 2013: The Physical Science Basis. Contribution of Working Group I to the Fifth Assessment Report of the Intergovernmental Panel on Climate Change* (Cambridge: Cambridge University Press, 2013), pp. 1153–7.
2. Intergovernmental Panel on Climate Change, *Special Report on the Ocean and Cryosphere, Summary for Policymakers* (Geneva: IPCC, 2019), p. 20.
3. Josh Holder, Niko Kommenda and Jonathan Watts, 'The Three-Degree World: The Cities that will be Drowned by Global Warming', *Guardian*, www.theguardian.com (3 November 2017).
4. IPCC, *Special Report on the Ocean and Cryosphere*, p. 5.
5. Ibid., pp. 20–27.
6. Ibid., p. 21.
7. Scott Kulp and Benjamin Strauss, 'New Elevation Data Triple Estimate of Global Vulnerability to Sea-level Rise and Coastal Flooding', *Nature Communications*, vol. 10, no. 1 (2019), pp. 1–12, at p. 5.
8. The term 'climate exiles' is adopted by Sujatha Byravan and Sudhir Chella Rajan, 'The Ethical Implications of Sea-Level Rise Due to Climate Change', *Ethics & International Affairs*, vol. 24, no. 3 (2010), pp. 239–60.
9. Anote Tong, 'Nation Under Threat', in *Climate 2020: Facing the Future* (London: United Nations Association, 2015), p. 76.
10. Rebecca Buxton, 'Reparative Justice for Climate Refugees', *Philosophy*, vol. 94 (2019), pp. 193–219, at p. 194.
11. David Miller, *National Responsibility and Global Justice* (Oxford: Oxford University Press, 2007), p. 221.
12. For a suggestion along those lines, see Mathias Risse, 'The Right to Relocation: Disappearing Island Nations and Common Ownership of the Earth', *Ethics & International Affairs*, vol. 23, no. 3 (2009), pp. 281–300, at p. 296.
13. David Owen, 'Refugees and Responsibilities of Justice', *Global Justice: Theory Practice Rhetoric*, vol. 11, no. 1 (2018), pp. 23–44, at p. 36.
14. Rory Walsh and Charlotte Stancioff, 'Small Island Perspectives on Climate Change', *Island Studies Journal*, vol. 13, no. 1 (2018), pp. 13–24, at p. 17.
15. Milla Emilia Vaha, 'Hosting the Small Island Developing States: Two Scenarios', *International Journal of Climate Change Strategies and Management*, vol. 10, no. 2 (2018), pp. 229–44, at p. 235.
16. Clare Heyward and Jörgen Ödalen, 'A Free Movement Passport for the Territorially Dispossessed', in Clare Heyward and Dominic Roser (eds), *Climate Justice in a Non-ideal World* (Oxford: Oxford University Press, 2016), pp. 208–26.
17. Clare Heyward, 'Climate Change as Cultural Injustice', in Thom Brooks (ed.), *New Waves in Global Justice* (Basingstoke: Palgrave Macmillan, 2014), pp. 149–69.

18. Submission of the Maldives to the Office of the UN High Commissioner for Human Rights under Human Rights Council Resolution 7/23, 'Human Rights and Climate Change' (25 September 2008) at p. 7.
19. Vaha, 'Hosting the Small Island Developing States', p. 232.
20. James Ker-Lindsay, 'Climate Change and State Death', *Survival*, vol. 58, no. 4 (2016), pp. 73–94.
21. Montevideo Convention on the Rights and Duties of States (1933), Article 1.
22. Rosemary Rayfuse and Emily Crawford, 'Climate Change, Sovereignty and Statehood', *Sydney Law School Legal Studies Research Paper*, 11/59 (2011), p. 5.
23. International Covenant on Civil and Political Rights, Article 1.
24. Anna Stilz, 'The Value of Self-Determination', *Oxford Studies in Political Philosophy*, vol. 2 (2016), pp. 98–127, at p. 100.
25. Alberto Costi and Nathan Jon Ross, 'The Ongoing Legal Status of Low-Lying States in the Climate-Changed Future', in Petra Butler and Caroline Morris (eds), *Small States in a Legal World* (Dordrecht: Springer, 2017), pp. 101–38, at pp. 108–9.
26. Rosemary Rayfuse, 'International Law and Disappearing States', *Environmental Policy & Law*, vol. 41 (2011), pp. 281–7, at p. 284. See also Ker-Lindsay, 'Climate Change and State Death'; Milla Vaha, 'Drowning Under: Small Island States and the Right to Exist', *Journal of International Political Theory*, vol. 11, no. 2 (2015), pp. 206–23.
27. Buxton, 'Reparative Justice for Climate Refugees,' pp. 169–70.
28. Cara Nine, 'Ecological Refugees, State Borders, and the Lockean Proviso', *Journal of Applied Philosophy*, vol. 27, no. 4 (2010), pp. 359–75, at p. 366.
29. Ibid., p. 359; Joachim Wundisch, 'Territorial Loss as a Challenge for World Governance', *Philosophical Papers*, vol. 48, no. 1 (2019), pp. 155–78, at p. 158.
30. See e.g. Cara Nine, 'Ecological Refugees, State Borders'; Avery Kolers, 'Floating Provisos and Sinking Islands', *Journal of Applied Philosophy*, vol. 29, no. 4 (2012), pp. 333–43.
31. Wundisch, 'Territorial Loss as a Challenge for World Governance'.
32. Nine, 'Ecological Refugees, State Borders'; Kim Angell, 'New Territorial Rights for Sinking Island States', *European Journal of Political Theory*, vol. 20, no. 1 (2021), pp. 95–115.
33. See Frank Dietrich and Joachim Wundisch, 'Territory Lost – Climate Change and the Violation of Self-determination Rights', *Moral Philosophy and Politics*, vol. 2, no. 1 (2015), pp. 83–105, at p. 88.
34. Jamie Draper has suggested that the redistribution of territory would bring in tow significant moral costs that we should seek to avoid if possible. Draper, 'Self-Determination and Territory in Small-Island States', draft paper.
35. Nine, 'Ecological Refugees, State Borders', p. 372.
36. Ibid.
37. Daniel Philpott, 'In Defense of Self-determination', *Ethics*, vol. 105, no. 2 (1995), pp. 352–85, at p. 353.
38. Nine, 'Ecological Refugees, State Borders', p. 372; Anna Stilz, *Territorial Sovereignty: A Philosophical Exploration* (Oxford: Oxford University Press, 2019), p. 180.
39. See https://www.parliament.nz/en/mps-and-electorates (accessed 8 May 2021).
40. See https://www.sametinget.se/english (accessed 6 May 2021).
41. Costi and Ross, 'The Ongoing Legal Status of Low-Lying States in the Climate-Changed Future', pp. 108–9.
42. Susin Park, *Climate Change and the Risk of Statelessness: The Situation of Low-lying Island States* (United Nations High Commissioner for Refugees, Legal and Protection Policy Research Series, 2011), pp. 3–4.
43. James Crawford, *The Creation of States in International Law*, 2nd edn (Oxford: Oxford University Press, 2006), p. 34.
44. Jörgen Ödalen, 'Underwater Self-Determination: Sea-Level Rise and Deterritorialized Small Island States', *Ethics, Policy & Environment*, vol. 17, no. 2 (2014), pp. 225–37.
45. Maxine Burkett, 'The Nation Ex-Situ: On Climate Change, Deterritorialized Nationhood and the Post-Climate Era', *Climate Law*, vol. 2 (2011), pp. 345–74, at p. 357.

46. Vaha, 'Drowning Under', pp. 213–15.
47. George Kacewicz, *Great Britain, the Soviet Union and the Polish Government in Exile (1939–1945)* (The Hague: Martinus Nijhoff, 2012).
48. Ödalen, 'Underwater Self-Determination'.
49. International Law Association, *International Law and Sea Level Rise: Report from the Sydney Conference* (London: International Law Association, 2018), p. 9.
50. Ibid., pp. 14, 19.
51. There are important questions about whether exiles would retain an EEZ down the generations, or whether their right to that EEZ would eventually fade away, if their descendants came to enjoy sufficiently good opportunities in their new home state.
52. See https://www.abc.net.au/news/2019-02-18/tuvalu-pm-slams-kevin-rudd-suggestion-as-neo-colonialism/10820176 (accessed 13 April 2019).
53. Polynesian Leaders Group, *Taputapuatea Declaration on Climate Change* (Papeete, 16 July 2015).
54. Delap Commitment, *Securing Our Common Wealth of Oceans* (Majuro, Marshall Islands, 2 March 2018).
55. Pacific Islands Forum Secretariat, *Our Sea of Islands, Our Livelihoods, Our Oceania. Framework for a Pacific Oceanscape*, Pacific Islands Forum (November 2010).
56. Karen McNamara and Carol Farbotko, 'Resisting a "Doomed" Fate: An Analysis of the Pacific Climate Warriors', *Australian Geographer*, vol. 48, no. 1 (2017), pp. 17–26, at p. 17.
57. Jason Titifanue et al., 'Climate Change Advocacy in the Pacific', *Pacific Journalism Review*, vol. 23, no. 1 (2017), pp. 133–49, at pp. 143–4.
58. Milan Loeak, quoted in McNamara and Farbotko, 'Resisting a "Doomed" Fate', p. 20.

9. A BLUE NEW DEAL

1. See https://www.gndforeurope.com/about (accessed 25 November 2020).
2. House Resolution 109, *Recognizing the Duty of the Federal Government to Create a Green New Deal*, 116th Congress, 1st Session.
3. Darren McCauley and Raphael Heffron, 'Just Transition: Integrating Climate, Energy and Environmental Justice', *Energy Policy*, vol. 119 (2018), pp. 1–7.
4. Abel Gustafson, 'The Green New Deal has Strong Bipartisan Support', *Yale Program on Climate Change Communication* (14 December 2018).
5. The House Resolution, for instance, contains one fleeting reference to ensuring that the oceans are protected, but does not recognise the potential of the ocean economy to play a role in the transition beyond carbon. House Resolution 109, p. 13.
6. Melanie Arter, 'Sen. Elizabeth Warren: "We Need a Blue New Deal as Well"', www.cnsnews.com (5 September 2019).
7. David Helvarg, 'A Blue New Deal for a Blue Marble Planet', https://mission-blue.org (10 July 2019).
8. Mimi Abramovitz, 'The Feminization of Austerity', *New Labor Forum*, vol. 21, no. 1 (2012), pp. 30–39.
9. Fergus Green and Ajay Gambhir, 'Transitional Assistance Policies for Just, Equitable and Smooth Low-Carbon Transitions: Who, What and How?', *Climate Policy*, vol. 20, no. 8 (2020), pp. 902–21.
10. Ahmet Atil Asici and Zeynep Bunul, 'Green New Deal: A Green Way out of the Crisis?', *Environmental Policy and Governance*, vol. 22 (2012), pp. 295–306, at 299.
11. House Resolution 109, p. 5.
12. This squares with the argument in Chris Armstrong, 'Decarbonisation and World Poverty: A Just Transition for Fossil Fuel Exporting Countries?', *Political Studies*, vol. 68, no. 3 (2020), pp. 671–88 – though I focus there on the global situation.
13. Green and Gambhir, 'Transitional Assistance Policies', p. 11.
14. Ibid., p. 6.

15. New Economics Foundation, *Blue New Deal: Good Jobs for Coastal Communities through Healthy Seas* (London: New Economics Foundation, 2015), p. 9.
16. Mary Zsamboky et al., *Impacts of Climate Change on Disadvantaged UK Coastal Communities* (London: Joseph Rowntree Foundation, 2011), p. 30.
17. Oxford Consultants for Social Inclusion, *Three Suggestions for the Coastal Regeneration Fund* (15 September 2011).
18. Elizabeth Rush, *Rising: Dispatches from the New American Shore* (Minneapolis, MN: Milkweed, 2018).
19. New Economics Foundation, *Blue New Deal*, p. 16.
20. Katy Wright, 'Resilient Communities? Experiences of Risk and Resilience in a Time of Austerity', *International Journal of Disaster Risk Reduction*, vol. 18 (2016), pp. 154–61.
21. Callum Roberts, *Ocean of Life: The Fate of Man and the Sea* (London: Penguin, 2012), pp. 120–28.
22. John Kaldellis et al., 'Environmental and Social Footprint of Offshore Wind Energy. Comparison with Onshore Counterpart', *Renewable Energy*, vol. 92 (2016), pp. 543–56, at p. 544.
23. New Economics Foundation, *Blue New Deal*, p. 22.
24. Patricio Bernal, J.S. Weis and K.E.A. Segarra, 'Salt Marshes', in the *First Global Integrated Marine Assessment* (New York: United Nations Division for Ocean Affairs and the Law of the Sea, 2016), pp. 887–92.
25. Katie Arkema et al., 'Coastal Habitats Shield People and Property from Sea-Level Rise and Storms', *Nature Climate Change*, vol. 3, no. 10 (2013), pp. 913–18, at p. 914.
26. David Read et al., *The Role of Land Carbon Sinks in Mitigating Global Climate Change* (The Royal Society, 2001).
27. Richard Page et al., *In Hot Water: The Climate Crisis and the Urgent Need for Climate Protection* (Amsterdam: Greenpeace International 2019), p. 14.
28. Joe Guinan and Martin O'Neill, *The Case for Community Wealth Building* (Cambridge: Polity 2020), p. 2.
29. Ibid., p. 30.
30. Lisa Campbell et al., 'From Blue Economy to Blue Communities: Reorienting Aquaculture Expansion for Community Wellbeing', *Marine Policy*, no. 124 (2021), 104361.
31. Rowan Jacobsen, 'Rebuilt Wetlands Can Protect Shorelines Better Than Walls', *Scientific American* (1 April 2019).
32. Arkema et al., 'Coastal Habitats', p. 916.
33. *Fast facts: Natural Infrastructure*, Office for Coastal Management, National Oceanic and Atmospheric Administration (12 August 2019).
34. Arkema et al., 'Coastal Habitats', p. 916.
35. World Bank Group, *Seaweed Aquaculture for Food Security, Income Generation and Environmental Health in Tropical Developing Countries* (2016).
36. Carlos Duarte et al., 'Can Seaweed Farming Play a Role in Climate Change Mitigation and Adaptation?', *Frontiers in Marine Science*, vol. 4 (2017), pp. 1–8, at pp. 3–4.
37. Lorenna Machado et al., 'Dose-Response Effects of *Asparagopsis Taxiformis* and *Oedogonium sp.* on In Vitro Fermentation and Methane Production', *Journal of Applied Phycology*, vol. 28 (2016), pp. 1443–52.
38. Duarte et al., 'Can Seaweed Farming Play a Role?', p. 4.
39. Qisheng Tang, Jihong Zhang and Jianguang Fang, 'Shellfish and Seaweed Mariculture Increase Atmospheric CO2 Absorption by Coastal Ecosystems', *Marine Ecology Progress Series*, vol. 424 (2011), pp. 97–104.
40. Diane Bailey and Gina Solomon, 'Pollution Prevention at Ports: Clearing the Air', *Environmental Impact Assessment Review*, vol. 24, nos. 7–8 (2004), pp. 749–74.
41. D.S.H. Moon, J.K. Woo and T.G. Tim, 'Green Ports and Economic Opportunities', in Lisa Loloma Froholdt (ed.), *Corporate Social Responsibility in the Maritime Industry* (Dordrecht: Springer, 2018), pp. 167–84, at p. 175.

42. Peter de Langen and Henrik Sornn-Friese, 'Ports and the Circular Economy', in Rickard Bergqvist and Jason Monios (eds), *Green Ports* (Amsterdam: Elsevier, 2018), pp. 85–108.
43. David Helvarg and Jason Scorse, 'Putting the Blue in the Green New Deal', *Mongabay* (13 March 2019).
44. Magnus Jiborn et al., 'Decoupling or Delusion? Measuring Emissions Displacement in Foreign Trade', *Global Environmental Change*, vol. 49 (2018), pp. 27–34.
45. Darrel Moellendorf, *The Moral Challenge of Dangerous Climate Change* (Cambridge: Cambridge University Press, 2014), chapters 1 and 5.
46. African Union, *Africa Blue Economy Strategy* (Nairobi: African Union, 2019), p. 13.
47. Page et al., *In Hot Water*, p. 9.
48. M.F. Adame et al., 'Avoided Emissions and Conservation of Scrub Mangroves: Potential for a Blue Carbon Project in the Gulf of California, Mexico', *Biology Letters*, vol. 14, no. 12 (2018), 20180400.
49. Vien Ngoc Nam et al., 'Carbon Stocks in Artificially and Naturally Regenerated Mangrove Ecosystems in the Mekong Delta', *Wetlands Ecology and Management*, vol. 24, no. 2 (2016), pp. 231–44.
50. For a fuller argument to this effect – which concentrates on the case of rainforests – see Chris Armstrong, 'Fairness, Free-riding, and Rainforest Protection', *Political Theory*, vol. 44, no. 1 (2016), pp. 106–30.
51. Mads Barbesgaard, *Blue Carbon: Ocean Grabbing in Disguise?* (Amsterdam: Transnational Institute, 2016).
52. Nathan Bennett et al., 'Blue Growth and Blue Justice: Ten Risks and Solutions for the Ocean Economy', *Marine Policy*, vol. 125 (2021), e104387.
53. Rajarshi DasGupta and Rajib Shaw (eds), *Participatory Mangrove Management in a Changing Climate: Perspectives from the Asia-Pacific* (Tokyo: Springer Japan, 2017).
54. Duarte et al., 'Can Seaweed Farming Play A Role?', p. 2.
55. Calvyn Sondak et al., 'Carbon Dioxide Mitigation Potential of Seaweed Aquaculture Beds (SABs)', *Journal of Applied Phycology*, vol. 29 (2017), pp. 2363–73, at p. 2368.
56. Torsten Thiele and Leah Gerber, 'Innovative Financing for the High Seas', *Aquatic Conservation: Marine and Freshwater Ecosystems*, vol. 27 (2017), pp. 89–99, at 91.
57. Amina Mohammed and Simon Zadek, 'From Green Bonds to Sustainable Development: The Case of Nigeria', in Raj Desai et al. (eds), *From Summits to Solutions: Innovations in Implementing the Sustainable Development Goals* (Washington DC: Brookings Institution Press, 2018), pp. 66–79, at p. 77.
58. John Broome and Duncan Foley, 'A World Climate Bank', in Inigo Gonzalez-Ricoy and Axel Gosseries (eds), *Institutions for Future Generations* (Oxford: Oxford University Press, 2016), pp. 156–69.
59. Thiele and Gerber, 'Innovative Financing for the High Seas', at p. 95.
60. Robert Hockett and Aaron James, 'Why Joe Biden Can Stop Worrying and Start Spending Like Crazy', *New Republic* (1 December 2020).

10. BEYOND THE BLUE NEW DEAL

1. For another argument that the advent of the Anthropocene might require us to rethink basic principles of oceanic governance, see Davor Vidas, 'The Anthropocene and the International Law of the Sea', *Philosophical Transactions of the Royal Society A*, vol. 369, no. 1938 (2011), pp. 909–25.
2. Camilo Mora et al., 'How Many Species are there on Earth and in the Ocean?', *PLoS Biol*, vol. 9, no. 8 (2011), e1001127.
3. See https://www.iucncongress2020.org/motion/069 (accessed 11 February 2021).
4. See https://www.un.org/bbnj/sites/www.un.org.bbnj/files/draft_text_a.conf_.232.2019.6_advanced_unedited_version_corr.pdf (accessed 30 September 2019).
5. See http://statements.unmeetings.org/media2/21996848/algeria-obo-african-group.pdf (accessed 6 March 2021).

6. See https://www.un.org/bbnj/sites/www.un.org.bbnj/files/revised_draft_text_a.conf_.232. 2020.11_advance_unedited_version.pdf (accessed 22 December 2020).

7. Zoe Scanlon, 'The Art of "Not Undermining": Possibilities Within Existing Architecture to Improve Environmental Protections in Areas Beyond National Jurisdiction', *ICES Journal of Marine Science*, vol. 75, no. 1 (2018), pp. 405–16.

8. See https://www.oceanographicmagazine.com/features/greenpeace-global-oceans (accessed 23 March 2021).

9. Klaudija Cremers et al., *A Preliminary Analysis of the Draft High Seas Biodiversity Treaty* (Paris: IDDRI, 2020).

10. *Marx and Engels Collected Works Volume 38* (London: Lawrence and Wishart, 1982), p. 503.

11. For an inspiring argument to this effect, see Deborah Rowan Wright, *Future Sea* (Chicago: Chicago University Press, 2021), chapter 5.

12. Quoted in Aline Jaeckel, Kristina Gjerde and Jeff Ardron, 'Conserving the Common Heritage of Mankind: Options for the Deep-Seabed Mining Regime', *Marine Policy*, vol. 78 (2017), pp. 150–57, at p. 157.

13. 1991 Protocol on Environmental Protection to the Antarctic Treaty, Article 2.

14. United Nations General Assembly, *Renewing the United Nations: A Programme for Reform* (New York, United Nations, 1997), paragraph 85.

15. Independent World Commission on the Oceans, *The Ocean, Our Future* (Cambridge: Cambridge University Press, 1998), p. 17.

16. See e.g. Christopher Stone, *Should Trees Have Standing? Law, Morality and the Environment* (Oxford: Oxford University Press, 2010); Mary Turnipseed et al., 'Using the Public Trust Doctrine to Achieve Ocean Stewardship', in Christina Voigt (ed.), *Rule of Law for Nature: New Dimensions and Ideas in Environmental Law* (Cambridge: Cambridge University Press, 2013), pp. 365–79, at p. 375; Cassandra Brooks et al., 'Challenging the Right to Fish in a Fast-Changing Ocean', *Stanford Environmental Law Journal*, vol. 33 (2013), pp. 289–324, at p. 321.

17. Turnipseed et al., 'Using the Public Trust Doctrine to Achieve Ocean Stewardship', p. 377; Turnipseed et al., 2013: 5–6; Mary Turnipseed et al., 'The Public Trust Doctrine and Rio+ 20', in *Third Nobel Laureate Symposium on Global Sustainability* (2012), pp. 1–7, at pp. 5–6.

18. Peter Sand, 'Sovereignty Bounded: Public Trusteeship for Common Pool Resources?', *Global Environmental Politics*, vol. 4, no. 1 (2004), pp. 47–71, at p. 57.

19. On the importance of indigenous knowledge about the ocean, and the role that it could play in a new treaty for High Seas biodiversity, see Clement Yow Mulalap et al., 'Traditional Knowledge and the BBNJ Instrument', *Marine Policy*, 122 (2020), 104103.

20. See also Prue Taylor, 'The Future of the Common Heritage of Mankind. Intersections with the Public Trust Doctrine', in Laura Westra, Prue Taylor and Agnes Michelot (eds), *Confronting Ecological and Economic Collapse* (London: Routledge, 2013), pp. 32–46, at p. 44.

21. Enric Sala et al., 'The Economics of Fishing the High Seas', *Science Advances*, vol. 4, no. 6 (2018), eaat2504.

22. See e.g. Crow White and Christopher Costello, 'Close the High Seas to Fishing?' *PLoS Biology*, vol. 12, no. 3 (2014), e1001826. See also Rashid Sumaila et al., 'Winners and Losers in a World Where the High Seas is Closed to Fishing', *Scientific Reports*, vol. 5, no. 1 (2015), pp. 1–6.

23. Sumaila et al., 'Winners and Losers in a World Where the High Seas is Closed to Fishing', p. 3.

24. Alexis Rife et al., 'When Good Intentions Are Not Enough . . . Insights on Networks of "Paper Park" Marine Protected Areas', *Conservation Letters*, vol. 6, no. 3 (2013), pp. 200–12.

25. Graham Edgar et al., 'Global Conservation Outcomes Depend on Marine Protected Areas With Five Key Features', *Nature*, no. 506 (2014), pp. 216–20.

26. For another attempt to 'think big' when it comes to ocean governance, see Enric Sala and Kristin Rechberger, 'Protecting Half the Ocean?', in Raj Desai et al. (eds), *From Summits to Solutions: Innovations in Implementing the Sustainable Development Goals* (Washington DC: Brookings Institution Press, 2018), pp. 239–62.

27. Since the ocean is a three-dimensional space, the focus on surface area in discussions of ocean protection should probably be replaced by a focus on volume. Given that the High Seas are typically much deeper than coastal areas, the proportion of the ocean *by volume* that would be strongly protected, in my proposal, would be well in excess of 95 per cent.

28. High Level Panel for a Sustainable Ocean Economy, *Transformations for a Sustainable Ocean Economy* (December 2020).

29. Henrik Österblom and Robert Blasiak, 'Oil Licences Undermine Norway's Ocean Leadership', *Nature*, no. 590 (2021), p. 551.

30. Chris Armstrong, 'Decarbonisation and World Poverty: A Just Transition for Fossil Fuel Exporting Countries?', *Political Studies*, vol. 68, no. 3 (2020), pp. 671–88.

31. David Symes and Jeremy Phillipson, 'Whatever Became of Social Objectives in Fisheries Policy?', *Fisheries Research*, 95 (2009), pp. 1–5.

32. For a discussion of some of the options, see Paula Casal and Nicole Selamé, 'Sea for the Landlocked: A Sustainable Development Goal?', *Journal of Global Ethics*, vol. 11, no. 3 (2015), pp. 270–79.

33. Anca Gheaus, 'The Feasibility Constraint on the Concept of Justice', *The Philosophical Quarterly*, vol. 63, no. 252 (2013), pp. 445–64.

34. Daniel Pauly, 'Anecdotes and the Shifting Baseline Syndrome of Fisheries', *Trends in Ecology & Evolution*, vol. 10, no. 10 (1995), p. 430.

35. Carlos Duarte et al., 'Rebuilding Marine Life', *Nature*, no. 580 (2020), pp. 39–51, at p. 39.

36. Doug Beare et al., 'An Unintended Experiment in Fisheries Science: A Marine Area Protected by War Results in Mexican Waves in Fish Numbers-at-age', *Naturwissenschaften*, vol. 97, no. 9 (2010), pp. 797–808.

37. Callum Roberts et al., 'Marine Reserves Can Mitigate and Promote Adaptation to Climate Change', *Proceedings of the National Academy of Sciences*, vol. 114, no. 24 (2017), pp. 6167–75.

38. Duarte et al., 'Rebuilding Marine Life', p. 43.

39. Alexandre Zerbini et al., 'Assessing the Recovery of an Antarctic Predator from Historical Exploitation', *Royal Society Open Science*, vol. 6, no. 10 (2019), 190368.

AFTERWORD

1. See https://radicaloceanfutures.earth (accessed 18 June 2021).

2. On the idea of a neoliberal ocean future, see Katherine Seto and Brooke Campbell, 'The Last Commons: (Re)constructing an Ocean Future', in William Cheung, Yoshitaka Ota and Andres Cisneros-Montemayor (eds), *Predicting Future Oceans* (Amsterdam: Elsevier, 2019), pp. 365–76, at pp. 372–3.

FURTHER READING

SCIENCE AND ECOLOGY

For an introduction to the ecosystem roles of the ocean, readers could do no better than start with Rachel Carson's classic *The Sea Around Us* (Carson would become famous for her book *Silent Spring*, but she was first and foremost a marine biologist). For more recent work on the fascinating science of oceans, in our world and beyond, try Jan Zalasiewicz and Mark Williams, *Ocean Worlds*, or Dorrik Stow, *Oceans: A Very Short Introduction*. Alex Rogers, *The Deep* provides an insight into the mysterious world of the deep sea. Sylvia Earle and Callum Roberts have contributed hugely to our understanding of ocean and the need for better protection. Try Roberts's *Ocean of Life* to begin with, or Earle's *The World Is Blue*. For an accessible introduction to the ecology of the shoreline, see Adam Nicolson, *The Sea is Not Made of Water: Life Between the Tides*.

HISTORY AND CULTURE

For a compendious account of our encounters with the ocean, which takes a great historical sweep and a truly global perspective, see David Abulafia, *The Boundless Sea: A Human History of the Oceans*. On sailing in particular, start with Lincoln Paine, *The Sea and Civilization: A Maritime History of the World*. On Pacific Islanders' experience of living in what they call Oceania, see Epeli Hau'ofa, *We Are The Ocean*. Christina Thompson's *Sea People: In Search of the Ancient Navigators of the Pacific* provides a historical perspective. For a survey of the ocean's representation in fiction, see Margaret Cohen, *The Novel and the Sea*.

SOCIOLOGY, ECONOMICS AND PSYCHOLOGY

Philip Steinberg's *The Social Construction of the Ocean* charts the different ways in which we have thought of the ocean as a space, offering many sociological insights along the way. In *Capitalism and the Sea*, Liam Campling and Alejandro Colás put the ocean back at the heart of the analysis of the modern economy. Though it is told on a smaller scale – concentrating on the Arabian Peninsula – Laleh Khalili's *Sinews of War and Trade* offers a fascinating account of the influence of capital, labour and geography in the contemporary maritime economy. Steve Mentz's *Ocean* provides some rich musings on what the ocean has meant to us and our societies. For a provocative account of the difference that living near water can make to our happiness and well-being, see Wallace Nichols, *Blue Mind: How Water Makes You Happier, More Connected and Better at What You Do*.

LAW AND GOVERNANCE

For an introduction to the contemporary Law of the Sea, read Yoshifumi Tanaka's *The International Law of the Sea*, or Donald Rothwell and Tim Stephens's book of the same name. For a good guide to ocean politics more broadly, see Mark Zacharias and Jeff Ardron, *Marine Policy: An Introduction to Governance and International Law of the Ocean*. There are surprisingly few imaginative accounts of what the ocean politics of the future could look like. For an engaging recent exception, see Deborah Rowan Wright, *Future Sea*.

HUMAN RIGHTS AT SEA

For more on the challenges faced by those who work at sea, try Alasdair Couper, Hance Smith and Bruno Ciceri, *Fishers and Plunderers: Theft, Slavery and Violence at Sea*. Ian Urbina's *The Outlaw Ocean: Crime and Survival in the Last Untamed Frontier* provides a very readable, and at times horrifying, account of abuses on the open ocean. Readers wanting a vivid insight into what it means for individual workers could do no better than to read Vannak Anan Prum's illustrated memoir *The Dead Eye and the Deep Blue Sea: A Graphic Memoir of Modern Slavery*. For an accessible account of the sometimes murky world of shipping, see Rose George, *Deep Sea and Foreign Going*.

FISHING

For a useful account of the emergence and development of the fishing industry, see Brian Fagan, *Fishing: How the Sea Fed Civilization*. For a clear-eyed account of the ecological impacts of the fishing industry, see Callum Roberts, *The Unnatural History of the Sea*. Daniel Pauly's work has been highly influential in fisheries science, and his *Vanishing Fish: Shifting Baselines and the Future of Global Fisheries* is well worth a look. For a critique of the impact fishing and aquaculture have had on the ocean, try Stefano Longo, Rebecca Clausen and Brett Clark, *The Tragedy of the Commodity: Oceans, Fisheries, and Aquaculture*.

CETACEANS AND OTHER OCEAN CREATURES

For insights into the life of cetaceans that roam the ocean, try Nick Pyenson, *Spying on Whales: The Past, Present and Future of the World's Largest Animals*, or Susan Casey, *Voices in the Ocean*. For more on their distinctive social and cultural practices, see Hal Whitehead and Luke Rendell, *The Cultural Life of Whales and Dolphins*. For a fascinating account of the distinctive intelligence of the octopus, see Peter Godfrey-Smith, *Other Minds: The Octopus and the Evolution of Intelligent Life*.

CLIMATE CHANGE AND SEA-LEVEL RISE

Elizabeth Rush's *Rising* provides a vivid account of the impact that climate change is already having on the American shore. For a more global perspective, see Jeff Goodell, *The Water Will Come: Rising Seas, Sinking Cities, and the Remaking of the Civilized World*. For the legal implications of sea-level rise, see Snjólaug Árnadóttir, *Climate Change and Maritime Boundaries*.

INDEX